2001
FOOD SECRETS
REVEALED

BY
DR. MYLES H. BADER
(The Wizard of Food)

2001 FOOD SECRETS REVEALED

Copyright 1997, Dr. Myles H. Bader

All Rights Reserved

No part of this book may be reproduced or transmitted in any form, or by any means, electronic or mechanical, including photocopy, recording, or by any information storage and retrieval system, without the written permission of the author.

Published by:
Northstar Publishing
1818 Industrial Rd., Suite 209
Las Vegas, Nevada, 89102
800-717-6001

Printed in the United States of America
First Printing September 1997
ISBN: 0-9646741-5-7

Illustrations by:
Deborah Rose Peek
707-994-7819

Desktop Publishing by:
Suzanne Merritt
Fax 760-931-9797

INTRODUCTION

This book will be the most unusual food book you will ever read. There are thousands of books available on food and nutrition but none of these books will really tell you about the secrets and the mysteries surrounding food. Most books provide you with the nutritional content of foods or tell you which foods are good or bad for you. Some books try to help you choose which foods will make you healthier or which to avoid if you have a medical problem and some will provide facts about foods.

Finally, after 21 years in the health and nutrition field, I have written a book that explains "why" foods react the way they do when they are cooked, what is the chemical nature of certain foods, how small alterations in a recipe can result in a spoiled dish, and why certain foods are not as safe as you think they are.

2001 Food Secrets Revealed will for the first time answer these questions and much, much, more.

Nutrition has always been an interest of mine since I received my public health degree in the 1970's. Previous books I have written have been on interesting food facts and chefs' secrets; grandmothers' and great-grandmothers' methods of preparing foods; how to repair foods; and generally those little tricks that will make working with foods more enjoyable and successful.

The more I have written books on these food facts, the more interested I have become in how everything really worked. What happens to dairy products that makes them spoil fast? Why does an egg go bad after 10 to 14 days? Why does hamburger turn brown in the center before the top? How does baking powder work in a recipe? Why does baking soda turn potatoes black?

During the last 20 years I have found that the public's awareness in food and nutrition has escalated to such a level that when I give a fact on radio or in a lecture I am bombarded with a multitude of questions about why foods and additives react the way they do. The research that went into this book was tremendous and will provide the public with more in-depth information regarding foods than they have ever had easy access to.

The facts in this book are usable and based on scientific investigation, and will provide insights that will not easily be found in any other book on food and nutrition.

This book is dedicated to my grandaughter, Veronica Peek.

A WORD ABOUT THE AUTHOR

Dr. Myles H. Bader (known by many as The Wizard of Food) has been interviewed on over 2,000 radio and television talk shows internationally during the past five years. These shows have included the Oprah Winfrey Show, Crook and Chase, America's Talking, The Discovery Channel, The Morning Exchange, and QVC, to mention just a few.

Dr. Bader received his doctorate in Health Science from Loma Linda University and is board-certified in Preventive Care. He has practiced weight control, nutrition, fitness, and cardiac rehabilitation in major clinics in California and Nevada for 21 years and has established prevention and executive health programs for hundreds of corporations.

Recently, Dr. Bader has formulated one of the finest supplement products to be released in the United States, combining a super-antioxidant formulation with a person's everyday vitamin and mineral needs into one unique product.

Current books he has authored include: *To Supplement or Not To Supplement, 8001 Food Facts and Chef's Secrets, The Ultimate Household Reference Guide, Grandmother's Kitchen Wisdom,* and *The Wellness Desk Reference.*

Presently, he lectures extensively throughout the United States and Canada and continues to appear as a guest on radio and television shows discussing his current books. He is regarded as one of the leading authorities in the field of preventive care, having made more than 3,000 presentations.

TABLE OF CONTENTS

CHAPTER 4—FOOD; FREEZING, STORAGE, & PRESERVATION . 75

CHAPTER 8— SUGAR AND SUGAR SUBSTITUTES . . . . — . . . 129

CHAPTER 13 —SUPERMARKETS **183**

CHAPTER 14 —BEVERAGES **189**

CHAPTER 1
BAKING SECRETS

Good Old Bread Box

The dry air in the refrigerator actually draws moisture from the bread. Bread does develop mold faster at room temperature than under refrigeration at approximately 45° F. However, the freshness of the bread is lost in half the time. Freezing maintains the freshness but liquid is released as cells burst from the freezing temperatures, and the texture of the bread is never the same as fresh. If the bread is kept tightly wrapped and stored in a bread box, it will be fresher and taste better than with any other method of storage.

Non-Crispy Bread Crust

Do you ever wish that you could bake a loaf of bread without the crust becoming too crispy? Well, the secret to a softer crust is to open the oven door and throw in a few ice cubes about midway through the baking time. This will produce a dense steam and provide just enough extra moisture to keep the crust from becoming hard and too crispy. It also will allow the bread to rise more easily, producing, a nice firm, chewy inside.

The Role of Salt in Bread-Making

Salt has never really been needed when making bread. It does, however, make the crust a little crispier as well as slowing down the growth of the yeast which will prevent the dough from increasing its volume too fast.

Why Does French Bread Get Stale So Fast?

French bread is made without fat. The fat content in breads tends to slow down the loss of moisture and keep them softer by reducing the percentage of gluten. This prevents forming as strong a structure. French bread will get stale after only five to seven hours, which is why the French purchase their bread supplies at least twice a day.

Do the Twist

In the year 600 A.D. in a monastery in Northern Italy, a monk made the first pretzel. It was during Lent and he was forbidden to use any type of fat, eggs, or milk, so he used flour, salt, and water. He formed the bread into the shape of what he thought were two arms crossed in prayer. He named the bread "pretiola," which is Latin for "little gift," and gave the treat to the town children as a special reward for saying their prayers.

Sweeteners' Role in Bread-Making

Sweeteners such as honey, molasses, and cane sugar are really not required in bread making. They do, however, tend to slow down the coagulation of the protein, allowing the dough to increase in volume and making a fluffier loaf. They do add a few more calories to the bread but they also extend the shelf life.

If you do plan to use honey or molasses, always add a small amount of extra flour to offset the liquid sweetener.

What Is America's Favorite Cookie?

It's no contest: America's favorite cookie is the Oreo, which was first marketed by the National Biscuit Company of Hoboken, New Jersey, in 1912. The "Oreo biscuit," as it was originally known, was described in the company literature as "a biscuit with two beautifully embossed, chocolate-flavored wafers with a rich cream filling." The company has manufactured 210 billion Oreos since they were introduced in 1912, which is an average of over 2.5 billion every year for 85 years. If you are a health advocate, that amounts to over 8 trillion calories.

The Rise and Fall of a Soufflé

A soufflé rises because of the air bubbles that are trapped in the egg whites as they are beaten. When the soufflé is placed in the oven, the air in the bubbles expands, causing the soufflé to rise. If the soufflé is punctured or shaken it will cause a premature release of the air and the soufflé will collapse and is ruined.

Who invented Twinkies?

Twinkies were invented by James Dewar in 1930 who attributed his long life of 88 years to the fact that he ate two Twinkies every day since he invented them.

What is Chess Pie?

This a regional specialty of the Southern United States. It has a rich, smooth, translucent filling made of eggs, sugar, and butter held together with flour. In the 1800's the pie was made with molasses since sugar was not that available. It is a thin pie and may be made using a variety of flavorings, such as pineapple or bourbon.

Dissolving Flour

Instant flour will always dissolve more readily than a regular flour. Regular flour may lump easily because the exterior of the flour molecule gelatinizes immediately when contact is made with a warm liquid, forming a protective shield that blocks the liquid from entering the flour's inner molecules. This forms lumps with dry insides and wet outsides. Instant flour is produced with irregular shaped molecules with jagged edges so that the liquid can enter. Since they are so irregular they are unable to clump together easily.

How Much Bread Does A Bread Plant Bake?

Most large bread baking companies can bake 20,000 loaves an hour. The typical plant uses raw materials by the trainload since they consume two million pounds of flour every week, delivered in steam-sterilized boxcars or specially equipped truck tankers. The flour is then stored in sealed silos until used, with each one carefully dated. Bakeries that use this much flour have very strict rules regarding sparks or the lighting of a match since flour dust may be ignited if the right conditions exist.

What Is A Mexican Wedding Cake?

This is really not a cake but a very rich, buttery, cookie filled with pecans or almonds. The cookies are coated with powdered sugar when they are warm and then again after they are cooled. They are sometimes found in bakeries and called Russian tea cakes.

How Does Bread Become Stale?

When the bread is baked, a large percentage of the water accumulates in the starch. As the bread ages, the water is released from the starch and the protein, allowing the texture of the bread to become more crumbly and firm. As the bread continues to age, the water content inside the bread is released and the water is absorbed by the crust, drying the crust (making it hard) through evaporation of the moisture into the air. Re-heating the bread allows the moisture that remains in the bread to be distributed back into the starch and partially gelatinized. When re-heating a bread it must be placed in a sealed container or wrapped in a damp non-flammable material to avoid any evaporation and prevent the crust from becoming too hard.

Why Sour Dough Bread Is Sour

The yeast used in bread is normally standard baker's yeast which does not work well in the acidic environment needed to produce sour dough breads. Baker's yeast works by breaking down maltose, which the acids used in sour dough bread cannot do. The acids that are found in sour dough bread are 75% lactic acid and the balance is acetic acid. The bacteria in sour dough breads also require maltose and do not break it down. The bacteria prefer a temperature of 86° F.(300° C.) and a pH of 3.8 to 4.5 as ideal. Standard bread prefers a pH of 5.5. Starters for sour dough have lasted for hundreds of years and are thought to be protected by bacteria that are related to penicillin mold in cheese.

How Does Baking Powder Work?

Baking powder is a mixture of a number of chemicals that will leaven breads. The main chemicals are calcium acid phosphate, sodium aluminum sulfate or cream of tartar, and sodium bicarbonate. This mixture of acids and bases produces a chemical reaction when water is added to it, producing carbon dioxide, a gas. When this occurs, the gas creates minute air pockets or will enter already existing ones in the dough or batter. When you then place the mixture in a hot oven or hot plate, the dough rises because the heat causes additional carbon dioxide to be released from the baking powder, as well as expanding the trapped carbon dioxide gas which creates steam. This pressure swells the dough or batter and it expands or rises for the occasion.

Does Storage Time Affect Baking Powder?

Baking powder does lose potency over time and if you are unsure of its freshness you should test it before using it. Place ½ teaspoon of baking powder in a small bowl, then pour ¼ cup of hot tap water over it. The more bubbling activity there is, the fresher the baking powder. The activity must be at a good active level or the dough will not rise sufficiently. Try this test on a box of fresh baking powder so that you will be familiar with the activity level of the fresh powder.

What Thickeners Work Best in Fruit Pies?

For apple pies you should not need a thickener. For all others the best thickening agent is a combination of 2 tablespoons each of cornstarch and tapioca. Just mix them with the sugar before adding to the fruit. When baking remember that cornstarch has twice the thickening power of flour.

Baking With Buttermilk As A Substitute For Milk

When you substitute buttermilk in place of milk you are adding additional acid to the dough and upsetting the ratio of acid and base needed for the leavening agent to cause the release of the maximum amount of carbon dioxide. This will reduce the amount of carbon dioxide that is generated. To offset the additional acid you need to add a small amount of baking soda in place of an equal amount of baking powder. The basic rule of thumb is to reduce the amount of baking powder by 2 teaspoons and replace it with ½ teaspoon of baking soda for every cup of buttermilk you use in place of the milk.

How Many Eggs Can A Baker Break, If A Baker Breaks Eggs?

Large baking companies will rarely have their bakers take the time to break open every egg. In some cases either the yolk or the white will be used and the baker would have to separate the eggs before he could go to work. Eggs are usually purchased frozen, which eliminates the problem. Especially if the bakery uses more egg yolk than whites (or vice versa), the financial saving could be substantial over the course of a year. Frozen eggs are delivered under refrigeration at -15° F. and must be thawed before they can be used. Defrosting takes six to eight hours in a special thawing tank of cool, running water.

What Can You Use To Replace Fat In Baked Goods?

First, we need to realize that fat has a number of important purposes in baked goods. It extends shelf life, tenderizes the product, adds flavor, and contributes to the texture. When fat is replaced the baked product may be altered to such a degree that the finished product will not be acceptable. Replacements include skim milk, egg whites, and certain starches and gums. These will all lower the fat content and reduce the total calories. The gums and starches cannot replace the fat completely; however, they do help to retain moisture.

Home Formula For Baking Powder

Following is the formula for making 1 teaspoon of baking powder. Use ½ teaspoon of cream of tartar and ¼ teaspoon of baking soda. If you plan on storing a quantity of the powder for a few days, add ¼ teaspoon of corn starch to absorb moisture from the air. This will prevent a chemical reaction from taking place before you are ready to use it. This formula tends to cause the release of carbon dioxide faster and the mixture should be used as fast as possible. Commercially produced powders work at a higher temperature, giving them a longer period of time before they react.

Solving the Mystery of Cake Problems

- Layer Cakes

If your cake has a coarse texture or is heavy and solid, you probably didn't beat the sugar and Crisco, margarine, or butter long enough. These ingredients need to be beaten together very thoroughly for the best results.

If your cake is dry, this may indicate over-cooking and failure to check the doneness after the minimum cooking time. Another reason this occurs is that you may have over-beaten the egg whites.

If your cake has elongated holes it is a sign of over-mixing the batter at the time the flour was added. Ingredients should be mixed only enough to combine them totally.

- Angel Food, Chiffon, And Sponge Cakes

If your cake has poor volume you may not have beaten the egg whites long enough. Beat them, however, only until they stand in straight peaks. They should look moist and glossy when the beaters are removed. Another problem occurs if you over-mix the batter when you add the flour. The ingredients should be gently folded in and combined until the batter is just smooth.

If your cake shrinks or falls, the egg whites have probably been beaten too long. Another problem may be that you forgot to cool the cake upside down, allowing the steam to dissipate throughout the cake and creating a lighter, more fluffy cake.

If your cake is tough, you probably over-mixed the batter at the time when the dry ingredients were added. Ingredients should be blended only until they are mixed.

If your sponge cake has layers, you didn't beat the egg yolks long enough. They should be beaten until they are thick and lemon-colored.

If your chiffon cake has yellow streaks, you have added the yolks directly into the dry ingredients instead of making a "well" in the center of the dry ingredients and then adding the oil and then the egg yolks.

If your chiffon cake has a layer, you probably have either over-beaten or under-beaten the egg whites. Beat the egg whites only until they are stiff and look moist and glossy.

How Do They Make Commercial Cakes So Light?

Commercial cakes are difficult to duplicate from scratch and are usually light and tender. The reason for this is that they use chlorinated flour and special fat emulsifiers. These items are available but not always easy to find in the supermarket unless you know what to look for. To produce the chlorinated flour, bleaching agents are mixed with chlorine gas. The chlorinated flour changes the surface properties of both the starch and flour fats, then inhibits the gluten proteins from coming together. This special flour can tolerate more structural damage by the sugar and shortening than normal flour, the result being a sweeter, more tender product.

Hard Water May Affect Your Baked Product

The high mineral content of hard water may retard fermentation by causing the gluten to become tough. The minerals will prevent the protein from absorbing water the way it normally would. To counteract this problem there are a number of methods you may wish to try, such as using a bottled water, adding a small amount of vinegar to reduce the pH, or using more yeast. Water that is too soft can cause the dough to be sticky. If you are having a problem, you may want to consider using a dough improver.

World's Greatest Pancakes! Here Are The Secrets!

There are a number of tricks that chefs use to prepare the best pancake batter. The first is to use club soda in place of whatever liquid the recipe calls for. This increases the amount of air in the pancake and makes it fluffier. The second is not to over-mix the batter; otherwise it will cause the gluten to over-develop, resulting in a tougher pancake. Over-mixing can also force out more of the trapped carbon dioxide that assists in the leavening. Most people tend to mix the batter until all the small lumps of flour are dissolved. This is overkill. Instead, stop mixing before this occurs and place the batter in the refrigerator. This slows the development of the gluten and the activity level of baking powder or yeast. Third, adding sugar to your recipe causes carmelization and produces a golden brown outside. The more sugar, the more carmelization will take place, and the more brown the pancake will be.

I Wonder Where The Yellow Went?

When flour is processed, it still tends to retain a yellowish tint which is not very appealing. This yellow tint is caused by a chemical group called "xanthophylls" which remains in the flour. Bleaching is needed to remove the yellow tint; however, when this is done it destroys the vitamin E in the flour. The yellow color is left in pasta, which is why semolina is never white. The bleaching is done by using chlorine dioxide gas. Better flours are naturally aged, allowing the air to bleach them.

What Is A Shoofly Pie?

Shoofly pie is an old Pennsylvania Dutch specialty, a very sweet spicy pie that has a standard bottom pastry shell and a custard filling made from molasses and boiling water. It is usually covered with a crumb topping made with brown sugar and a variety of spices. Sometimes the custard is on top and the crumbs are inside. The name originated because of the flies that would hang around the pie trying to get at the molasses.

The Hot Griddle Bouncing-Water Test

Pancakes should be cooked on a griddle that is approximately 325° F. for the best results. To be sure of having the proper temperature, just dribble a drop or two of cold water on the hot griddle. The water should bounce around on the top of the griddle, close to the spot you dropped it, because steam is generated and gravity forces the water back down to the griddle. If the griddle is too hot, the water drops will be propelled off the griddle. This usually occurs at about 425° F.

The Blind Oreo Test

Tufts University conducted a "blind" test on 36 consumers who agreed to taste Oreo cookies to see if they were able to tell the difference between the regular Oreo and the new reduced-fat version. The reduced-fat version barely won the test, with 18 tasters favoring the reduced-fat and 17 preferring the regular Oreo. The reduced-fat Oreo has 47 calories and 1.67 grams of fat per cookie, compared to 53 calories and 2.33 grams of fat in the regular Oreo cookie. The difference is so minor that people will not easily be able to perceive it.

A Fool Makes A Great Dessert

This is actually a classic British dessert made from fruit and whipped cream. The "fool" is usually made with a cooked fruit purée which is chilled, sweetened, and then folded into the whipped cream and served like a parfait, layered in a tall glass. The fruit of choice is the gooseberry and the "fool" probably originated in the 15th century.

Yeast And Its Baking Uses

A block of yeast is composed of millions of one-celled fungi that will multiply at a fast rate given their favorite carbohydrate food, which is either sugar or starch in a moist environment. Yeast reproduces ideally at 110° to 115° F. except when used for bread dough, which does best at 80° to 90° F. Yeast causes the carbohydrate to convert into a simple sugar, glucose, which then ferments into alcohol and carbon dioxide. It is the carbon dioxide that will leaven the baked goods, similar to the reaction of baking powder in expanding the air and creating steam. There is no risk of the production of alcohol, since the heat from the baking evaporates the alcohol as well as killing the live yeast cells.

A Slump You Can Really Get Into

A "slump" is a New England dessert that dates back to the 1700's and is a deep-dish fruit dessert topped with a biscuit-like crust. It is similar to the "grunt" except that it is baked instead of steamed. The dough used for the "slump" is a dumpling dough which will stay moist on the inside while becoming crispy on the surface. The name of the dessert was derived from the fact that the dessert does not hold its shape well and usually slumps over when served.

Will Bread Rise In A Microwave?

It is possible for bread to rise in a microwave oven in approximately one-third of the time it would take through normal methods. The only problem is that it may affect the flavor somewhat because the slower it rises, the more time there is to develop the flavor and have it permeate the dough. If you do decide to use this method, your microwave needs to have a 10% power setting. If you try to use any higher temperature, the dough will turn into a half-baked glob. To raise dough for one standard loaf, place ½ cup of hot water in the back corner of the oven. Place the dough in a microwave bowl that is well greased and cover it with plastic wrap, then cover the plastic wrap with a damp towel. Set the power level to 10% and cook the dough for 6 minutes, then allow it to rest for 4 to 5 minutes. Repeat the procedure if the dough has not doubled its size.

Why Aren't Your Biscuits Light And Fluffy?

Check your baking powder for freshness and make sure that you sift all the dry ingredients together. This will provide you with the texture you desire. If you don't have a sifter, then just place all the ingredients into a large sieve and shake them all out. It's the even blending of the ingredients that is the key. Shortening is also the preferred fat over butter since shortening is a more refined product and adds lightness. Butter will make a biscuit more solid.

Is Kneading Really Kneaded?

Kneading is required to evenly distribute the yeast and other ingredients throughout the dough. If this is not done adequately the dough will not rise evenly, resulting in a product with a shorter shelf life. Dough-kneading machines make this chore easy and if you knead dough frequently a machine is a necessity.

What Is Fondant Icing?

Fondant icing is produced from glucose, sucrose, and water that is cooked to 240° F., then quickly cooled off to 110° F. and quickly worked until it has a white, creamy, smooth texture. To ice with the mixture, cool it down to 100° F. and it will flow smoothly. It is normally used as a base for butter cream icing.

What Is A Snickerdoodle?

The "snickerdoodle" is a true American cookie that originated in the 1800's in the northeastern United States. It is a buttery, cookie filled with dried fruit, nuts, and spices, usually nutmeg or cinnamon. The top of the snickerdoodle is sprinkled with powdered sugar before it is baked, producing a crinkly top. It may be found either hard or soft.

The Cure For Dome-Top Cakes

This problem is usually the result of adding too much flour to your batter. Thick batter does not circulate in the pan well and the batter around the edges tends to set before the batter in the center. This causes a reduction in the amount of heat that is transferred to the center and the center will take too long to harden, thus allowing the center more time to rise into a dome.

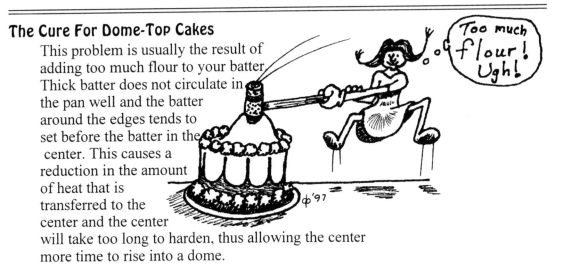

What Is Arrowroot?

Arrowroot is derived from the root stalks of a South American tuber which is finely powdered and used as a thickener. Its thickening power is about one to two times that of all-purpose flour and, like cornstarch, it should be mixed with adequate cold water to produce a paste before adding it to a hot mixture. One of the best features about arrowroot is that it will not impart a chalky taste if it is over-cooked. It's best not to over-stir a mixture that contains arrowroot or it will revert and become thin again. If your recipe calls for arrowroot and you don't have any, just use 2¼ teaspoons of cornstarch or 1½ tablespoons of all-purpose flour in place of 1 tablespoon of arrowroot.

Removing Breads and Cakes from Pans

When breads and cakes are baked, they build up steam inside which needs to be released after they are removed from the oven. If the steam is not allowed to escape it will convert to water as it comes in contact with the cooler air and be absorbed back into the product, making the product soggy. To avoid this problem, remove the pan from the oven and allow the product to remain in the pan to rest for a few minutes. The product should then be removed and placed on a cooling rack, which will allow more of the area to release additional steam and prevent any moisture that has gone to the bottom of the product from making the bottom soggy.

Dry And Compressed Yeast

Compressed yeast has a higher level of moisture, about 70% compared to the standard dry yeast at 8%. Compressed yeast should be stored in the refrigerator and lasts for about only two weeks before losing its effectiveness. Dry yeast should always be stored in as airtight a container as possible since it absorbs water rather easily. The yeasts are interchangeable, with 1 packet of the active dry yeast equaling the leavening power of 1 cake of the compressed yeast.

Chocolate Cakes Need To Be Leavened With Baking Soda, Never Baking Powder

Chocolate has a high acid level, so high that it would upset the balance between the acid (cream of tartar) and the base of baking powder. When baking soda (sodium bicarbonate) is used, it may make the chocolate cake too basic. Most recipes also call for the addition of a sour-milk product such as yogurt or sour cream to assure that the batter will not be too alkaline (basic). If the batter did become too alkaline, the cake would turn red instead of brown and it would taste bitter.

The Secret to Making Fluffy Biscuits

Whatever recipe you are using probably calls for you to use yeast. Instead of the yeast, substitute 1 teaspoon of baking soda and 1 teaspoon of powdered ascorbic acid (vitamin C). By doing this you will not have to wait for the dough to rise. The addition of these products will react with the other ingredients and the dough will rise naturally during the baking process.

What is Cream of Tartar?

Tartar is derived from grapes during and after the process of fermentation. Two pinkish crystalline sediments remain in wine casks after the wine has fermented. They are "argol" which collects on the sides of the cask and "lees" which collects on the bottom. These substances are actually crude tartar. The crude tartar is then de-crystallized by cooking it in boiling water and allowing the remains to crystallize again. This substance is then bleached pure white and further crystallized. As this process concludes, a thin layer of very thin white crystals is formed on the surface. The name "cream of tartar" is derived from this thin top layer that looks like cream. It is used to produce baking powder when mixed with baking soda.

What Is Baking Soda?

Baking soda is actually bicarbonate of soda which is derived from the manufacture of common washing soda, also known as "sal soda." Baking soda is composed of carbon and oxygen molecules which combine to form carbon dioxide gas. If a batter is sufficiently acidic then only baking soda is needed to produce carbon dioxide. If the batter does not have sufficient acid then baking powder, which carries both acid and alkali, is needed. All baking soda in North America is mined from the mineral trona, which is found in Green River, Wyoming. The large deposit was discovered in the 1930's. Trona is actually composed of sodium bicarbonate and sodium carbonate, a very close relative.

The ore is removed from deep mines, crushed, rinsed, and heated to produce sodium carbonate. The sodium carbonate is then dissolved in water and carbon dioxide is forced through the solution, releasing the sodium bicarbonate crystals, which are then washed, dried, and packaged as baking soda.

Sodium bicarbonate is also produced in the human body to assist in maintaining the acidity (pH) level of the blood. It is also found in saliva and will neutralize plaque acids which might otherwise dissolve our teeth. Another action in the body is to neutralize stomach acids so that we don't get ulcers, as well as assisting in the breathing process by transporting carbon dioxide from the tissues to the lungs for disposal.

Making A Turkish Delight

This is a chewy, rubbery textured dessert made from fruit juice, honey, and a number of different sugars, cornstarch, or gelatin. It is colored a pink or green and usually contains a variety of nuts to add texture. It is found in squares and covered with powdered sugar.

What Is Ammonium Carbonate?

This product is similar to sodium bicarbonate; however, it needs neither acid nor alkaline mediums to produce carbon dioxide. The addition of moist heat causes the reaction to occur. Since it decomposes rapidly, it is usually used only in cream puffs and soft cookies when a fast release and expansion of carbon dioxide gas is needed.

Poorly Rising Dough: Your Problem?

One of the most frequently encountered problems is that yeast dough doesn't rise adequately. There are a number of reasons for this. First, the dough may be too cool and reduce the level of yeast activity. The temperature needs to be between 80° and 90° F. for the best results. Second, the yeast may have been prepared with water that was too hot, which is a frequent problem. The water must be below 140° F. for optimum results. Third, you may have forgotten to test the yeast and it was over the hill.

Jumble, Jumble: It's Not A Dance Craze

It's a great-tasting cookie that was first introduced in the United States 200 years ago and is still being sold today. It is a sugar cookie baked in a ring shape, flavored with sour cream and then scented with rose water. Sometimes nuts are added to the top.

Yeast: Dead or Alive?

Yeast should be tested before you use it. Just mix a small amount in ¼ cup of warm water that has ¼ teaspoon of sugar mixed in. The mixture should begin bubbling (happy yeasties) within about 5 to 7 minutes. If this does not occur, they are either dead or too inactive to provide the leavening function.

The Composition Of Pasta

Pasta is composed of two main ingredients, water and either standard flour or the coarsest part of the wheat which is called semolina. Pasta dough needs to be very stiff and is therefore only 20% water, compared to bread dough which is about 40% water. Durum wheat semolina is the choice for most of the better-quality pastas and contains a very low percentage of starch and a high percentage of protein. The gluten matrix is very strong since the protein does not have to compete with the starch for the moisture. Because the protein is strong, it can be extruded by machine without falling apart. Standard flour pasta is easily broken and is the poorer-quality product.

The Napkin Test

There is an easy method of determining whether a baked goods product has a high fat level which is simply called the "napkin test." Place the baked goods in a paper napkin or a piece of paper towel; if the product leaves a grease stain, it contains more than three grams of fat. If you would like to reduce the fat content of pizza, dab a napkin on the surface of the pizza to absorb some of the fat.

Hermits Are Chewy

This type of hermit is a chewy, spicy cookie that is usually flavored with brown sugar, cinnamon, nutmeg, and cloves. Occasionally, raisins and nuts are added and they are either drop or bar cookies.

Unbleached vs. Bleached Flour

Unbleached flour would be the best choice for most baking projects that call for one or the other. The unbleached will have a more natural taste since it lacks the chemical additives and bleaching agents used in bleached flour. Bleached flour is less expensive to produce since it doesn't require aging, which strengthens the gluten content of the unbleached flour. It's best not to skimp when buying the unbleached flour; not all companies may allow the flour to age adequately.

Why Doesn't Bread Collapse Once The Steam Is Released?

The structure of the bread is supported by the coagulation of the proteins and the gelatinization of the complex carbohydrates. If this did not occur, all baked goods would collapse once they start to cool as the steam and carbon dioxide dissipate.

What is a Bath Bun?

It is a yeast-risen type of roll that is filled with candied citrus peels and raisins or currents. They are usually topped with powdered sugar and occasionally caraway seeds. They are commonly found in England and originated in the town of Bath. The creator of the popular roll was Dr. W. Oliver Bath in the mid-1800's when the town was a popular vacation spa.

Making It With A Twist

Pretzels are made from a stiff, thin, yeast-raised dough which is baked so that the pretzel will have a hard surface. Once the pretzel dough is shaped, it is sprayed with a 1% solution of lye (sodium hydroxide) or sodium carbonate that is heated to 200° F. It is this process of spraying and heat that causes the surface starch to become gelatinized. The surface is then lightly salted or left plain and baked in a high heat oven for 4 to 5 minutes. The gelatinized starch will harden and leave a shiny surface. The lye creates an alkaline condition on the surface which causes the intense brown color. The lye reacts with carbon dioxide while it is cooking to form a harmless carbonate substance. The final cooking stage takes about 25 minutes and dries the pretzel out; less cooking time will produce a soft pretzel.

Cookie Facts

Cookies are made from doughs that are high in sugar and fats and lower in water content than other types of doughs. Because of this, there is a shortage of available water for starch granules and gluten protein. The sugar will draw moisture from the mixture more than other ingredients and between this and the fact that a cookie dough mixture is not mixed the same as other doughs, the gluten development is minimized. If you desire a cookie with a cake-texture, this can be achieved by mixing the shortening, eggs, sugar, and liquid together, then gently folding in the flour and leavening agent. To prepare a more dense cookie, just mix all the ingredients together very slowly. Because of the way cookies are mixed and the limited use of liquid, the starch is able to gelatinize only slightly.

What Happens When You Use Margarine In Cookies?

When margarine is used to make cookies, the firmness of the dough will depend on the type of margarine you use. One of the most important things to remember when choosing margarine for cookies is that the package must say "margarine," not "spread." If the margarine is made from 100% corn oil, it will make the dough softer. When using margarine you will need to adjust the "chilling time" and you may have to place the dough in the freezer instead of the refrigerator. If you're making "cutout" cookies, the chilling time should be at least 5 hours in the refrigerator. Bar and drop cookie doughs do not have to be chilled.

You've Got To Love A Grunt

This "grunt" was first introduced in the late 1700's in America and is a type of cobbler. It was made with berries or other fruit and topped with a biscuit pastry dough, then steamed in a kettle with a lid while hanging over an open fire. Water was added to the fruit and as it steamed sugar was added to the grunt, forming a syrup on top of the fruit. The name originated in Massachusetts and the "grunt'" comes from the sound that the fruit makes as it releases the steam. Grunts are still served in the New England states, with ice cream on the side.

Sources for Baking Equipment

Albert Uster Imports, Inc.
9211 Gaither Rd.
Gaithersburg, MD 20877
(800) 231-8154

Dean & DeLuca
560 Broadway
New York, NY 10010
(800) 221-7714

The Kitchen Witch Gourmet Shop
127 N. El Camino Real Ste. D
Encinitas, CA 92024
(619) 942-3228

Williams-Sonoma
P.O. Box 7456
San Francisco, CA 94120
(800) 541-2233

C.A. Paradis, Inc.
1314 Bank St.
Ottawa, Ontario, K1S 3Y4
Canada
(613) 731-2866

Why Different Baking Times For Different Baked Goods?

Baked goods should always be baked at high temperatures such as 425° to 450° F. This will allow the expanding gasses to sufficiently increase the dough's volume before the protein has a chance to coagulate, which sets the structure for the food. Small biscuits, because of their size, can easily be baked at the above temperatures without a problem. However, a lower temperature is preferred for breads (about 400° F.) since the higher temperature would probably burn the crust before the insides were baked. If you are baking a bread with a high sugar content, you need a lower temperature of about 325° - 375° F. since sugar will caramelize at a very high temperature and cause the crust to turn black.

What Is The Fastest-Growing Baked Good Product?

The baking industry today is gearing up for tortillas and tortilla chips. Americans are consuming more tortillas than they are bagels, English muffins, and pitas combined. In 1996 we consumed over 60 billion tortillas (not including tortilla chip sales) totalling over $2 billion in sales, according to the Tortilla Industry Association. This works out to 225 tortillas per person annually.

How Old Is the Bagel?

The name bagel comes from the German word "beugel" meaning a round loaf of bread. The first mention of the bagel was in 1610 in Krakow, Poland, where it was mentioned in a piece of literature that it would be given to women in childbirth. The earliest picture of a bagel was in 1683 by a Jewish baker in Vienna, Austria.

Who Makes the Best Sour Dough Bread in America?

Baldwin Hills Bakery in Phillipston, Massachusetts, owned by Hy Lerner, makes the finest 100%, all natural, sourdough bread. Studying in Europe, he learned a method of fermenting wheat to form a special sour dough starter. He uses a wood-fired oven that holds 2,000 loaves and the water comes from a 500-foot deep artesian well. All the ingredients used are organically grown, even the sesame seeds and raisins. He imports his sea salt from France. The finest spring wheat is purchased from the Little Bear Trading Company in Winona, Minnesota. He does not use sweeteners; however, the bread has a light, sweet flavor. To order the bread call (508) 249-4691.

What Is A One-Bowl Cake?

It is a layer cake which is made by mixing the batter in one bowl. When this is done, you omit the step of creaming the shortening or butter with the sugar. Using the one-bowl method, you add the shortening, liquid, and the flavorings to the dry ingredients, and beat. Then add the eggs and beat the batter again.

Where Can You Find The World's Best Macaroons?

The best macaroons are made by White Oak Farms and are called the St. Julien Macaroons. They are named after a 14th-century mystic, St. Julien. The macaroons are fat-free, low in calories and are made French-style with crushed almonds, egg whites, sugar, and flavorings. They need to be kept cold due to the lack of preservatives. To order the macaroons, call (508) 653-5953.

What Is A Moon Pie?

A Moon Pie is simply marshmallow between two vanilla cookies or graham crackers. Because of its round shape, people thought it resembled the moon. It was originally called the Lookout Marshmallow and was know as the largest 5¢ snack cake on the market. Later the name was changed to the Lookout Moon Pie. It was a regional bakery novelty that had its origins in Chattanooga, Tennessee, at the Chattanooga Bakery. It was only sold in the southern United States. The snack cake caught on nationally and has sold over 2 billion since its creation in 1917. The Moon Pie is still manufactured by the Chattanooga Bakery on King Street. The bakery produces 300,000 Moon Pies every day. The company does no advertising due to its loyal following over the years.

Does Your Pastry Have Puffy Ends?

Puff pastry dough is made from flour, butter, and water. A small amount of butter is placed between the layers of dough before it is folded several times, which may produce as many as 700 layers. When the dough is cut, be sure to only slice the dough with a very sharp knife and cut straight down. Never pull the knife through the dough or cut the dough at an angle. If you do, it will cause the ends to puff up unevenly as the pastry bakes.

America's Greatest Fruitcake

The best fruitcake in the United States is made by the Gethsemani Monks at their farm in central Kentucky. The fruitcake is a dark cake, made with cherries, raisins, dates, pineapple, and high-quality nuts. Almost all ingredients are grown in their own gardens and if you expect to purchase the fruitcake for Christmas you need to order early at (502) 549-3117.

What Different Liquids Create Different-Textured Breads?

Liquids tend to impart their own significant characteristics to breads. Water, for instance, will cause the top of the bread to be more crisp, and significantly intensifies the flavor of the wheat. Water that remains after potatoes are boiled (potato water) will add a unique flavor and make the crust smooth as well as causing the bread to rise faster due to the higher starch content. Any liquid dairy product will change the color of the bread to a richer, creamy color and leave the bread with a finer texture and a softer, brown crust. Eggs are capable of changing the crust so that it will have a moister texture.

Any liquid sweetener used (such as molasses, maple syrup, or honey) will make the crust dark brown and keep it moist. A vegetable or meat broth will give the bread a special flavor and provide you with a lighter, crisper crust. Alcohol of any type will give the bread a smooth crust with a flavor that may be similar to the alcohol used, especially beer. Coffee and tea are commonly used to provide a darker, richer color and a crisper crust.

What Is The Baker's Secret To Grease And Flour?

Recipes for a variety of foods may call for you to "grease and flour" the pan before adding any ingredients. The standard method is to grease the pan with an oil and then spinkle flour in and tap the pan or move it around to allow the flour to distribute as evenly as possible. However, sticking still may occur unless you place a piece of waxed paper on top of the grease, then grease the waxed paper and then flour. One of the professional chef's secrets is to use what is known as the "baker's magic" method, which is to prepare a mixture of ½ cup of room temperature vegetable shortening, ½ cup of vegetable oil, and ½ cup of all-purpose flour. Blend the mixture well and use it to grease your pans. If stored in an airtight container, it will keep for up to 6 months in the refrigerator.

CHAPTER 2
FOOD PREPARATION AND COOKING

Digital Cooking?

We are all aware that if you place your hand into a pot of boiling water at 212° F. you will definitely get burned. However, when you place your hand into a 325° F. oven all you feel is the intense heat and do not get burned. The reason for this is that air neither transfers nor retains heat as well as water.

The Dangers Of Fats In The Fire

Barbecuing is one of our summer pastimes and charcoal is the fuel of choice. Americans spend over $400 million each year on charcoal briquettes. When fat drips down on these briquettes, a chemical reaction takes place and the smoke that rises contains a chemical called a benzopyrene (a carcinogen). The black coating on your meats may contain enough of this carcinogen to equal the risk of smoking 15 cigarettes. It would be best to scrape the black material off or use artificial briquettes or a gas grill.

The Chemistry Of Cooking

When you use heat to cook food, basically you are increasing the speed of the molecules of that food. The faster they move, the more they collide, the more heat is generated, and the hotter the food gets. This changes the texture, flavor, and even the color of the food. For every 20° F. you raise the temperature over the normal cooking temperature, you will actually increase the molecular activity by 100%, not 20%.

Cake Pans Must Rise To The Occasion

Cake pans are a very important part of making a cake. Some factors will influence the outcome more than others. The thickness of the pan, for example, is not very important. However, the finish of the pan and its volume relative to the size of the cake are very important. If a cake is heated faster, the gas cells will expand faster and the batter will set better. The perfect pan for the job should be the actual size of the finished product. If the sides of the pan are too high, the unused area can shield the batter from needed radiant energy, slowing the rate at which the batter is heated and making the cake drier. This is also the cause of humps in the cake. Never use a baking pan with a bright surface, since it will reflect radiant heat and transmit the heat too slowly, thereby slowing the baking process.

Dangerous Butcher Blocks

Any cutting surface has the potential of harboring dangerous bacteria. Hot pots are often placed on cutting boards and especially butcher-block surfaces. When this occurs, some of the heat is transferred to the surface and into the board where bacteria may be lurking. Bacteria like the heat and it may activate them for a longer period of time or provide a place for them to survive as you are preparing foods.

Moist Heat Or Dry Heat?

Foods such as meat that contain a large percentage of connective tissue, or foods that have a tough fibrous structure like that found in certain vegetables, should be cooked using moist heat. Since for the most part these foods are not naturally tender, they will be tenderized by the use of the moist heat. There are, of course, exceptions to the rule, one of which is if the meat is heavily marbled or if frequent basting is done.

Quick, Shut The Door

If anyone has ever driven you crazy because you opened the oven door when something was cooking, this is your chance to tell them that when the door is opened or left ajar for a few minutes it only takes 40 to 50 seconds for the temperature to return to the pre-set temperature. It is not really a big deal and will not affect the food.

Who Barbecues, Mom or Dad?

When it comes to slaving over the hot barbecue in the back yard, it's dad who gets the chore 60% of the time. However, it's mom who chooses what is to be barbecued almost 100% of the time. The most common items to barbecue are hamburgers, chicken, hot dogs, and corn on the cob.

Put A Lid On It

When you are boiling water, place a lid on the pot and the water will come to a boil in a shorter period of time. However, this is only true after the water reaches 150° F. Before this point it doesn't matter if the pot has the lid on it or not. The water will not produce enough steam until it hits the 150° level and at that level it is best to trap the steam in the pot. To raise 1 gallon of water from 60° to 212° F. (boiling) on a gas range top takes 23 minutes with the lid on. Without the lid it takes about 35 minutes.

Cooking In A Recreational Vehicle: It May Be A Hazard

In 1995, over 250 Americans were killed and thousands have become ill from carbon monoxide (CO_2) poisoning while cooking and using heaters on motor homes. The odorless gas is produced from faulty heating and cooking units. Every motor home should be equipped with a CO_2 detector which sounds an alarm like a smoke detector and costs $40 to $80.

The Secret of World-Class Gravy

One of the most frequent problems with gravy is that the cook is tempted to use too much flour to thicken the gravy. When this is done it tends to detract from the gravy's flavor, which is dependent on the small amount of drippings. Chefs rarely use flour and usually deglaze the roasting pan with water to trap the drippings that have adhered to the bottom of the pan, add a small amount of butter and reduce the mixture over heat, stirring frequently, until it is thick. Try not to prepare gravy too thick since it will thicken as it cools, and may be relatively solid by the time it is poured.

Are There Different Temperatures of Boiling?

When we see water bubbling either lightly or more rapidly, the temperature will always be the same, 212° F. (100° C.) There is the possibility of a difference at times but for the most part it remains constant. The only difference in the rapidly boiling water is that the food may cook somewhat faster due to the increased activity of the heat-carrying molecules. The food will cook more evenly and food will retain more nutrients if the water is not rapidly boiling. Hard water, because of its high mineral content, will boil 1° to 2° F. above soft water.

Never Salt Foods To Be Fried

Salt tends to draw moisture from foods. If a food is salted before it is placed in the fryer, it will draw moisture to the surface and cause spattering in the hot oil.

Never Re-Use Frying Oil

When oil is used for frying, the temperature is raised to such a high level that a percentage of the oil is broken down (begins smoking) and decomposes into trans-fatty acid oil as well as turning a percentage of the polyunsaturated oil into a saturated oil. Trans-fatty acids, though edible, tend to cause an increase in free radicals (abnormal cells) in the body, which may raise the bad cholesterol levels and lower the good cholesterol levels. It's best to use new oil every time you fry.

Smoke, Flash, And Fire Points Of Oils

The smoke point of an oil is the point at which the oil starts deteriorating. All oils have different smoke points, canola oil having one of the highest and therefore one of the best for frying. Flavor would be another determining factor in using an oil with a lower smoke point. The smoke point is the point at which the oil is starting to convert a percentage of the oil into trans-fatty acids. The flash point is the point the oil starts to show a small amount of flame emanating from the surface of the oil; this usually occurs at about 600° F. and should tell you that the oil has reached a dangerous level. The fire point is about 700° F. and this is the point where you should have a fire extinguisher. Do not try to use water on a grease fire. The fire needs to be smothered to extinguish it.

Smoke Points of Fats

FAT	SMOKE POINT
Canola Oil	525° F.
Safflower Oil	510° F.
Soybean Oil	495° F.

FAT	SMOKE POINT
Corn Oil	475° F.
Peanut Oil	440° F.
Sesame Oil	420° F.
Animal Lard	400° F.
Vegetable shortening	375° F.
Unclarified Butter	250° F.

Just How Hot Is Hot?

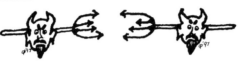

Your gas range at home will burn at 300° F. It is easily controlled heat and therefore the heat of choice for almost all chefs. Electric ranges will heat up to only 200° F. and small temperature changes are more difficult to control. Depending on the dish this can become a problem, especially with boil-overs. Frying temperatures need to be kept within a range so as not to cause a deterioration of the oil to a point when it will start smoking and break down. Therefore you need to know the smoke point of the type of oil you wish to use and use a thermometer to check the temperature at frequent intervals if you wish to use the upper ranges of the fat.

Cooking Stuffed Turkey

The best temperature for cooking turkey is 325° F. since a lower temperature will allow bacteria in the stuffing to multiply for too long a period. Higher temperatures may shorten the cooking time too much and prevent the stuffing from cooking thoroughly. Slow overnight cooking with the dressing in the bird has been the cause of numerous cases of food poisoning.

Never Crowd When Deep-Frying

Adding food to hot oil tends to lower the temperature of the oil. Foods will absorb too much oil when this occurs unless the oil is returned to the normal frying temperature within a very short period of time.To reduce the effects of a lower frying temperature, either of two methods is recommended. First, don't add too much food to the oil at one time. It not only lowers the temperature but causes overcrowding and prevents all the food from frying evenly. Second, start the temperature about 15° F. above the recommended frying temperature so that when you do add the cold food it will still be approximately the desired temperature. Whenever possible, food should be left out for a short period before placing it into the fryer; the closer to room temperature the food is, the higher the oil temperature after the food is added. If the food is too cold, the oil may drop down to the greasy range of about 300°-325° F. and may never get to the proper temperature.

Candy-Making Secret

Sugar crystallization is one of the more frequent problems when making candy. This usually occurs when the slightest grain of sugar that may be trapped on the side of the pan falls down into the syrup mixture. This can easily be prevented by heating the sugar over low heat; do not stir until the sugar is completely dissolved. To dissolve any sugar crystals that are still clinging to the sides of the pan, tightly place the lid on the pan and continue cooking the syrup for 3-4 minutes. The steam that is generated will melt the clinging sugar grains.

Hot Spot, Cold Spot

Your cooking pans should be made of a material that will dissipate the heat evenly throughout the bottom of the pan so that the food will cook evenly. Unfortunately, many pans do not have this ability and develop cold spots. To check your pan, place a thin layer of about 4-5 tablespoons of sugar that has been mixed with 2 tablespoons of water on the bottom of your pan and spread it out as evenly as you can. The sugar over the hot spots will caramelize and turn brown, forming a pattern of the hot spots. Hopefully, you will not have a pattern and all the sugar will caramelize at about the same time. If you do have a problem, use a heat diffuser under the pan or try the same test using a lower heat setting.

Testing Your Metal

There are a number of materials that are used to produce pots and pans, many of which do not really do the job adequately. Certain metals are still the best all-around cookware. Remember: the thicker the gauge of the metal, the more uniformly it tends to distribute the heat. The finish on the metal will also affect the efficiency of the cookware.

- Copper: One of the worst types of cookware is the thin, stamped, stainless steel pots with a thin copper-coated bottom. The copper coating is approximately $\frac{1}{50}$ of an inch in thickness and too thin to distribute the heat efficiently and uniformly.

  The "real" copper cookware provides excellent, even heat distribution on the bottom as well as the sides of the pan. The copper, however, needs to be kept clean and if black carbon deposits form to any degree it will affect the heat distribution significantly. These pots are usually lined with tin, which must be replaced if it wears out; otherwise, excess copper may leach into the food, causing a health risk. Foods that are high in acid will increase the release of copper. The metal ions in copper will also react with vitamin C and reduce the amount available.

- Aluminum: Aluminum cookware stains very easily, especially if you are using hard water to cook with. Certain foods, such as potatoes, will also cause the pans to stain easily. If you cook a high-acid-content food, such as tomatoes, onions, or wine, or if lemon juice is used in aluminum, it will probably remove some of the stain. However, if the pan is stained when the acidic foods are cooked it may transfer the stain to the food, possibly turning your foods a brownish color.

  Aluminum pans also tend to warp if they are subjected to rapid temperature changes, especially if they are made of a thin-gauge aluminum. If they are made of a thick gauge, they will have excellent heat-flow efficiency and will not rust, making the thick gauge type excellent cookware.

- Cast Iron/Carbon Steel: These are both non-stainless steel, iron-based metals that have a somewhat porous, jagged surface. These pots need to be "seasoned." To accomplish this you need to rub the cooking surfaces with canola oil and heat it at 300° F. for about 40-50 minutes in the oven, then allow it to cool to room temperature before using. The oil has the ability to fill and seal the pores and even provides a somewhat non-stick surface. Another factor is that when the oil is in the pores, water cannot enter and possibly cause rust.

- These pots should be washed daily using a mild soap and dried immediately. Never use salt to clean the pot, since this may cause rusting. If a cleanser is needed, be sure it is a mild one. Iron pots tend to release metal ions that react with vitamin C and reduce its potency.

- Teflon and Silverstone: These non-stick surfaces are the result of a chemically inert fluorocarbon plastic material being baked on the surface of the cookware or other type of cooking utensil. Silverstone is the highest quality of these non-stick items. The food is actually cooked on jagged peaks that protrude from the bottom. This prevents the food from sticking to a smooth surface. The surface is commercially "seasoned," producing the final slick surface.

The major contribution of the non-stick surfaces is that you can cook without the use of fats, which reduces the caloric intake of total dietary fat. The less expensive non-stick cookware usually has a very thin coating and will not last very long with everyday use. With heavy use and continual cleaning, the coating will eventually wear thin on any coated piece of cookware or utensil.

- Multi-Ply Pans: The bottoms of these pans usually have 3 layers. They are constructed with a layer of aluminum between two layers of stainless steel. Stainless steel does not have the hot-spot problem and the heat will be more evenly diffused by the aluminum. You will also not have to worry about the aluminum discoloring.

- Enamel Cookware: While the enamel does resist corrosion, it is still a metal coated with a thin layer of enamel. The coating is produced by fusing powdered glass into the metal surface, which is in most cases cast iron. The cookware can chip easily if hit against another object and can even shatter if moved from a very hot range into cold water.

- Glass Cookware: Rapid temperature changes may cause the glass to crack or break in many brands. Glass has a very low "heat-flow" efficiency rating and when boiling water is pouring into the glass cookware, the actual heat that is transferred from the boiling water to the bottom of the cookware will travel slowly back to the top of the pot. Because of this, the bottom of the pot will swell and the top of the pot does not expand, creating a structural type of stress. A crack is very possible. Corning ware and Pyrex, in that order, would be the only choices for glass cookware, since both will resist most stresses.

Cruciferous Cooking

When you cook a cruciferous vegetable such as cauliflower, never use an

aluminum or iron pot. The sulfur compounds will react with the aluminum to turn the cauliflower yellow. If cooked in an iron pot, the cauliflower will turn brown or a bluish-green.

The Pressure of Pressure Cooking

Pressure cooking is more desirable for people who live at higher altitudes, since water boils at 203° F. at 5,000-foot elevations instead of the standard 212° F. at or near sea level. Normally, a food would take longer to cook at the higher elevations. A pressure cooker allows the water to reach a temperature of 250° F. by increasing the atmospheric pressure in the pot and using the steam to cook the food faster. Steam conducts heat better than air and forces the heat into the food.

Cooking In A Brown Bag? Don't Even Think Of It

When grandma cooked her turkey in a brown bag years ago, the quality of the brown bag was totally different from the ones we get today from the supermarket. The majority of the brown bags of today are produced from recycled paper using a number of harmful chemicals. When heated, these chemicals may be released into the foods and may produce free radicals.

Cooking With Alcohol

The boiling point of alcohol is 175° F., much lower than the boiling point for water of 212° F. When alcohol is added to a recipe it will lower the boiling point until it evaporates. For example, if you decide to change your recipe by adding some wine to replace some of the water, you will need to increase your cooking time by about 10%.

Salting Your Cooking Water

If you add 1 teaspoon of salt to your cooking water, it will raise the temperature 1-2° F. Sugar and many other ingredients will also raise the temperature of the water. Unless the recipe calls for this increase, it is best not to add salt because salt has the tendency to cause toughness in many foods.

Boiling Point vs. Altitude

As the altitude increases, the atmospheric pressure decreases, placing less pressure on water that is trying to boil. When this occurs, it is easier for the water to boil and the water molecules are able to be released more easily. Water will boil at a lower temperature at the 5,000-foot elevation. For every additional 1,000 feet, water will boil at approximately 2° F. less than at sea level.

ALTITUDE (feet)	FAHRENHEIT	CELSIUS
0	212	10
1,000	210	99
2,000	208	98
3,000	207	97

ALTITUDE (feet)	FAHRENHEIT	CELSIUS
4,000	205	96
5,000	203	95
10,000	194	90

High-Altitude Baking

When you are baking at an altitude of over 3,500, feet it will be necessary to increase your oven temperature 25° F. for each additional 1,500 feet. You should also add 1 tablespoon of flour to your recipe for every 1,500 feet over the 3,500 elevation. The leavening agent also needs to be adjusted. If 1 teaspoon is called for at sea level, you will need to reduce the leavening agent by ⅓ teaspoon for every 1,500 feet of elevation up to 6,500 feet.

How A Convection Oven Works

The standard oven and the convection oven work very similar to each other. The notable difference in the convection oven is that it has a fan that increases the distribution of the heat molecules, providing heat to all areas faster and more evenly. Because of the fan and the efficiency of the heat circulation, a lower temperature is usually required. This saves energy. Roasts, especially, do well in a convection oven. Because of the lower heat, the meat tends to be juicier.

Making The Breading Stay Put

Preventing the breading from falling off foods can sometimes create a real headache unless you follow a few simple rules. First, make sure that the food that is to be breaded is very dry, and use room temperature eggs. Over-beating the eggs will also cause a problem. Second, after you apply the breading place the food into the refrigerator for 1 hour before allowing the food to remain out for 20 minutes before frying. Homemade bread crumbs are the best. Because of their uneven texture they tend to hold better.

Why Pans Warp

Metal pans have a higher heat-flow efficiency rating than other materials as well as having a tougher internal structure. Metal pans warp due to structural stress caused by sudden changes in temperature. The thinner the metal pan, the more easily it will warp. The thicker the pan, the less likely it is to warp.

How Does Heat Cook Food?

There are 3 main methods of transferring heat to food: radiation, convection, and conduction. Basically, you are transferring heat from a hot object to a cold one. Radiant heat is in the form of electromagnetic waves, such as those from a toaster to the toast. It does not require any assistance from air and water. The energy travels at 186,000 miles per second, the speed of light. Convection cooking employs circulating molecules which are propelled by either gas or liquid. The heat is placed at the bottom of the food or liquid and, as the heat rises, it allows the colder food or liquid to fall toward the heat. The air or water currents provide the convection cooking as a vehicle for the heat. Conduction cooking utilizes an oven where the hotter molecules pass along the heat from the surface to the interior of the food. When an aluminum spike is inserted in a potato, the heat is allowed to pass more easily to the inside and heat the food from both the inside and the outside at the same time.

Never Use Plastic Wrap In A Microwave

When foods become hot, chemicals from plastic wrap may be released and migrate into the food. The wrap may also stick to the food, especially fatty or sugary foods. Waxed paper, paper towels, or a plate work well.

Solving Problems That May Occur In Sauce Bearnaise

Sauce Bearnaise is one of the most popular sauces in United States restaurants. It is an emulsion sauce that combines oil and water. It was developed in France in the 1830's and goes well with meats and fish dishes. When preparing the sauce, the most frequent problem is that of over-heating. One of two problems may occur. The first is that if the egg proteins are overheated they tend to coagulate, forming small curds in a liquid that is supposed to be creamy. The second problem is that over-heating may cause a breakdown of the emulsion, which causes it to separate. To prevent the protein from coagulating, try placing a small amount of vinegar in the sauce to lower the pH.

Why Chefs Leave The Broiler Door Ajar

When the door is left ajar, it will actually improve the broiling process and reduce the roasting process. When the door is left ajar, the pan and the air inside the broiler do not become as hot as they normally would. This reduces the effects of conduction-heat cooking. It still allows the same heat intensity to occur and improves the flavor and imparts a more crusty texture to meats.

Why Your Pot Lid May Stick

When you are cooking a food, the air space that is inside the pot increases in pressure and raises the lid very slightly. This allows the heated air (gas) to escape. When the heat is turned off, however, the pressure and temperature are decreased; water molecules sealing around the rim of the lid pull the lid tightly shut. The longer the lid is left on, the tighter the seal. If this occurs, never place the pot in cold water. Just place the pot on moderate heat for a minute or so to return the pressure to a more equal level with the outside.

Should You Zap It Or Gas It?

There is no contest here. It is definitely gas that wins. Because you are able to change the temperature quickly, as well as have instant heat control, it is preferred by almost all chefs. Boil-overs are more easily controlled than with electric in all instances. The range, however, is a different story. Electric ovens will reach the desired temperature more rapidly and hold it more evenly with excellent accuracy.

Microwave Magic?

A microwave oven actually works by emitting high-frequency electromagnetic waves from a tube called a "magnetron." This type of radiation is scattered throughout the inside of the oven by a "stirrer." The "stirrer" is a fan-like reflector which causes the waves to penetrate the food, reversing the polarity of the water molecules billions of times per second, causing them to bombard each other and creating the friction that heats the food.

Do I or Don't I Microwave It?

Microwave cooking is less expensive than most other methods of cooking; however, it is desirable only for certain types of foods. If you are baking a dish, it will rise higher in a microwave oven; however, meats do not seem to have the desired texture and seem a bit mushy. When it comes to placing something frozen in the microwave, it will take longer to cook since it is difficult to agitate the water molecules when they are frozen.

Can't Top A Restaurant Wok

The big difference is in the more intense heat that is developed in a professional wok. Your home gas range is only capable of producing less than 10,000 BTU's. The BTU's produced in a professional wok are almost twice that high due to a larger gas feeder line and larger burner opening diameters. Also, the specially-built wok has a series of burners, not just one. The higher heat tends to seal the juices and flavors in. Since less juice remains in the wok, the juices that are there stick to the vegetables more readily. Beware of special woks built with flat bottoms for electric ranges. The flat bottoms make it very difficult to stir and cook the vegetables properly.

Self-Cleaning Ovens: It's Hotter Than Hades

Electric ovens are capable of much higher temperatures than gas ovens. Since the electric ovens go as high as 1000° F. during the self-cleaning phase, it literally disintegrates any food or grease particles and turns them into dust that only needs to be wiped away.

As Igor Would Say, Wok This Way

Cooking in a wok originated in China over 2,000 years ago during the Han Dynasty. It was prompted by the lack of cooking oil. It cooked the food fast and was an energy saver. There are a few things that every cook should be aware of when stir-frying foods:
- Before cooking beef, pork, or chicken, partially freeze the meat for about 1 hour so that it will be easy to slice thin, even-size pieces.

- Place the meat in a marinade for great flavor for a few minutes while you are preparing the vegetables. Adding a small amount of cornstarch to the marinade will protect the meat from the high heat and make it more tender and juicy.

- Vegetables should be cut into uniform bite-size pieces to insure that they will cook evenly. If vegetables are preferred in different sizes, then they will have to be added at different times, which makes the cooking more difficult.

- Oil should be used very sparingly. Approximately 1 tablespoon is all that is needed for 4 servings, which is just enough to place a thin coating on the bottom of the wok.

- For the best results, never stir-fry more than ½ pound at a time.

Woks: A Good Source of Iron?

Most woks are made from steel which is 98% iron. A study performed at Texas Tech University found that if you stir-fry in a steel wok it will increase the iron content in foods by as much as 200-500%. The amount of iron in a 3½ ounce portion of vegetables may rise from 0.4 to 3.5 mg when cooked in a wok. If the wok is made of stainless steel, it will only release an insignificant amount of iron.

Quick Quiche Me

Quiches should be served right from the oven to the table and never allowed to cool. Quiches are usually made with onions and mushrooms, both of which have a high water content. Because of this the quiche will lose a large amount of moisture as it cools. This causes the crust to become soggy and weepy.

When Was The Microwave Oven Invented?

In 1946 Dr. Percy Spencer, an engineer at Raytheon Laboratories, was working with a magnetron tube which produces microwaves. He had a candy bar in his pocket which he went to eat and found that it had melted though there was no heat source for that to occur. The only thing he could think of that would cause this to occur was the magnetron tube he was working with. He then tried placing a small amount of popcorn near the tube and the popcorn popped in a few seconds. He then tried focusing the beam through a box at an egg, which exploded on one of his associates, much to the surprise of both. The result was the first microwave oven, called the Amana Radar Range. It was introduced in 1977. The word "radar" was used since the actual beam was invented in England and used as microwave radar to detect Hitler's planes in 1940.

Who Invented The Toaster?

The first people to toast bread were the Egyptians in 2500 B.C., using long-handled forks. The inventor of the toaster as we know it today was Charles Strite, who received a patent for the toaster in 1919. However, the toaster didn't really work as well as he would have liked and it took him a few more years after poor field tests to produce the first pop-up toaster in 1926, with the brand name of Toastmaster. The toaster had a darkness timer and sales went wild. Congress was so impressed, it declared March 1927 as National Toaster Month.

Crock Pot a.k.a. Slow-Cooker

The Crock Pot was invented in 1971 by Rival. Many consumers still question whether the pot is safe or a breeding ground for bacteria, since it is used for all-day cooking at a low temperature. The fact is that most slow cookers have settings that range from 170°-280° F. Bacteria die at 140° F., which is below the lowest possible temperature that can be used. However, if the lid is left off it may cause a problem with food not being fully cooked and harboring bacteria that are still alive. To minimize the risk of food poisoning, these rules should be followed:

- All foods should be at refrigerator temperature. No frozen or partially thawed foods.

- Cook only cut-up pieces of meat, not whole roasts or fowl, to allow the heat to penetrate fully.

- Make sure that the cooker is at least ½ to ⅔ full or the food will not absorb enough heat to kill any bacteria.

- The food must be covered with liquid to generate sufficient steam.

- The original lid should always be used and should be tight-fitting.

- When possible, allow the cooker to cook on the high setting for the first hour. It can then be reduced.

- Never use the cooker to re-heat leftovers. A number of bacteria are usually found on leftovers and it takes a high heat to kill them.

- Always follow the manufacturer's directions for temperature settings.

The Cutting Edge

One of the most important utensils in a kitchen is your knife. There are a number of different materials used in knife blades, many of which are relatively new and need to be evaluated as to which will suit you best. Make sure the handle is secured with at least 3 rivets. It should feel comfortable and you should avoid all plastic grips. When cutting foods, the best surface would be a soft wooden cutting board. Hardwoods and plastic boards tend to dull the blade faster and also reduce the life of the knife.

Carbon Steel: This is by far the best. It takes the sharpest edge and is the preferred knife for the serious chef. However, if the blade is not constantly kept dry it will rust. Acids in foods may also take their toll and turn the blade black, which can be imparted back to foods.

Superstainless Steel: This not one of the better quality blades. Once it dulls and loses its original well-honed sharpness it is almost impossible to restore to a decent level of sharpness. It does resist rust and staining.

Stainless Steel: Has the ability to resist rust and the acid effects from foods. It will take a sharper edge than the superstainless steel, but will dull and does not really take a very sharp edge.

High-Carbon Stainless Steel: This is the most expensive of the four types mentioned here and will not rust or stain. It does not have to be washed and dried continually when in use. It can be sharpened to a sharper edge than either of the other stainless steel knives.

How Do You Sharpen A Knife?

The one method that should never be used on a good kitchen knife is that of allowing a coarse grinding wheel to be used. If you do this, the blade will only last a few years and will become thinner and thinner. Rotating steel disks are not recommended, either. The preferred method is the "butcher's steel." This is just a rough-surfaced, hard metal rod with a protective handle. If the butcher's steel is used frequently it will keep the edge on the knife. If you have a problem keeping the edge, it may mean that you are not using the sharpener as frequently as you should and you may have to use a "whetstone" to return the edge. The whetstone is made of silicon carbide (carborundum).

What Is The Proper Way To Store A Knife?

One of the best ways to store a quality knife is to keep it in a wooden counter-top knife holder that was made for the knife. However, not all wooden holders are quality ones and the holder should not have a hard surface for the blade to lie on. The higher quality holders will have a protective liner that allows the edge of the blade to rest free. When a knife is stored in a drawer with other utensils it will end up with small nicks on the blade. This will ruin a high quality knife.

What Should I Look For When Buying A Knife?

Purchasing a knife is an investment that you need to make. It is a kitchen tool that is indispensable and unless you buy a quality knife you will not have it very long and will not be very satisfied with the results. Purchase either carbon-steel or high-carbon steel knives. The manufacturer should be a recognized name such as Trident, Wusthof, or Heckles. Be sure that the blade and the handle are one piece and that the handle is not attached to the blade. If the knife has a plastic hilt, it is not recommended.

Boiled Foods Take Longer To Cook On Bad-Weather Days

When the weather is bad and stormy, the atmospheric pressure goes down. The lower the pressure gets, the lower the boiling temperature of water gets. The temperature decrease is usually about 1°-2° and it will take a little longer to cook boiled foods.

Why Is It Safe To Place My Hand In The Oven Without Getting Burned?

The skin is in a constant state of moisture evaporation which cools it. When you place your hand into an oven you have a short period of time before the heat starts to affect your skin, especially if you wear a protective glove. On the other hand, when you place your hand into a pot of boiling water, you will be burnt almost instantly since the small amount of cooling effect is lost immediately.

How to Check Your Oven Temperature Without a Thermometer

Place about 1 tablespoon of flour on the bottom of a cookie sheet and place it into a preheated oven for about 5 minutes. When the flour turns a light tan the temperature is between 250° and 325° F. If the flour turns a golden brown, the oven is between 325° and 400° F. When it turns a dark brown the temperature is 400° to 450° F. When it is almost a black color, the oven will be 450° to 525° F.

CHAPTER 3
FRUITS AND VEGETABLES

Fruits and Vegetables

Fruits and vegetables are the easiest targets for loss of nutrients due to their soft skins. The skins are easily damaged and their meat is easily damaged by the air, light, or heat. When cooking or preparing produce for a meal, it is best to leave the produce in pieces as large as possible until you are ready to serve it. Exposing the surface of any fruit or vegetable will cause nutrients to be lost immediately and the longer the surfaces are exposed, the higher the losses. In some fruits the vitamin C can be totally lost in less than 1 hour of exposure.

Wax Coatings On Fruits and Vegetables

 A thin coating of wax helps seal the moisture in and extends the storage times. Retaining more moisture reduces the weight loss, providing a higher profit. A secondary benefit to the industry is that it gives the produce a sheen which is eye-catching. The wax coating is safe to eat, but may give the produce an off-flavor. One of the drawbacks is that it does make it more difficult to clean the produce, especially if pesticide residues remain under the wax coating.

How Green I Am

Have you ever heard someone say that if you leave the pit in the guacamole it will not turn black? I'm sure you have, and you have probably tried it to no avail unless you covered the entire dish tightly with plastic wrap. The plastic wrap, not the pit, did the trick, because it would not allow oxygen to oxidize the guacamole, which turns it black. Guacamole will oxidize on the surface in about 60-90 minutes if left out uncovered. The area under the pit was not exposed to the air, which is why it never turned black. The air is not our friend when it comes to exposed foods. Another method that works is to spread a thin layer of mayonnaise on the top of the guacamole dip.

Throw The Lettuce In The Washing Machine

Greens need to be thoroughly washed before they are used in a salad and they are not always as dry as they should be if you are in a hurry to prepare the salad. When this happens, just put the greens in a clean pillowcase and place them in the washing machine on the fast spin cycle for just 2 minutes.

What Makes Popcorn Pop?

When the popcorn kernel is heated, the moisture inside turns to steam. As the pressure builds, it has to vent and bursts the kernel. The explosion forms the fluffy white starch. Normal corn will not explode because it does not have as high a moisture content as special popcorn. When the popcorn is popped, it is best to open the bag or remove the lid as soon as possible. This prevents the popcorn from absorbing the steam and becoming soggy. Popcorn should always be stored in a well sealed container so that it will retain as much of its moisture as possible.

Fresh Corn: The Best Corn

If you want to taste the sweetest corn ever, then it needs to be as fresh as possible, no more than 1-2 days at the most from the farm to you. The sugar in corn will start converting to starch as soon as the corn is picked. This reduces its sweetness. When you heat the corn, it also speeds up the sugar conversion. Refrigeration will slow the process down. Salt should never be placed in the water when cooking corn, as it will toughen the kernels, since table salt contains traces of calcium. Salt in the water will also toughen almost all types of legumes.

Salad Dressing Soaks Into Lettuce. Why Won't Water?

Lettuce leaves as well as many plants have a waxy cuticle, which is a mixture of various chemicals that are all related to repelling water and preventing the leaves from becoming water-logged. This cuticle also protects the leaves from losing too much of their internal moisture. The oils in salad dressing, however, are related to the chemicals that keep the water out. Water molecules also tend to bead up and fall off the leaf, while the oil spreads out and coats the surface.

To Tear It Or To Cut It

Recently, I saw two different cooking shows on television and watched one chef tear the lettuce and the other cut the lettuce with a knife. The chef that tore the lettuce mentioned that tearing it would extend the life of the lettuce before it would turn brown. After trying this I found out that it makes no difference at all whether you tear or cut lettuce. It will brown and oxidize in the same amount of time.

Hot Potato, Baked Potato

When baking a potato, many people tend to wrap the potato in aluminum foil, thinking that it will speed up the cooking time. After trying to bake potatoes a number of different ways to see which method was the fastest, I was surprised to find that when oiling the skin with vegetable oil the skin reached a higher temperature faster and baked the potato faster than when it was wrapped in aluminum foil. The only other method that did speed up the cooking time was inserting an aluminum nail into the center of the potato.

Flatulence Levels of Common Beans

The following list provides information that was released by the USDA's Western Laboratory in Berkeley, California. The list of beans is in the order of those that produce the most gas, or are higher in the sugar that causes the problem, to the beans that are lower, rated on a scale of 1-10.

Soybeans	10
Pea Beans	9
Black Beans	8.5

Pinto Beans	8.5
California Northern Beans	8
Great Northern Beans	7
Lima Beans	6.5
Garbanzos (chickpeas)	6
Black-Eyed Peas	5

The Eye In Popeye

Spinach contains 2 special antioxidants that belong to the carotenoid family, lutein and zeaxanthin. In recent studies, these antioxidants are proving to be important in an age-related disease of the eye known as macular degeneration. This form of blindness is prevalent in people over 65 and is the leading cause of blindness. Experts believe that overexposure to sunlight, pollution, and smog over a period of years may contribute to this problem. Consuming foods that are high in these carotenoids (such as kale, collard greens, spinach, sweet red peppers, mustard greens, and hot chili peppers) may significantly lower the risk by as much as 75%.

Cooking Onions And Garlic Together

When sauteeing onions and garlic together, be sure to sauté the onions first for at least ½ their cooking time. If the garlic is placed in the pan at the same time, it will over-cook and possibly burn, and release a chemical that will make the dish bitter.

Goodbye To Flatulence

When it comes to eating beans, many of us have a problem with flatulence (gas). The gas is produced by the fermentation of the complex sugar oligosacchaide found in beans and some other vegetables, such as cabbage and broccoli. The small intestine does not have the proper enzyme to break this sugar down and it passes into the large intestine where bacteria break it down and unfortunately ferment the sugar, producing hydrogen, methane, and carbon dioxide gases.

There is a simple method of de-gassing beans at home and that is to just add a tablespoon of fennel to the water the beans are soaking in to neutralize the complex sugar. However, when you are in a Mexican restaurant eating refried or black beans, you don't stand a chance unless you consume an equal amount of rice. Rice has the ability to neutralize the gas in the beans. We found this out in Mexico when we asked a restaurant owner why no one ever seems to have a gas problem in Mexico when they consume large quantities of beans daily. We were told about the rice and have tried it with perfect success every time.

Pop Goes The Onion, Insides Only

Have you ever cooked a whole onion only to have the insides pop out and ruin the appearance of the dish you are preparing? This is a very common occurrence and happens almost every time unless you pierce the onion with a thin skewer once or twice, which allows the steam to escape. Another method is similar to one that is used on chestnuts so they won't explode: cut an "X" on the stem end which will release the steam without damaging the onion.

X Marks The Spot

If you cut an "X" on the stalk end of each Brussels sprout with a sharp knife before cooking them, the sprout will retain its shape and not fall apart. The small opening will allow the steam to be released through the bottom instead of being forced through the leaves.

MSG, The Flavor of Mushrooms?

The unique flavor of fresh mushrooms is caused by glutamic acid, the natural version of the same flavor-enhancer used in monosodium glutamate (MSG). Mushrooms, however, do not have any sodium.

Ethylene Gas vs. Apples And Bananas

Never store an apple near a banana unless you wish to ripen the banana in a very short period of time. Apples tend to give off more ethylene gas than most other fruits (except green tomatoes) and will hasten the ripening of many fruits and vegetables.

Ethylene gas is a natural gas that is released by all fruits and vegetables as they ripen. Ethylene has been used for centuries to ripen fruits and vegetabless. Fruits and vegetables are commonly gassed as they are trucked to market. Ethylene increases the permeability of the cell membrane which allows the cell to respire more. This uses up carbon dioxide up to five times faster than it ordinarily would. This increased activity of the cell causes the fruit or vegetable to ripen faster.

The Secret To Making A Smooth Or Chunky Applesauce?

Whether you prepare a smooth or chunky applesauce depends on when the sugar is added. If you prefer a chunky applesauce, then add the sugar before cooking the apples. If you prefer a smooth applesauce, add the sugar after the apples are cooked and mashed.

Shedding A Tear For Onions

When you slice into an onion, a gas is released that affects the lachrymal glands in the eyes and causes a defensive reaction by the body against the chemical propanethiol S-oxide which reacts with the fluid in your eyes, forming sulfuric acid. The body protects itself from the acid by tearing and washing out the eyes, thus ridding itself of the irritant. One of the best ways to prevent this is to store onions in the refrigerator and wear solid plastic goggles when slicing them. This tends to slow down the release of the fumes.

Grapefruit And Drugs: Do They Mix?

Recent studies have shown that grapefruit will increase the absorption rate of a number of drugs. A researcher at the University of Western Ontario found that grapefruit juice caused a three-fold absorption rate for a blood pressure medication. An enzyme in the gastrointestinal tract has a negative effect on certain medications, which reduces their absorption rate. A chemical in the grapefruit juice tends to neutralize that enzyme. Some of the drugs that are affected are calcium-channel blockers (Procardia, Adalat), antihistamines (Seldane), immunosuppressants (cyclosporine), short-acting sedatives (Halcion), and estrogens (Estinyl). The race is now on worldwide to isolate the actual ingredient that is causing the reaction.

Cooking An Onion

Cooking an onion will actually turn the sulfurs contained in the onion into sugars, which is why onions tend to have a sweeter flavor after cooking. As onions are browned, the sugars and protein change and become a deep brown color and caramelize, which also intensifies the flavor. The reaction is called the Maillard reaction. Onions will change color when cooked and turn a creamy white color from the chemical anthocyanin. This chemical should not come into contact with metal ions from aluminum or iron pots or it will turn brown. When onions are sliced with a carbon-steel knife, the same reaction takes place and changes the color of the onion.

The No-Waste Orange

The orange juice industry uses every bit of every orange it processes. The residues, from the production of orange juice is a multi-million dollar industry. Everything including the pulp, seeds, and peel is used in food products such as candy, cake mixes, soft drinks, paints, and even perfumes. Over 100 million pounds of "peel oil" is sold for cooking uses. It is also made into a synthetic spearmint base for the Coca Cola company which uses it as a flavoring agent.

Cucumber: Bitterness Remover

This fact really surprised me, and I thought it was just another old wives' tale that had been passed down through the years and really didn't work. To my surprise it actually worked. The next time you purchase a standard cucumber (not the long, skinny, English variety) cut about 1 inch off one end and then rub the two exposed areas together in a circular motion while occasionally pulling them apart. This will cause enough suction to release a substance that causes the cucumber to sometimes have a bitter taste. Then throw away the small end you used to release the bitterness.

Kernel Corn

Choosing fresh corn can be a difficult task unless you have some "corn knowledge." If the corn still has its husk, it will be necessary to peel back a small area and examine the kernels. The kernels should be packed tightly together with no gaps between the rows. Gaps between rows mean that the ear is over-mature. If the tip has no kernels, the corn was picked too soon and not allowed to mature. The kernels should always be plump and juicy and should spurt a milky, starchy, liquid when broken. If the center of the kernel is sinking inward, it is drying out and will not be as sweet.

Why Soak Celery And Carrots?

A number of vegetables tend to lose their moisture before you are able to use them up and they become limp. There is no need to discard them when all you have to do is immerse them in a bowl of ice cubes and water for 1 hour in the refrigerator. The cells will absorb the water and swell, forcing them close together again and making the vegetable hard and crisp. Soaking fresh vegetables, however, may have the opposite effect because of excess water build-up in the spaces between the cells.

How Does Fruit Ripen In A Brown Paper Bag?

Fruit normally gives off ethylene gas, which hastens its ripening. Some fruits give off more gas than others and ripen faster, while other fruits are picked too soon and need a bit of help. When you put a piece of unripe fruit into a closed container such as a brown paper bag, the ethylene gas that is given off does not dissipate into the air but is trapped and builds to a higher concentration, causing the fruit to ripen faster. One fruit that tends to give off the gas at a more significant level is an apple. Apples should always be stored by themselves or they may cause other fruits, such as a banana, to ripen faster than you may desire.

Grapefruit White-Out

The white material just under the skin of a grapefruit may be easily removed either by immersing the grapefruit in very hot water for 5-6 minutes or by placing it in boiling water for 3 minutes. However, this material is very high in an antioxidant known as carotene and is worth eating even though it may be a bit bitter.

Why Are Cucumbers Waxed?

Cucumbers tend to shrink during shipping and storage. The wax coating is to prevent the shrinkage and is edible. The skin should never be removed until you are ready to eat the cucumber or it will lose most of its vitamin C content. The cucumber is capable of holding 30 times its weight in water and is a member of the gourd family. If you can remember back to the 1930's, "cucumber" was slang for a $1 bill.

Old Potato, New Potato, Best Potato?

A new potato will have more moisture than an old potato; however, they are used for different dishes. A new potato should be used for dishes such as potato salad since they will absorb less water when boiled and less mayonnaise when prepared, both of which add less fat to the potato. They are stronger and won't break as easily when a salad is stirred. Idaho and other varieties of older potatoes are best for baking and French fries. They are drier, meatier, and starchier. Because of this they will bake fluffier and have a lighter texture. When French fries are made, an older potato will splatter less because of its lower water content. When baking a potato, make sure you pierce the potato to allow steam to escape. Otherwise it may become soggy.

Why Fruits Turn Brown When Exposed To Air

Fruits contain a "phenolic" compound which is responsible for turning the exposed meat of fruits brown when they are cut up or bitten into. This happens fairly rapidly, especially to apples, bananas, pears, potatoes, and avocado. The browning is caused by the enzyme polyphenoloxidase, which causes the oxidation (breakdown by oxygen) of the phenolic compound in the cells and the conversion to a brown color. This is a similar action that occurs when you tan from the sun. Citrus fruits, melons, and tomatoes lack the enzyme and therefore can't turn brown through this chemical reaction. However, if they are allowed to sit out with their flesh exposed to oxygen for any length of time they will turn brown through normal oxidation.

The browning can be slowed down, even if the flesh is exposed by refrigerating the fruit at 40° F. However, boiling will actually destroy the enzyme. Salt also will slow down the enzyme but will negatively affect the flavor. Placing the fruit in cold water will slow the process by keeping the surface from the air, and so will brushing lemon juice on the surface or spraying the surface with an ascorbic acid spray (vitamin C mixed with water).

Why Does Corn Occasionally Turn Rubbery?

When corn is cooked, the protein goes through a chemical change called denaturization which simply means that the chains of amino acids (proteins) are broken apart and re-form into a network of protein molecules that squeeze the moisture out of the kernel. This turns the corn rubbery. The heat also causes the starch granules to absorb water, swell up and rupture the kernel, releasing the nutrients. Corn should be cooked just long enough to cause the kernels to barely rupture, which allows the protein to remain tender and not tough. When corn is boiled in water, 50% of the vitamin C is destroyed; however, if you cook it in a microwave without water almost all of the vitamin C is retained.

How Does A Pickle Get Pickled?

It all starts with a fresh cucumber arriving at the pickle factory. Three processes control their fermentation. The first type of processing starts with the "curing" stage where the cucumbers are stored for up to 3 years in large tanks filled with a salt-brine mixture. Next, they are washed and placed in a vat of fresh water, then heated to remove any excess salt residues. After being cleaned, they are packed in a final "liquor" solution and will end up the dark green color we expect them to be.

The second type of processing is for "fresh pack" pickles, which eliminates the holding tanks and speeds the cucumbers into a flavored brine or "syrup," then immediately into pasteurization. The pickles emerge less salty than the cured pickles and are a lighter green in color.

The third method of processing is done totally under refrigeration. These special pickles are known as "deli dills." They are cleaned and graded and proceed right to the flavored brine without any further stages. They are never cooked or pasteurized and remain very cucumber-like in flavor and texture. These pickles are always found in the refrigerated section of the market and must be kept in the refrigerator.

Sour pickles are completed in a solution of vinegar and special spices. Sweet pickles are just sour pickles that have been drained of all traces of brine and bathed in a mixture of vinegar, sugar, and spices. The most popular is the gherkin.

Are Green Potatoes Safe To Eat?

When you see a potato with green spots or with a greenish tint, it would be best not to purchase it. Overexposure to light causes a chemical reaction that increases a chlorophyll build-up and the production of the chemical solanine. Solanine will impart a bitter taste to the potato and high levels can actually cause serious medical problems, such as interfering with nerve impulse transmission, abdominal discomfort, nausea, and diarrhea. It is best to store potatoes in a dark location to avoid solanine build-up. They may also be a risk factor for people with arthritis.

Why Soak Fries In Water

The surface of a cut potato deteriorates very quickly when exposed to air. When this occurs, a layer of sticky starch is formed as soon as the potatoes are placed into the frying vat. The potatoes may stick to each other as well as the pan and it will be almost impossible to serve them. If you soak the potatoes in ice water for 5-7 minutes before frying them, it will wash off a large percentage of the surface starch and the problem will not occur. They should also be drained on paper towels and should be good and dry when you fry them. Otherwise you will have hot oil splatter.

What Is The New Freedom II Squash?

The Asgrow company of Michigan has developed a new strain of squash called the Freedom II squash that is resistant to viruses transmitted by aphids. This is expected to make more squash available and lower the prices due to less pesticide use. The company is also developing virus-resistant cantaloupe, watermelon, and cucumbers.

Should Spinach Be Eaten Raw?

While most vegetables should be eaten raw, especially to retain their enzymes, spinach has a tough cellular wall that will only release the maximum number of nutrients and in sufficient quantity if it is cooked. Carrots are actually better cooked as well. Our digestive systems cannot break these two vegetables down sufficiently to gain the most from them.

Are Chips Made From Vegetables Healthier Than Other Chips?

The number of calories in a vegetable chip such as the new carrot chip is about the same as in any potato chip, since it is fried in oil. Any chip that is fried will be high in calories and fat and almost void of any nutritional value. If the chip is baked, it will have fewer calories. However, because of the high-heat processing that is used, the nutritional value is reduced significantly.

Eggplant Bitter? Salt It

Since eggplants will last only a few days even under refrigeration, it is best to use them the same day or no later than the next day after they are purchased. Eggplants tend to be a bit bitter and the easiest method to eliminate this problem is to slice them into ½ inch slices and then lightly salt the slices and allow them to drain on a wire rack for 30 minutes.

Never Serve A Cold Tomato

Cold temperatures, especially those in the refrigerator, will affect the flavor and aroma of tomatoes. The cold tends to reduce the level of conversion of the linolenic acid in the tomato to a  substance called z-3 hexenel which gives the tomato its aroma and flavor. For the best flavor, leave the tomatoes at room temperature for at least an hour before serving them.

The Best Dried Fruit And Tomatoes, Anywhere

The finest, all-natural fruits and tomatoes can be found at Timber Crest Farms in Healdsburg, California. All products are unsulfured and packaged without any preservatives or additives. The farm is owned by Ron and Ruthie Waltenspiel, who have been producing the finest quality products for 32 years. Almost all the products are grown on their ranch, with most being grown under the strict organic regulations of the California Health and Safety Code. This one of the cleanest operations of its kind I have ever had the privilege of visiting. To order or receive a catalog call (707) 433-8251 or write to Timber Crest Farms, 4791 Dry Creek Road, Healdsburg, California 95448.

Mashed Potato Education

There are a number of hints to follow when preparing mashed potatoes. First, never pour cold milk into the potatoes, it has a tendency to mix with the starch that has been released through the mashing process and may make the potatoes heavy, soggy, and even create lumps. The milk should be warmed in a pan with a small amount of chives for flavor before being added. Buttermilk will give the potatoes a great flavor. A pinch or two of baking powder will give them extra fluff. Second, never over-mix or over-cook the potatoes. Both will cause the cell walls to rupture, releasing an excess of starch and producing a soggy, sticky product. Potatoes should be stirred with a vertical motion and never with a circular one. This will lessen the damage which occurs by crushing the cells on the wall of the bowl. Never put baking soda in potatoes; it will turn them black.

Skinny French Fries: Is There A Reason?

A number of the fast food chains like McDonald's serve their French fries thinner than most other restaurants. When raw potatoes are pre-cut thin, exposing the surface, a percentage of the complex carbohydrates has time to convert to sugar. The extra sugar causes the French fries to brown faster and the thinner fry will cook faster. If they tried to serve normal size fries, they would be too brown or under-cooked.

Tenderizing Vegetables

The major component in the cell wall of fruits and vegetables is a complex carbohydrate called cellulose. The higher the cellulose content, the firmer the fruit or vegetable will be. To tenderize the cellulose, heat and moisture are used. However, certain vegetables have different degrees of cellulose in their various parts. Stems have more than tips, which is why it is necessary to remove the outer covering with a vegetable peeler before cooking broccoli or asparagus; otherwise the tips will be mushy if the stalks are tender. When heat or moisture is applied to the vegetable, it tends to destroy the cell's ability to retain and release moisture, which causes a structural breakdown resulting in tenderness. It also dissolves some of the pectin which is active in holding the cells walls together.

What Is A NewLeaf Potato?

The Monsanto Company has genetically engineered a potato that provides the potato with natural resistance to the Colorado potato beetle, reducing the need for additional pesticides. They are also working on a new potato that will absorb less fat when fried into French fries.

Can A Potato Explode In The Oven?

It is not unusual for a white potato to explode in the oven if the skin is not pierced. It doesn't really explode; however, it may crack open and make a mess since potatoes are very high in water content and build up a good head of steam as they bake. It is best to pierce the skin with a fork before baking potatoes.

Losing Color In Vegetables

The color lost by vegetables is the result of loss of the pigment by a chemical reaction of the pigment with the acid that is being released by the cooking process. A variety of colors may actually appear in the same vegetable, depending on the length of time it is cooked. After a period of cooking, the liquid medium may deplete the acid and turn alkaline, changing the color of the vegetable again. In green vegetables, the acid that is released reacts with the chlorophyll, lightening the color. In cabbage, the pigment chemical anthocyanin may be changed from red to purple depending on the acid or alkaline nature of the liquid. Baking soda placed in the water will help reduce and neutralize the effects of the acid and keep most vegetables their natural color, but it will also destroy a number of vitamins, especially C and thiamine. The best method of retaining color is to steam your vegetables.

Onions And Potatoes Not Good Friends

Onions should never be stored in the same bag with potatoes. Onions tends to release gases that will alter the flavor of a potato. Cooking the two together is not a problem unless you overdo the quantity of onions and they take over the flavor and aroma of the potato.

Can Vitamin C Survive In Commercially-Prepared Products?

The methods of preparation and packaging will determine the level of vitamin C that will remain in a commercial product or juice that has been placed in a container for a market. Frozen orange juice loses only about 2% of its vitamin C content over a 3-month period of home freezer storage. If the juice is sold in glass bottles it will retain almost 100% of the vitamin C; however, if it is stored in plastic or waxed cardboard containers, oxygen will be able to pass through and reduce the potency, depending on the storage time. The best juice to buy is the juice that is squeezed and sold fresh in the market. All commercially prepared bottled juices are pasteurized and the natural enzymes are killed by the heat.

Peas Are Best When Used In Soups Or Stews

The difference between fresh green peas and dried split peas is that the dried peas are actually mature seeds and usually have twice as much starch as the fresh peas. Dried peas contain an excellent source of protein. It is best not to soak split peas before using, since the water you will discard will contain a good percentage of the B vitamins. When you use the split peas for soups or stews, you will normally consume the liquid which will have some of the B vitamins still available for use.

Why Won't The Color In Yellow Or Red Peppers Fade?

Green peppers contain chlorophyll as the coloring agent which is sensitive to the acids in the pepper. When the pepper is cooked it is released and causes discoloration. Red and yellow peppers rely on carotenoid pigments for their color. These pigments are not affected by the acids or the heat from cooking.

Why Do Cooked Potatoes Have More Nutrients Available?

Raw potato nutrients are very difficult for the body to obtain. The potato cells tend to hold the nutrients until the potato is softened and cooked, and our digestive systems are unable to break the cell walls down in sufficient quantity. Potatoes should never be cooked in aluminum or iron pots or they will turn yellowish, nor can they be sliced with a carbon-steel knife. It's best to cook potatoes in a glass or enamel pot if you wish them to be a nice pale color.

Can Prunes Really Relieve Constipation?

Prunes contain the organic chemical diphenylisatin which is a related to another compound, biscodyl, that is the active ingredient in some of the over-the-counter laxatives. Biscodyl tends to increase the secretion of fluids in the bowel and will stimulate contractions of the intestines, thereby pushing the waste material on its way.

What Are Duchess Potatoes?

They are a light, fluffy combination of mashed potatoes, egg yolk, sweet cream butter, and seasonings to taste. The mixture is then placed into a pastry tube and piped around meats, poultry, casseroles or fish dishes as a decorative touch.

Brown Spots On Bananas Tell The Sugar Content

Bananas are always picked when they are green. If they are allowed to ripen on the tree, they tend to lose their taste and become mealy. As soon as the banana is picked, the sugar content increases from 2% to 20%. The more yellow the skin becomes, the sweeter the banana. Brown spots are the result of the sugar level increasing over the 25% level. The more brown, the higher the sugar content. Presently, we are consuming 25 pounds of bananas per person annually. Banana imports top 15 billion bananas a day which amounts to a $5-billion business in the United States. Bananas are mainly grown in tropical climates; however, they are also grown in Iceland in soil heated by volcanic steam vents.

What Happens When You Sprinkle Sugar On A Strawberry?

Strawberries can easily be sweetened by sprinkling powdered sugar on them and allowing them to stand for a short while. The sugar on the surface of the berry mixes with the moisture that is naturally being released, producing a solution that is somewhat denser than the liquid inside the berry. Through osmosis the liquid with the less density flows toward the liquid which is more dense, placing the sugar inside the strawberry cells and sweetening the berry.

Pop Goes The Cranberry

Cranberries will not handle a great amount of heat before the water inside produces enough steam to burst the berry. When the cranberry pops and bursts, it is time to stop the cooking process, otherwise the cranberry will become bitter and very tart due to chemical changes. The addition of lemon juice and a small amount of sugar to the water will help to preserve the color, since the heat will cause the pigment (anthocyanin) to be dissolved and turn the cooking water red.

Is Cranberry Juice Helpful For Bladder Problems?

Recently, researchers at Youngstown University found the "cranberry factor," which may interfere with the ability of bacteria to adhere to the surface of bladder cells as well as the urinary tract. The factor tends to show up in the urine of humans and animals within 2-3 hours after drinking cranberry juice and stays active for about 12 hours. Research is continuing and may show promise that there is actual scientific data that proves cranberries will be a benefit in urinary infections.

Do Cucumbers Sweeten After They Are Picked?

Cucumbers do not contain any starch. Therefore they are unable to produce sugar to sweeten them. They will, however, get softer as they age and absorb more moisture into the pectin. If the cucumber gets too soft, just soak the slices in lightly salted cold water to crisp them up. The reaction that occurs removes the unsalted, lower-density water from the cells and replaces it with the higher-density salted water.

Why Is Eggplant Always Served In A Puddle Of Oil?

The cells in a fresh eggplant have a very high air content that will escape when the eggplant is heated. When you cook an eggplant, in oil the air escapes and the cells absorb a large quantity of oil. The cells fill up with oil and, as the eggplant is moved about, they eventually collapse and release the oil. Eggplant parmigiana is always served in a pool of olive oil for this reason. Eggplant should never be cooked in an aluminum pot, which will cause the eggplant to become discolored.

Is It True That Figs Can Tenderize A Steak?

It is a fact that figs have the ability to tenderize meats. Fresh figs contain the chemical ficin which is called a proteolytic enzyme, one that is capable of breaking down proteins with an action similar to that of papain from papayas or bromelin from pineapples. Ficin is effective in the heat ranges of 140°-160° F., which is the most common temperature used to simmer stews. If fresh figs are added to the stew, it will help to tenderize the meat and impart an excellent flavor as well. However, if the temperature rises above 160° F. ficin is inactivated. Canned figs will not work since they have been heated to very high temperatures during their sterilization process.

How The Tomato Became A Vegetable

The United States Supreme Court set a precedent in 1893 by ruling that a tomato for purposes of commerce will be declared a vegetable, even though botanically it is a seeded fruit.

Male And Female Asparagus Stalks?

The male asparagus flower has a stamen that will produce a spore. The female asparagus flower has a pistil, or ovary. The male asparagus stalks are thinner, while the female stalks are fatter. The darker the color of asparagus, the more tender it will be; the greener or the whiter, the better.

Removing Indigestion From Potato Pancakes

For some reason a number of people have a problem tolerating fried potato pancakes and always get indigestion. This problem is easily solved by adding 1 teaspoon of baking soda to the potato pancake batter.

Can Organic Fruits and Vegetables Harbor Bacteria?

Even the most serious vegetarian or organic-only eater needs to take precautions against dangerous bacteria. Most organic fruits and vegetables are grown using natural manures which may harbor the bacteria *E. coli. E. coli* is found in the intestinal tract of animals and may be found in manure. It is necessary to wash your organic produce well before consuming it.

What Is A Designer-Label Tomato?

A new tomato is making an appearance in supermarkets everywhere. Called the FlavrSavr tomato, it is a genetically engineered tomato that can be shipped vine-ripened without rotting. This is the first whole food to be born of biotechnology. Most tomatoes are shipped green and gassed with ethylene gas to turn them red before they get to the market. The only downside is that the new tomato will cost about $2.00 per pound.

A Mole That Tastes Good

A "mole" is actually a Mexican sauce made from chili peppers and tomatoes. The combination of ingredients, especially the variety of chili pepper, will determine whether the mole is spicy or mild. The most popular mole is mole poblano, which is a spicy red sauce that even includes unsweetened chocolate and is served over turkey. Green mole is made from green chiles and cilantro.

A Coconut Separation

To easily separate the outer shell of a coconut from the inner meat, just bake the coconut for 20-25 minutes at 300° F., then tap the shell lightly with a hammer. The moisture from the meat will try to escape in the form of steam and establish a thin space between the meat and the shell. This separates the two. The coconut milk (which unlike the coconut and the meat is low in saturated fat) should be removed first by piercing 2 of the 3 eyes with an ice pick. One hole will allow the air to enter as the milk comes out the other one.

Why Is The Beta-Carotene Increasing In Carrots?

According to the USDA, scientists have been improving carrots to such a degree that they presently have twice the beta-carotene level that they did in 1950. By the year 2000 the beta-carotene level is expected to double again, thanks to genetic research.

Why Is It That The Longer I Cook Broccoli, The Worse It Smells?

Broccoli and Brussels sprouts contain a natural chemical called mustard oil (isocyanates). This chemical, when heated, breaks down into a foul-smelling sulfur compound, hydrogen sulfide and ammonia. In fact, you should never cook these vegetables in an aluminum pot or the reaction will cause an even more intense smell. The longer you cook the vegetables, the more chemicals are released and the smellier the kitchen. If you keep a lid on the pot and place a piece of fresh bread on the top of the broccoli or Brussels sprouts while they are cooking, the bread will absorb some of the odor. Then discard the bread.

Sauerkraut To The Rescue

Sauerkraut was popularized by Genghis Khan when his marauding hordes brought the recipe back from China. The recipe found its way throughout Europe and to Germany where the cabbage was fermented with salt instead of wine and given the name "sauerkraut." However, sauerkraut became a real hero in 1772 when Captain James Cook, who had heard of its possible health properties, decided to bring 25,000 pounds of it on his second journey to explore the Pacific Ocean. Since sauerkraut has vitamin C,, he lost only one sailor to scurvy in over 1,000 days at sea. The sauerkraut supply lasted one year without going bad.

Does Cooking Change Garlic?

When garlic is heated, the chemical that gives garlic its unique flavor is partially destroyed. The chemical is diallyl disulfide, which is a sulfur compound. If garlic is allowed to sprout, most of the diallyl disulfide goes into the new sprouts and the garlic will become milder.

Orange Juice And Antacids Do Not Mix

If you take an antacid that contains aluminum, avoid drinking any kind of citrus juice. A 4-ounce glass of orange juice can increase the absorption of aluminum found in antacids tenfold. Aluminum can collect in the tissues and high levels may affect your health. Allow at least 3 hours after taking an antacid before drinking citrus juice.

How Do You Make An Orange Juice Fizz?

A fun drink for children is to add ¼ teaspoon of baking soda to 8-10 ounces of orange juice, lemonade, or other acidic fruit drink. Stir the drink well and it will do a great deal of fizzing, much to the kids' delight. It will also reduce the acidity level of the drink.

What Is The Chinese Lantern Fruit?

The fruit is the physatis, a round berry that is encased in a pod that exactly resembles a Chinese lantern. It is also known as the Cape gooseberry and is used as an ornamental garden plant. The berry is cultivated in South Africa and Peru. It is an extremely rich source of vitamin A and excellent source of vitamin C.

Apples As A Stress Reliever?

Researchers at Yale University recently discovered that the fragrance of apples will relax a person. A calming effect was noted in a number of instances when the person sniffed apple spice fragrance. When they smelled mulled cider or baked apple it actually reduced anxiety attacks. Try it; you'll like it!

Dried Pineapple From Taiwan

Most of the dried pineapple that is sold in the United States is being imported from Taiwan and is saturated with refined sugar instead of pineapple juice. The sugar-sweetened pineapple will be very plump and will have a coating of sugar crystals, while the naturally sweetened pineapple will look somewhat mottled, fibrous and will lack the surface crystals.

Hairy Fruit?

The rambutan is one of the most unusual looking pieces of fruit you will ever see. The fruit resembles a small lime in shape and is covered with what looks like hair. The name of the fruit is from the Malayan word for "hairy." The skin, however, is harmless and peels off easily, the fruit is usually sold in cans.

Is Is Safe To Eat Fiddlehead Fern?

The fiddlehead fern is a member of the ostrich fern family. They are shaped like a musical note with a long stem and a circular bottom. They are about 2-5 inches long and about 2 inches in diameter. The texture of the fern is similar to green beans, with a flavor between asparagus and green beans. They are usually used in salads, stir-fried, or steamed. Fiddlehead fern should never be eaten raw or lightly sautéed. A number of people have become ill due to a toxin that is only destroyed if the fern is boiled for 10 minutes before it is consumed. All illnesses were in upstate New York and Banff, Alberta, Canada, and in all cases the fiddlehead was eaten raw or only partially cooked.

Pucker Up!

If you have ever bitten into a piece of fruit that was not ripe or tried eating a lemon, or even took a sip of strong tea, then you have experienced a reaction known as astringency that results in dryness of the mouth, puckering, and constricting of the lips. It is how your mouth feels as it comes in contact with a class of phenolic compounds called tannins. The tannins affect the protein in the saliva and mucous membranes of the mouth, resulting in puckering.

De-Gassing The Sunroot

The Jerusalem artichoke or sunroot contains a number of indigestible carbohydrates that cause flatulence in susceptible individuals. These annoying carbohydrates can be almost entirely eliminated naturally from the vegetable by a month of cold storage in the refrigerator before being used. About half of the remaining carbohydrates can be eliminated through cooking if the sunroot is sliced and boiled for 15 minutes. The only way to eliminate all the problem carbohydrate is to cook the whole root for about 24 hours which will break the carbohydrates down to fructose. Sunroot is very high in iron which may cause them to turn gray with cooking. If you add ¼ of a teaspoon of cream of tartar to the boiling water 5 minutes before they are done, it will prevent the discoloration. If you add 1 tablespoon of lemon juice to the boiling water when you first start cooking, it will keep the root crisp and eliminate the color change.

What Is Flatulence?

Flatulence or intestinal gas may be caused by a number of foods that contain sugars that promote excess gas production. The problem of flatulence was studied when it became a problem for pilots since the gas expand as the altitude increases and can cause pain and discomfort. At 35,000 feet the gas will expand to 5.4 times more than at sea level. Almost 50% of the gas is nitrogen, with about 40% being carbon dioxide produced by aerobic bacteria in the intestinal tract. The remainder is a combination of methane, hydrogen sulfide, hydrogen, ammonia, and the really bad odor-makers, the indoles and skatoles. In the late 1960's, astronauts had to be selected who would not produce large amounts of gas. The two beans that cause the most problems are Navy and Lima beans, with pinto beans coming in a close third.

The Sweet Nature Of Sweet Potatoes

Sweet potatoes cook somewhat differently from regular white potatoes in that they tend to become sweeter the more you cook them. A percentage of the starch in a sweet potato tends to convert to sugar when the potato is heated. The cells in a sweet potato are not as strong as those in a white potato and when it is boiled it will easily absorb water and swell up.

Carrots Easier To Digest When Cooked

Carrots are not affected to any great extent by heat and cooking, therefore there is almost no loss of the vitamin A content. Carrots will retain their color, which is the result of the chemical carotene. When carrots are cooked, a percentage of the hemicellulose (fiber) will become softer, making the carrot more easily digestible and allowing the digestive juices to reach inside the cells and release the nutrients for easier utilization by the body.

Celery Strings

Celery is easy to cook. The pectin in the cells will easily break down in water. However, the "strings" which are made of cellulose and lignin are virtually indestructible and will not break down under normal cooking conditions. The body even has a difficult time breaking them down and many people cannot digest them at all.

Can You Cook An Avocado?

No! Never cook an avocado, because a chemical reaction will take place that releases a bitter chemical compound. It will be rare to ever see a recipe that calls for cooked avocado. When restaurants do serve avocado on a hot dish they will always place the avocado on the dish just before serving it. If you slice an avocado, an enzyme called phenoloxidase is released from the damaged cells and converts phenols into a brownish compound. Ascorbic acid will neutralize this reaction for a period of time, slowing the browning.

Can An Apple Seed Poison You?

Apple seeds do contain the poison cyanide, which is a deadly poison. However, the poison is encased in a seed that cannot be broken down by the body and goes harmlessly through the body. If the seed were to split open, the amount of cyanide that would be released would not place you at risk. Other fruit seeds also contain cyanide those are apricots and peaches. These seeds are more easily split; however, they do not pose any health risk to a healthy person.

Medical Concerns With Celery?

Celery contains the chemical limonene which is an essential oil and known to cause contact dermatitis in susceptible individuals. This chemical is also found in other foods such as; dill, caraway seeds, and the peelings of lemons and limes. Photosensitivity has also been a problem with workers who handle celery on a daily basis unless they wear gloves. The chemical that is responsible for this problem is furocoumarin (psoralens) and increased contact may make your skin sensitive to light.

Going For A Physical? Don't Eat Carrots

There are two effects that your physician needs to be aware of if you consume a large amount of carrots. The first is that your skin may have a somewhat yellow tinge due to the excess amount of the carotenoids you are consuming. You may appear to have jaundice. The second problem may appear if you are asked to take a guiac test for occult blood in your feces. The active ingredient in the guiac slide is alphaguaiaconic acid which turns blue in the presence of blood. Carrots contain the enzyme peroxidase which causes a chemical reaction to take place with the alphaguaiaconic acid, turning it blue and giving you a false-positive test showing that you have blood in your feces.

Why Is It So Hard To Find A Fresh Apricot?

Apricots are mainly grown on 17,000 acres in the Santa Clara Valley in California. They were introduced by Spanish missionaries in the 1700's when they were establishing their missions along the California coast. Because they are so fragile, apricots do not transport well or last very long once they ripen. Barely 5% of the United States population has ever tasted a ripe apricot since they are unable to travel the thousands of miles to Midwest and Eastern markets.

Red Peppers vs. Green Peppers

Nutritionally speaking, sweet red peppers are superior by quite a bit. They are 11 times higher in beta-carotene and have one and a half times more vitamin C than a sweet green pepper. Hot red peppers contain about 14 times more beta-carotene than a hot green pepper; however, the vitamin C content is the same.

Some Vegetables May Form Carcinogens From Nitrites

Certain vegetables contain nitrites. These include beets, celery, eggplant, radishes, spinach, and collard and turnip greens. When they enter the stomach, they may convert to nitrosamines which are a known carcinogen. The problem can become even worse when these vegetables are left at room temperature for any length of time, allowing the microorganisms to multiply and convert more of the nitrites into nitrosamines. A normal healthy adult with a healthy immune system does not have a problem with these foods normally; however, some may not be recommended for infants. In moderation these vegetables are not a problem.

What Is The Oldest Known Citrus Fruit?

To date the oldest records of a citrus fruit dates back to 500 B.C. The citron originated in Hadramaut, which is located in a mountainous region of the Arabian peninsula. The citron is frequently confused with other fruits, especially the citron-melon. The fruit resembles a knobby lemon and may be sold in a variety of sizes depending on the country where it is grown. There are a number of varieties, one of which is the "etog" which is used in the Jewish festival of Sukkot. They may be found in most supermarkets from September to March.

What Is A Feijoa?

It is a small green-skinned fruit with a taste similar to a guava. The feijoa is popular in the southwestern United States as well as South America and New Zealand. It has black seeds and red pulp and is available throughout the summer months.

Some Russian Recipes Call For Cornels. What Are They?

Cornels are members of the dogwood family and resemble olives. The trees are mainly found in southern Europe. They are frequently used in Russian cooking and have a taste similar to a sour cherry. They tend to give dishes a sweet and sour taste, especially when used in meat and dessert recipes. The French pickle cornels like olives and also make them into a unique preserve.

What Is An Acerola?

The acerola is a fruit that resembles a cherry. It grows on a thick bush that is used as hedge in some tropical and sub-tropical areas. It is a native to the Caribbean and has become very popular in Florida. Recently, it has become an important fruit to nutritionists in that it is the richest fruit source of vitamin C. Approximately 4,000 mg of vitamin C can be found in 3½ ounces of the fruit. The acerola is sometimes called the Surinam cherry but is too sour to be eaten raw.

The Myth Regarding Lime Juice

A recent article in the *New York Times* referred to cooking raw meats and fish in lime juice without heat. This concept is also used in Latin America where people think that the acid in lime juice is "strong enough to kill bacteria." A Latin American dish called ceviche is fish or shellfish which is only marinated in lime juice before being consumed. Lime juice will not kill *E. coli* nor will it kill any parasites that are in the fish. If the raw fish is commercially frozen well below 0° for 3 days then it may be safe to eat.

What Is A MOG Inspector?

Grapes that are shipped from the orchard to wineries are routinely inspected for MOG (material other than grapes). These people are called MOG inspectors and look for leaves, rocks, and snakes. If these items are found, the orchards are fined.

Baked Potato May Not Be A Good Choice

Carl's Jr. has outdone itself by serving the worst baked potato in the United States. Carl's Jr.'s bacon and cheese baked potato has 730 calories and 43 grams of fat, 15 of which are saturated. A Burger King Whopper would be better with 630 calories and 39 grams of fat, 11 of which are saturated. Not that either is a very healthy meal. If you want a good baked potato have a Rax Cheese-Broccoli at only 280 calories and zero fat.

Cancer-Causing Fern That Looks Like Asparagus

An asparagus lookalike called bracken fern is sometimes difficult to distinguish from real asparagus and contains a powerful cancer-causing agent. Occasionally cows will eat the fern and develop bone marrow damage as well as inflammation of the bladder membranes.

Who Invented Potato Chips?

In the summer of 1853, a Native American by the name of George Crum was the chef at the Moon Lake Lodge in Saratoga Springs, New York. A guest ordered French fries and complained that they were too thick. Chef Crum sliced up another batch of potatoes, somewhat thinner, and served then. The guest rejected those, too, which upset the chef who then decided to slice the potatoes paper thin. The guest was delighted with the thin potatoes. They became a hit and the trademark of the restaurant and were called "Saratoga Chips." In 1996 the Frito-Lay Company used 7 million pounds of potatoes a day, in 35 plants, to keep us supplied with potato chips.

Removing The Pucker From Persimmons?

Persimmons are a very astringent fruit due to their natural level of tannins. When the fruit becomes ripe, the tannins are somewhat bound up and the fruit is edible. If carbon dioxide is present in larger quantities, however, the astringency can be reduced before the fruit is soft. Just wrap the persimmon as tightly as you can in 3 layers of a quality plastic wrap (such as Saran Wrap) and allow it to remain in a very warm location for at least 12 hours. Return the persimmon to room temperature for another 12 hours. If you don't have a very warm location, allow the wrapped persimmon to be placed in a gas oven with only the pilot light on overnight . If an electric oven is used leave the light on overnight. Or you can place a pot of boiling water in the oven with it to provide heat. Freezing a persimmon will also remove most of the astringency. Leave the fruit in the freezer for about 2 months before eating it.

What Is A Jackfruit?

This is the largest fruit known to exist and can measure up to 3 feet long, 20 inches across, and weigh up to 90 pounds (40 kg). The jackfruit is actually a combination of many different fruits which have fused together. It has a hard green-colored skin with pointed warts. The large seeds can be roasted and are similar to chestnuts. The seeds have a high calcium content and contain 12% protein. The fruit originated in India and East Africa.

Berry, Berry Interesting

The largest producer of blueberries in the United States is New Jersey, followed by Michigan. Blueberries are second only to strawberries in berry consumption.

Is There A Black Raspberry?

Raspberries actually are grown in three colors. The traditional red is what we see in the markets during the summer. Black and golden or yellow raspberries are sold in different areas of the country but are relatively common.

What Is Chowchow?

Chowchow is a relish made from chopped vegetables, usually cabbage, peppers, cucumbers, and onions. It is the packed in a sugar-vinegar solution and seasoned with special mustard and pickling spices. Serve it with meats and sausages.

The Color And Hotness Of Chili Peppers

The color of chilies is an indication of the level of ripeness of the vegetable. If the chili is picked before full maturity it will be green and contain more chlorophyll than a red chili that has matured and lost its chlorophyll. The highest concentration of capsaicin (hot stuff) is located in the white ribs to which the seeds are attached. If you remove the ribs and seeds and wash the insides a few times in cold water, you will eliminate 80-90% of the hotness. When the chili is then fried or boiled, it will lose even more. People who consume chilies frequently are less susceptible to the hot effects and tend to become immune to the bite. Remember that two liquids will neutralize the hot bite; they are whole milk and beer.

The hotness of chili peppers is attributed to the chemical capsaicinoids which act directly on the pain receptors in the mucosal lining of the mouth and the throat. A single drop of this pure chemical diluted in 100,000 drops of water will still cause a blister to form on a person's tongue. This chemical is measured in parts per million which are converted into heat units called Scoville units. This is how the degree of hotness of a hot a chili pepper is measured. One part per million of capsaicinoid is equal to 15 Scoville units. The hottest known pepper, the Habaneros, has a 200,000-300,000 Scoville unit rating.

Babaco As A Meat Tenderizer?

One of the latest arrivals in supermarket produce departments is the fruit babaco. It is an exotic tropical fruit and is presently grown for export by New Zealand. It is a relative of papaya and has a yellow-green skin when ripe, with pale yellow flesh. The fruit, however, has no pips (small black seeds) and the skin is edible. Babaco is high in vitamin C, has a low sugar content, and contains the enzyme papain that is used as a meat tenderizer.

Fresh Produce vs. Harmful Bacteria

As more and more produce is being imported from foreign countries, more outbreaks of food-borne illness are being reported, especially with the same bacteria that caused major concerns related to under-cooked hamburger, *E. coli*. This deadly strain of bacteria is usually the result of fecal contamination of meats during the slaughtering and processing. However, the strain is now showing up on vegetables and fruits. In 1996 four outbreaks related to lettuce were reported by the Centers for Disease Control and Prevention. Salmonella has been found on melons and tomatoes and other dangerous bacteria have been found on cabbage and mushrooms. In one instance more than 245 people in 30 states became ill from cantaloup.. Seventy percent of all produce is now imported from Third World countries.

When it comes to buying fresh produce, make sure you purchase only what you need for a short period of time. If bacteria are present, the longer you store it, the more they will multiply. Wash your hands before handling produce and wash the produce thoroughly before cutting it with a knife. Wash the produce in cold water or a special organic produce cleaner from a health food store.

An Apple For The Teacher

A survey performed by *USA Today* asked teachers what apple they would prefer if a student brought them one. The results were as follows:

Red Delicious	39%
Golden Delicious	24%
Granny Smith	20%
McIntosh	10%

Sweet and Sour Fruit

The main source of energy for a fruit is its sugar content, which is also utilized for the manufacture of the fruit's organic materials. The sugar content of most fruits averages 10-15% by weight. The lime, however, has only 1% compared to the date which is over 60%. The sugar is produced by starch which is stored in the plants leaves, and as the fruit ripens, the starch is converted into sugar. As the fruit ripens the acid content of the fruit declines and the sourness is reduced. Most fruit is sour before it ripens. A number of organic acids are responsible for the plant's acidic nature. These include citric, malic, tartaric, and oxalic acid. Almost all fruits and vegetables usually do, however, end up as slightly acidic.

Where Did The Fuzzy Peaches Go?

Peach fuzz was a term given to young boys when they were nearing the age to start shaving. The term came from the fuzz on the outside of peaches, which was a nuisance to many people who loved peaches but hated the fuzz. The peach industry was unable to develop a fuzzless peach so they have developed a machine that mechanically gently brushes the surface of the peach, removing most of the fuzz. Sales of peaches rose almost 50% after this was done.

Dangerous Citrus Peels

Unless the citrus is organically grown it would be wise not to eat any product that uses citrus peels, including orange and lime zests which are often grated into desserts. According to the EPA, citrus crops in the United States are routinely sprayed with a number of carcinogenic pesticides, which tend to remain in the skin. These include acephate, benomyl, chlorobenzilate, dicofol, methomyl, 0-phenylphenol, and even parathion. Even a thorough cleaning and scrubbing will not remove many of these chemicals.

Jujube: Chewy Candy or Date?

A jujube is also known as a Chinese date which has no relationship to the date we are used to seeing in the market. It is not even a member of the same botanical family even though it does look similar in both color and texture. Is is higher in vitamin C, calcium, iron, and potassium and is sold as a dried fruit.

Kiwi, A Great Meat Tenderizer

While we are familiar with the tenderizing properties of the enzymes in papaya and pineapple, we rarely hear about kiwi. Kiwi contains the enzyme actinidin which is an excellent meat tenderizer. Fresh kiwi needs to be puréed and can be used as a marinade for any type of meat, poultry, or pork. If you prefer, the pureed kiwi may be rubbed on the meat before cooking. Just allow the meat to sit in the refrigerator for about 30 minutes before cooking it. The meat will retain its own flavor and not pick up the kiwi flavor. Actinidin will also prevent gelatin from setting up, so you will have to add kiwi to a gelatin dish just before serving, preferably on the top. Cooking the fruit, however, will inactivate the enzyme.

Watermelon Popcorn?

In China, watermelon seeds are a treat and are roasted, salted, and eaten like popcorn. However, it is a high-fat treat, with 65% of the 535 calories in a 100 g serving coming from fat.

Paul Bunyan's Fruit and Vegetables

The largest watermelon that has ever been grown weighed 262 pounds. The world's longest zucchini grew to almost 70 inches. The world's largest squash was 654 pounds. The largest cabbage was 123 pounds. The world's largest lemon was 5 pounds 13 ounces. And the world's largest tomato was 4 pounds 4 ounces.

Green Oranges?

Florida oranges normally have more green tint than oranges from California or Arizona. This occurs due to the warm days and nights that allow the orange to retain more of the chlorophyll. A number of companies that sell Florida oranges may dye the oranges, since we are not used to purchasing green oranges and think that they are not ripe. When oranges are dyed they must be labeled "Color Added" on the shipping container. The cooler nights in California and Arizona remove the green; however, both states have laws prohibiting adding any color to citrus fruits.

What Is A Johnnycake?

Johnnycake is a homemade cornmeal bread that may be made in a bread form or in a pancake shape. It is made from cornmeal, salt, and cold milk or boiling water. It originated with the American Indians and the word derived from the Indian word "joniken." Purists believe that johnnycake can be made only with a special type of low-yield Indian corn from Rhode Island.

Cooking Fruits

The last thing a cook wants is mushy fruit. This frequently encountered problem can be resolved by adding some sugar to the cooking syrup. This will strengthen the cell walls with an artificial sugar "cell" wall. The sugar will also have the effect of drawing some of the fluid back into the cell to slow the drying-out of the fruit and retain the desired appealing consistency.

How Is Bean Curd, a.k.a. Tofu, Made?

Tofu is prepared by boiling soybeans in water, then grinding the beans into a paste and adding calcium sulfate to coagulate the curd and make it a better source of calcium than soybeans. However, most Japanese and Chinese tofu is made without the addition of the calcium sulfate. Instead, an acid such as lemon juice or vinegar is used. The protein in bean curd is 90% digestible, which is close to milk.

Poisonous Lima Beans?

Lima beans tend to produce an enzyme called cyanogen, which is a form of cyanide. Some countries have laws that restrict certain varieties of Lima beans from being grown. European and American farmers have developed new breeds of Lima beans that do not produce as much of the toxin and are safer to eat. These potentially harmful toxins may be removed by boiling the beans in a pot without a lid. This allows the hydrogen cyanide gas to escape with the steam. Neither raw Lima Beans nor their sprouts should ever be eaten.

Legumes: A Pain In The Abdomen?

Almost all legumes, including beans, peas, and lentils (fresh or dried), contain a toxin called a lectin which is capable of causing abdominal pain, nausea, diarrhea, and severe indigestion. To destroy this toxin, legumes must be cooked at a rolling boil for 10 minutes before lowering the heat to a simmer. Peas and lentils need to boil for only 2-3 minutes to kill the toxin.

Chili-Making: It's Bean A Secret

The first aim is to soften the bean and turn it into mush, without its falling apart. The cell wall needs to be weakened and the starch granules need to be gelatinized. Initially, beans are soaked in water containing 1-2 teaspoons of fennel seed for 3-4 hours. This will soften the beans and allow the fennel seed to neutralize the complex sugars that cause flatulence. The beans are then cooked in boiling water until they are tender but not overly mushy. The texture of the bean will remain more stable if the cooking is performed in a somewhat alkaline solution instead of an acidic one. This is why you should add ⅛ teaspoon of baking soda to the cooking water. Chili sauce is too acidic a solution for the bean until it is fully cooked, since it will not soften any further in the acidic environment. Many cooks try to save time by relying on the acidic chili sauce to complete the cooking of the bean and end up with hard beans.

Roasted Beans

Only two legumes, soybeans and peanuts, are commonly roasted. This is because of their high oil content which compensates for their dryness. When roasted, both legumes tend to change flavor and texture. The low water content and the high temperature used for roasting are responsible for the browning of the outer coating. Unless you desire a very hard bean after it is roasted, it is best to partly cook the bean first. This will partly gelatinize the starch, making it more crisp than hard. Beans are similar to nuts when it comes to roasting and they should be roasted slowly at 250° F. (121° C.) to avoid burning the surface before the insides are done.

Reduce The Risk Of Stroke

Eight hundred middle-aged men who participated in the Framingham Heart Study reduced their risk of stroke by 22% by eating three servings of vegetables daily.

Aromatic Vegetables

A number of relatives of the carrot family have strong scented oils. This includes over 3,000 species. These include coriander, anise, cumin, dill, caraway, fennel, and parsley. Garlic has no aroma until the tissues are disturbed and the sulfur-containing amino acid cysteine is released to react with an enzyme that converts it into diallyl disulfide, which is the main component that causes the unique garlic aroma.

What Are The Best Greens?

The following vegetables are in descending order of nutritional value.

BETA-CAROTENE CAROTENOIDS	VITAMIN C
Dandelion Greens	Kale
Kale	Arugula
Turnip Greens	Mustard greens
Arugula	Turnip Greens
Spinach	
Beet Greens	
Mustard Greens	
CALCIUM	**IRON**
Arugula	Beet Greens
Turnip Greens	Spinach
Dandelion Greens	Dandelion Greens
	Swiss Chard
	Chard
	Kale

FIBER	
Kale	
Spinach	
Turnip Greens	
Mustard Greens	

Odoriferous Cruciferous?

We have all smelled broccoli, cabbage, Brussels sprouts, and cauliflower cooking, and it is not a pleasant aroma. Heating these vegetables causes a chemical to break down and release a strong-smelling sulfur compound composed of ammonia and hydrogen sulfide (rotten egg smell). The more you cook them, the more intense the smell, and the more compounds that are released. If you cook broccoli too long the compounds will react with the chlorophyll (the green color) and turn the broccoli brown. If you cook broccoli in a small amount of water it will slow down the reaction.

Preserves And Pectin

Many a cook still believes that preserves acquire their smooth, semi-solid consistency from the amount of sugar that is added. Actually, the consistency is controlled by the level of pectin which is extracted from the cell wall of the fruit. Pectin is similar to cement in that it holds the cell wall together and then forms a string-like network that traps liquids and converts them into a solid. A number of fruits, such as grapes and a few varieties of berries, contain enough of their own pectin to gel without the addition of added pectin, while other fruits such as apricots, peaches, and cherries need additional pectin to gel. The most popular sources of pectin are either apples or the white layer of citrus fruits found just under the skin. The balance between sugar and pectin is a very delicate one and the optimum pH (acid/base balance) is between 2.8 and 3.4. The pectin concentration needs to be no more than 0.5-1.0% with a sugar concentration of no more than 60-65%. Due to the obvious complexity of these exacting percentages, it would be best to stick to your recipe to the letter and not make any changes. Low-cal preserves are made with a special pectin that gels using very little sugar and contains calcium ions.

Making The Perfect Pickle

A cucumber needs to be either cooked or placed in an 8% brine solution to draw the moisture which will dilute the vinegar. It is then placed in a solution of vinegar and spices and brought to a 1-1.5% acidity level. The vinegar and brine is used to retard the bacterial growth and provide the pickle with its flavor. A fermented pickle such as a dill pickle is placed in a milder brine solution, one that will still allow some bacteria to grow and produce lactic acid which allows fermentation to occur. Sauerkraut is made in the same manner.

The Proper Way To Eat An Artichoke

This large globe-like vegetable tends to scare people away and many people never get to taste one. If you do eat an artichoke, remember that the best part to eat is at the base of the leaves, since the rest of the leaf is bitter and tough. Place the leaf into your mouth and draw the leaf through your teeth, removing the tender meat. After eating all meat on the leaves you will be left with the "choke" or the heart of the artichoke which can be eaten with a fork and is the most succulent portion of the vegetable.

Artichokes: A Real Sweet Treat

Artichokes contain the chemical cyanarin. Any food that is consumed immediately after eating artichokes will taste sweeter because of this substance, Cyanarin stimulates the taste buds that are involved in the sweet taste and keeps them stimulated for 3-4 minutes after you have eaten the artichoke. However, when you heat an artichoke the chlorophyll in its green leaves reacts with the acids in the artichoke or those in the cooking water and forms the compound pheophytin, which turns the leaves brown. The combination of the pheophytins and yellow carotenes may actually make the artichoke appear bronze. If you cook the artichoke fairly quickly this reaction will not take place and the artichoke will remain green.

Asparagus A Foul Odor; Beets Are Colorful

Asparagus contains a sulfur compound that is converted during the digestive process into a foul-smelling sulfur compound. When some people urinate after eating asparagus their urine may have a foul smell. Almost 40% of all people who eat asparagus have this problem, a harmless reaction that is caused by a specific gene. Beets contain a pigment called betacyanin which will harmlessly turn the urine and feces red. Only 15% of the population have the problem of not being able to metabolize this substance.

Jack-O-Lantern Miracle

One of the biggest problems every Halloween is that the pumpkin will get soft and mushy only a few hours after it has been carved. The problem is that when air is allowed to come in contact with the inside flesh, bacteria start to grow at a rapid pace. Spraying the inside of the pumpkin with an antiseptic spray will slow down the bacterial growth and increase the time it takes to deteriorate. Make sure you do not eat the pumpkin or the seeds after it has been sprayed.

How Do Fruits And Vegetables Make Vitamin C?

All plants manufacture vitamin C from sugars which are derived from the leaves and produced by photosynthesis. The more light a plant gets, the more sugars are produced and the more vitamin C the plant can produce. Another factor is that the more light a plant receives, the more chlorophyll and carotenoids the plant needs to handle its energy input, which causes the leaves to be darker. The darker the leaves of a vegetable, the more potential it has to produce vitamins A and C.

Veggie States

The following are the latest 1996 statistics on a few of the vegetables we consume in sufficient quantity to be worth even talking about:

VEGETABLE	POUNDS PER YEAR
Potatoes	83
Lettuce	28
Onions	15
Tomatoes	14
Carrots	8
Sweet Potatoes	4
Broccoli	3

What Is A Kiwano?

The kiwano is a member of the cucumber family and is actually an African horned melon. It is exported by New Zealanders who gave it a name similar to the kiwi for easier recognition and so that it would be more associated with New Zealand. The shape of the fruit is similar to a large gherkin; however, it is bright orange with a number of small horns protruding from the skin. The flavor is similar to that of a mango and a pineapple combined. It is very tasty and should become more popular and less expensive as more people purchase the fruit.

Can A Sweet Lemon Be Grown?

There is a fruit called a limetta or sweet lemon that is grown in Italy and California. It resembles a cross between a lemon and a lime and is so sweet that you will never pucker. The California variety is called the "millsweet" but has not really been that popular at the markets yet. They taste like lemonade and are excellent for lemonade, pie filling, and lemon sauces.

What Is The Most Popular Chinese Fruit?

There is really no contest, even though China does grow many great fruits: the lychee is definitely the most popular. In one report an ancient Chinese poet bragged about his lychee habit, claiming to eat 300 every day and as much as 1,000 in a day. The first fruit culture book ever written was in 1056 and was solely devoted to growing lychee. The skin is tough, brown, and scaly with a slight red tinge; however, it peels easily. They may be found either fresh or dried, especially in Chinese markets.

What Is The Difference Between Apple Juice And Cider?

In both products the apples are pressed and the juice extracted. However, apple juice is sterilized by pasteurization, whereas apple cider is not. Apple cider is sold at roadside stands and in markets without the protection of pasteurization. Occasionally when apples fall to the ground they come in contact with fecal material from farm animals and may be contaminated with the bacteria *E. coli*. Pasteurized cider may be available in some markets and should be the cider of choice. Cider needs to labeled "cider." If it does not have that name then it is just apple juice in a gallon jug. In 1991, 23 people drank apple cider produced at a small cider mill in Massachusetts and were infected with *E. coli*. If you do decide to purchase cider from a stand, be sure to inquire whether the apples were washed and inspected before being used for cider.

Why Does An Apple Collapse When Cooked?

If you place a whole apple in the oven and bake it, the peel will withstand the heat and manage to retain its shape as long as it can. The peel contains an insoluble cellulose and ligan which reinforce the peel and keep it intact. The flesh of the apple, however, will partly disintegrate as the pectin in its cell walls is dissolved by the water being released from the cells. The cells rupture and the apple turns to applesauce. The reason apples stay relatively firm in apple pies is that bakers add calcium to the apples.

Do Apples Have Any Medicinal Use?

Apples have been used for hundreds of years as a folk remedy for diarrhea. Thinly sliced raw apple contains an excellent level of pectin which is one of the main ingredients in over-the-counter anti-diarrheals such as Kaopectate. The pectin also tends to interfere with the body's absorption of dietary fats. Pectins tend to produce a type of fat-absorbing gel in the stomach when it comes into contact with the stomach acid.

Okra Is An Excellent Thickener

Okra is actually a vegetable that consists of numerous unripe seed capsules. It is a very high-carbohydrate food that is high in fiber and starch and contains a good amount of pectin and gums. The combination of these food elements provides an excellent thickener for soups and stews. As okra is heated, the starch granules absorb water and increase in size. They soon rupture and release amylose and amylopectin molecules, as well as some of its gums and pectin. These then attract additional water molecules and increase the volume, thus thickening the food.

Tomato Aroma Only Lasts For 3 Minutes?

If you like the aroma of fresh tomatoes in your salad, don't refrigerate them. Tomatoes should be left at room temperature if they are going to be used within 2-3 days after purchase. They should never be sliced or peeled until just before you serve them. The aroma is produced by the chemical z-3-hexenel which is released when the tomato is sliced open. The aroma chemical only lasts at the "maximum aroma" level for 3 minutes before it starts to lose its scent. If you refrigerate a tomato the chemical becomes dormant, but if you allow it to return to room temperature before you slice it the aroma will still be active.

What Is The Eggplant Of The Mushroom World?

Puffballs can be found dried or picked from the forest during the hot, humid summer months. They are called the "eggplant of the mushroom world" because they are very large, oval shaped and white.

What's A Zester?

The sweet flavor in a citrus fruit is contained in the outer rind or "zest." The tool used to remove the rind is called a zester. It removes only the rind, not the bitter white pith. The thin blade is used to remove only the extreme outer layer.

Can You Get High From Smoking Banana Peels?

Banana peels became very popular during the 1960's when scientists announced that they contained minute amounts of certain psychoactive compounds such as serotonin, norepinephrine, and dopamine. Banana peels were dried, ground up into a fine powder and rolled in paper cigarette wrappers. However, the fad didn't last too long since the effects were so weak that few people were actually getting high. The majority of the bananas being imported to the United States today are from Ecuador.

What Pie Is Served Near The Kilauea Volcano?

On the big island of Hawaii a special fruit called the "ohelo" is grown. The berry is a relative of the cranberry; however, it is much sweeter and is used to prepare jams and pies and is served at the Volcano House on the rim of the Kilauea crater. Be sure to try this unique pie if you are ever visiting the island of Hawaii.

How Do You Reduce Acidity In Tomato Products?

Some people are unable to eat spaghetti sauces and other tomato-based foods due to the higher acidic content of the tomato. When chopped carrots are added to any of these dishes, it will reduce the acidity without affecting the taste. The high fiber content of the carrot seems to do the job.

Purple Carrots?

Carrots were purple until the early 17th century when the orange color variety was developed in England. The beta-carotene levels were not always as high as they are today. Carrots were then developed with a higher level of beta-carotene to help the World War II British aviators acquire better night vision. The iron supply in carrots is also absorbed more efficiently than most other vegetable sources.

What Are The Top 20 Nutritious Vegetables?

The following list of vegetables starts with the most nutritious, calculated from the nutrient levels of 10 of the most important nutrients. They must contain all 10, which are protein, iron, calcium, niacin, vitamins A and C, potassium, phosphorus, thiamine, and riboflavin.

1. COLLARD GREENS
2. LIMA BEANS
3. PEAS
4. SPINACH
5. SWEET POTATOES
6. TURNIP GREENS
11. MUSTARD GREENS
12. SWISS CHARD
13. PARSLEY
14. TOMATOES
15. CORN
16. BEET GREENS

7. WINTER SQUASH
8. BROCCOLI
9. KALE
10. BRUSSELS SPROUTS

17. PUMPKIN
18. OKRA
19. POTATOES
20. CARROTS

CHAPTER 4
FOOD, FREEZING, STORAGE, AND PRESERVATION

Was Napolean Responsible For Food Preservation?

Napoleon's army was becoming sick and many of his men were dying from scurvy and other diseases related to lack of essential nutrients. Because of their long marches far from the food sources, all they could bring with them was salted meats. Napoleon talked the rulers at the time into offering a reward equal to $250,000 in today's money if anyone could develop a method of preserving foods. Nicholas Appert, a Paris confectioner, after 14 years of trial and error, finally invented a method of preservation. His method was to place food in a glass jar, allowing for expansion, and place a hand-hewn cork in the jar attached firmly with a piece of wire. Each jar was then wrapped in a burlap sack and lowered into a pot of boiling water. The time the jar was left in seemed to vary with the type of food. He was successful in preserving eggs, milk products, fruits, vegetables, and meats. He was awarded the prize money in 1810 by Napoleon and was labeled as " the man who discovered the art of making the seasons stand still."

Who Made The First Tin Can?

Canning was invented in 1810 by Peter Durand, an Englishman, who called the container a "tin canister." This would be an improvement over the glass jar, especially for transportation to outlying areas without breakage. The first "tin cans" had to be made by hand, with workers cutting the can from sheets of tin-plate and then soldering them together, leaving a small hole in the top to place the food in. The hole was then covered with a small tin disc and soldered closed. A tin worker was able to produce about 60 cans a day. The United States started a canning operation in the 1820's and within 20 years canning of foods was being done all over the country. In 1860 Isaac Solomon in Baltimore found that if he added calcium chloride to the water when it was boiling, he could raise the temperature from 212° F to 240° F. and thus reduce the processing time from about 6 hours to 45 minutes. A processing plant could now produce 20,000 cans a day instead of 2,500.

Who Came Up With The Name "Birdseye"?

The Birdseye food company was founded by Clarence Birdseye, an American businessman who invented the process of freezing food in small packages. He discovered the process by accident while hunting in Labrador in 1915. Some portions of caribou and fish were frozen by the dry Arctic air and when thawed were tender and still tasty. He developed a process that duplicated the Arctic conditions and started a company. Birdseye Seafoods was founded in 1923 and by 1929 had expanded his product line. In 1929 he sold out to General Foods.

Negative Effects Of Freezing Foods

When food is frozen a percentage of the cells tends to burst, releasing their liquids. This will occur in all foods regardless of the method of freezing or the type of wrap. Ice crystals are formed from the lost liquid and the food never has the same texture or exactly the same flavor as it originally had when it was freshly prepared. Biologically, the process that occurs is referred to as osmosis. Osmosis is the process by which a liquid passes through a semi-permeable membrane (cell wall) in order to equalize the pressure. When the food is frozen, the solids inside of the cell cause the water to become more concentrated, allowing the liquid from outside the cell to enter, form crystals and eventually cause a number of the cells to burst. Since some of the flavor of the food is contained in each cell, a percentage of the flavor is also lost. Meats, fruits, and most seafood are more negatively affected than vegetables.

Fruits And Vegetables vs. Refrigeration

The majority of fruits and vegetables are able to handle cold fairly well, with the exception of tropical fruits whose cells are just not used to the cold. Bananas will suffer cell damage and release a skin browning chemical and avocados will refuse to ripen in the cold when stored below 45° F. Oranges will develop a brown spotted skin. The best temperature for squash, tomatoes, cucumbers, melons, green peppers, pineapple and most other fruits and vegetables is actually at about 50° F. A few exceptions are lettuce, carrots, and cabbage which prefer 32° F. The humidity is a big factor and most fruits and vegetables need to be stored in the storage drawers which will protect them from drying out.

Tomatoes Do Not Like To Be Cool

Tomatoes do not like to be stored in the refrigerator until they are almost overripe. If the storage temperature is below 50° F. it will interfere with the ripening process and stop it cold. Even if the tomato does turn from green to red, it will still not be ripe. Tomatoes should be kept at room temperature or in a cool pantry and never on the windowsill in direct sunlight or they lose a percentage of their nutrients. Freezing tomatoes is not a problem as long as they are well sealed in a plastic bag. They will, however, lose some of their firmness and be a little mushy.

Are Your Cucumbers Gasping For Air?

Cucumbers should be stored unwashed in a plastic bag with holes to allow air to circulate around the cucumber, or should be placed in the vegetable drawer if your refrigerator has one. Cucumbers will only keep for 3-5 days and do best in the warmest part of the refrigerator around 40° F. Cucumbers do not freeze well because of their high water content. Too many cells tend to burst which makes the cucumber mushy.

Bean Cooking Times vs. Loss Of Nutrients

Many people worry about the loss of nutrients due to the long cooking and soaking times for beans and other legumes. Studies performed by the USDA, however, have proved that legumes, even if they require 1-1½ hours of cooking time, will still retain from 70-90% of their vitamin content and almost 95% of their mineral content. The most affected were the B vitamins; about 45-50% were lost.

Spud Storage

Potatoes are actually an enlarged stem called a "tuber" that extends from the plant underground and is the storage depot for the plant's excess carbohydrates. The potato plant actually is a plant that bears a vegetable similar to a small mini-tomato that is not that good to eat. If potatoes are stored below 40° F, they tend to release more sugar and turn sweet. Potatoes will last longer and remain solid longer if they are stored in a cool, dry location, preferably at 45°-50° F. Air must be allowed to circulate around potatoes. Moisture will cause them to decay. Potatoes do not freeze well. A large majority of the cells tend to burst and the potatoes become mushy and watery when thawed. Commercially processed potatoes will freeze.

How Sweet It Is

Sweet potatoes, unlike white potatoes, will freeze without becoming mushy if fully cooked, either boiled or baked. They need to be placed in a well sealed plastic container with as much air as possible bled out. The container then needs to be placed into a large sealed plastic bag. They will keep for 10-12 months.

Off With Their Tops

Carrots and beets need to have their tops removed before they are stored. The tops will draw moisture from the vegetable and reduce its storage life. However, you should leave about two inches of the root, if it is still there, to keep the bottom sealed. Carrots and beets need to be stored in a sealed plastic bag in the refrigerator. Both are very susceptible to a number of microbes that will cause them to decay. Carrots will freeze well with only minimal blanching. Beets should be boiled until they are fork tender before freezing.

Be Smart When Freezing Foods

There are a number of important rules that should be adhered to if you wish to freeze foods successfully:

- When preparing any vegetable for freezing, be sure to under-cook it. Re-heating will complete the cooking.

- Freezing tends to intensify the flavor in spices such as garlic, pepper, oregano, and cloves, so you should use less, and then add more before serving.

- Additional onions can be used since freezing tends to cause the flavor to be lost.

- Salt should be used in moderation or not at all. Salt tends to slow down the freezing process.

- Never use quick-cooking rice in a dish that will be frozen, as it tends to become mushy. Use regular or converted rice.

- Artificial flavorings and sweeteners do not do well when frozen.

- Cooked egg whites turn rubbery and cannot be frozen.

- Toppings should always be added before serving. Cheeses and bread crumbs on foods do not do well.

- Freezing causes old potatoes to fall apart. Always use new potatoes in dishes that are to be frozen.

- Gravies and sauces need to be made somewhat thicker than normal since they will usually separate.

- Cool foods first in the refrigerator before freezing.

Storing Cauliflower

One of the most important things to remember is never bump or injure the florets. This will cause the head to loosen and spread too fast and cause discoloration. Store the head in a plastic bag that is not wrapped too tightly around the head and store it in the vegetable crisper. Never wash the cauliflower before it is stored and it should keep 4-6 days. Wash the head thoroughly before eating since a number of chemicals are often used to preserve freshness. To freeze, just cut the cauliflower into small pieces, wash in lightly salted water, then blanch in salt water for 5 minutes. Drain and chill them before placing them into a plastic bag.

Storing Broccoli

Broccoli should be stored in a plastic bag in the refrigerator. It will keep for only 3-5 days before the florets start opening and a loss of nutrients occurs. To freeze broccoli, the leaves need to be removed and the stalks peeled. The broccoli should be cut into small lengthwise strips and blanched for 5 minutes, chilled and drained well and sealed in a plastic bag. It can be frozen for 10-12 months at 0° F.

A recent study at the University of Kentucky compared the vitamin C content of whole broccoli and plastic wrapped broccoli. Broccoli that was left out in the air lost 30% of its vitamin C content in 4 days, while the broccoli that was wrapped in plastic only lost 17% and retained its color better. The respiration rate of the broccoli was slowed down, which conserved the nutrients.

Storing Popeye's Favorite

Spinach will keep for only 2-3 days, providing it is stored in a sealed plastic bag. Do not wash it or cut it before you are ready to serve it. When purchasing spinach that has been prepackaged, be sure to open the bag and remove any brown or darkened leaves since they may cause the balance of the leaves to deteriorate at a faster rate. When freezing spinach, do not freeze the stems but only the whole leaves. This will allow the leaf to retain more of the moisture. Spinach should be washed in cold water, dried carefully and thoroughly with a paper towel, and stored in the freezer in an airtight bag. It should keep for 10-12 months if the freezer is kept at 0° F.

Why Is A Full Freezer More Energy Efficient?

A freezer that is full will use less energy than a half-full freezer because frozen foods retain cold air for a long period. The freezer will run fewer hours per day and save considerable money in electricity.

Storing Lettuce

All types of lettuce love the cold and the closer the temperature gets to 32° F. without going below that, the longer it will keep and the crispier it will be. Most refrigerators range between 35° and 40° F. which is good, but not the ideal temperature for lettuce. The lettuce should be stored without washing in a sealed plastic bag with a small hole or two for ventilation. Lettuce will turn brown easily if allowed to remain near most other fruits or vegetables due to the level of ethylene gas given off. Iceberg lettuce will remain fresher than any other type of lettuce due to its higher water content and will store for 7-14 days. Romaine lasts for 6-10 days and butterhead for only 3-4 days. If you need to crisp lettuce leaves, place them in the freezer for no more than 2-3 minutes; any more and you may have to discard them.

Blanching Before Freezing: A Must

When vegetables are frozen, enzymes may still remain active and cause changes in the color, texture, and taste in the vegetable even if they have been previously stored under refrigeration. Freezing will slow the changes down. However, it will not totally inactivate the enzymes. If vegetables are blanched by either boiling them in water that has boiled for 2 minutes first (to release oxygen) or steaming them for 3-4 minutes, they will not be cooked but the enzymes will be inactivated, and they will retain their color, texture, and taste. Of course, the enzymes are important to good nutrition and it would be more desirable to purchase only enough for a few days at a time.

Storing Cooked Vegetables

The best method of storing vegetables that have been cooked is to store them in a well-sealed plastic container in the refrigerator. They will last about 3-5 days. If you wish to freeze them, then seal them in an airtight bag or a container from which most of the air can be removed. Since cells will burst, releasing some of their liquid, they will be somewhat soggy but can be used in soups and stews. They will last from 8-12 months and still be edible.

Chest Freezer vs. Upright Freezer

This debate has been around for a long time; however, the answer has always been a fairly simple one. The chest freezer, even though the door may be larger, will retain its cold setting longer when the door is opened since cold air is heavier than hot air and tends to stay put. The upright freezer tends to release most of its cold air the minute the door is opened. Chest freezers will maintain and hold the preferred 0° F. freezer level to maximize food storage times before spoilage.

Origin of Canning

Preserving foods by placing them into a sealed container was originated in 1810 by the Frenchman Nicholas Appert who discovered that when sealing food in a container and then heating the container, the food would last longer and still be edible. Canned meat stored for 114 years has been eaten safely.

Problems With Aluminum Foil

Foods wrapped in aluminum foil may be subject to two problems. The first is that since aluminum foil is such a great insulator it tends to slow down the heat transfer and the food will not freeze as fast as you may want it to. The second is that when you crinkle the aluminum foil to place it around the food, micro-cracks develop which may allow air and moisture to penetrate the food. If you plan on storing food for more than 2-3 days in the refrigerator in aluminum foil, you should probably wrap the food in plastic wrap first. Aluminum foil will also react with foods that are acidic or salty and may impart a strange taste to the food.

Frozen Prehistoric Burgers

Russians claim to have recovered edible meat from a mammoth frozen in the ice of Siberia. The mammoth is estimated to be 20,000 years old. If they decide to clone it, we may be eating mammoth burgers. In the Yukon, frozen prehistoric horse bones estimated to be 50,000 years old were discovered in the ice. The marrow was determined to be safe to eat and was served at an exclusive New York dinner party.

Salt, The Microbe Inhibitor

For thousands of years salt has been used to preserve foods by inhibiting microbial growth. Salt has the ability to draw liquids from tissues, freeing bound water by breaking down proteins. The mechanism involves salt's ability to create a concentration of ions (electrically charged particles) outside of the bacteria and mold cells that encompass the microbe, drawing out its water and either drying it up and killing it or slowing down its replication. It is the drying-out feature of salt that makes it such a good preservative. To preserve meats in England the meat was covered with very large grains of salt that resembled corn, hence the name "corned beef."

Smoke Curing Foods

The use of smoke to cure foods is one of the oldest methods of food preservation and one that provides a number of risks to the body from the toxins that may be placed into the food from the smoke. Smoke may contain as many as 200 different chemical components which include alcohols, acids, phenolic compounds, pyrobenzine, and other carcinogenic chemicals. Many of these toxic substances do, however, retard microbial growth. Salt curing methods and smoking are frequently combined to minimize the oxidation of the fats which causes rancidity.

Butter B-Ware

When storing butter it will be more important where you store it than how long it will last. Butter tends to absorb odors more efficiently than any other food. If you store it near onions it will take on an onion smell. If it's around fish it will smell fishy. If butter is refrigerated it will retain its flavor for about 3 weeks. After that it starts losing flavor rather fast. If you desire a rich butter flavor it would be wise to date your butter package. Butter will freeze if you double-wrap it in plastic and then foil to keep it from absorbing freezer odors. It will last for 9 months if fresh when frozen and must be kept at 0° F.

Storing Celery

Celery should be stored unwashed in a plastic bag and should last for up to 2 weeks. Celery does not freeze well due to its high water content and will become mushy when thawed out. It can be re-crisped by placing the stalks in a bowl of ice water for 1 hour.

Asparagus Loses Sugar

Fresh asparagus loses sugar very rapidly and each day it is stored in a plastic bag in the refrigerator it will lose about 10-15% of its natural sugar. As the natural sugars are lost, the asparagus will also become tougher. The tips should be kept as dry as possible or they will become mushy and fall apart when they are cooked. To tenderize the stalks, just use your potato peeler and remove the first layer of the stalk. To freeze asparagus, remove the last 2 inches of the stalk and then blanch it in boiling water for 2-4 minutes (depending on the thickness of the stalks). If you steam it, blanch it and then add 1 minute. Tray-freeze before placing it into a plastic bag to keep the tips in good condition.

The Correct Method Of Freezing Bread

Always freeze bread in its original wrapper. Bread will release moisture when frozen which collects inside the wrapper. Be sure to never unwrap the bread when you defrost it; always leave the wrapper intact and sealed so that the bread can re-absorb the lost moisture and retain the original fresh taste.

Don't Store Corn

Corn is one vegetable that is always better if eaten when it is fresh, preferably the same day you purchase it. As soon as corn is picked it immediately starts to convert the sugars to starch. The milky liquid in the kernel that makes corn sweet will turn pulpy and bland in only 2-3 days. This is the reason that many people add sugar to the water when cooking corn. This guarantees the taste which was probably lost during just a few days of storage. Leftover fresh corn should be cooked for a few minutes just to inactivate the enzymes. Store the ears in a sealed plastic bag for 1-2 days before using. If you plan on freezing corn, clean it and blanch it for 4 minutes in boiling water. Allow the water to drain and tray-freeze, leaving space between the ears so that the kernels will retain their shape and not be crushed. Then seal it in plastic bags. Frozen corn will keep for 1 year.

Little Sprouts

When purchasing fresh sprouts, remember that they can be stored in the refrigerator for only 7-10 days, providing they are placed in a plastic bag and lightly moistened before it is sealed.Too much water in the bag will cause decay. Remember: the shorter the tendril, the more tender and younger the sprout. Sprouts cannot be frozen successfully; they become mushy and bland.

Storing Tofu

Tofu or soybean curd is produced from mashed soybeans, cultured similarly to cottage cheese and then pressed into small white custardy squares. It should be stored in the original container, and the liquid should be replaced daily with fresh, cold water. If this is done, tofu will last for 3-5 days from the "sell date" and possibly 2 weeks if it is very fresh when purchased. If you are going to freeze tofu it should be frozen as soon as it purchased, in its original water and container. It can be frozen for about 2 months at 0° F. After it is thawed it will, however, be a little bit more fragile and will disintegrate unless added to dishes just before serving.

Storing Dried Legumes

If legumes are kept in a dry, cool location below 70° F. they will last for up to 1 year and retain most of their nutrient content. They may be stored in their original bag or container or transferred to a sealed glass jar. Never mix old beans with new beans as they will not cook evenly. It is not necessary to freeze dry beans; this will not preserve their nutrient content any longer. Beans in cooked dishes may be frozen; however, they may be somewhat mushy when thawed.

Grapes, The Biggest Industry In The World

The grape industry is reported to be the largest single food industry in the world. This includes table grapes, raisin grapes, wine grapes, and juice grapes. Grapes need to be stored in a plastic bag and in the coldest part of the refrigerator. They should not be washed before being stored, but need to be washed very well before being eaten. Grapes do not freeze well since they are high in water content and become mushy when thawed. They can be eaten frozen or used in dishes and will freeze well for about 1 year.

Cherry Picking Time

Cherries should be stored in a refrigerator with as high a humidity as possible. For the best flavor, they should be placed unwashed in a plastic bag and allowed to stand at room temperature for 30 minutes before being eaten. Cherries will last about 4 days in the refrigerator. If you freeze cherries they must be pitted first and sealed airtight in a plastic bag; otherwise they will taste like almonds.

Storing Apples

Apples will ripen very quickly at room temperature. If you are not sure of their level of ripeness, just leave them out for 2-3 days before refrigerating them. Apples should be stored in the refrigerator to stop the ripening process. They may be washed, dried and placed into a plastic bag. When refrigerated, apples will stay fresh for 2-4 weeks. Apples may also be stored in a cool, dry location in a barrel that has sawdust in it. The apples should never touch each other and will last 4-6 months. To freeze apples, they need to be cored, peeled, washed, and sliced. Spray them with a solution of 2 teaspoons of ascorbic acid (vitamin C) in 12 tablespoons of cold water, then place them in a container, leaving ½ inch of space at the top.

Avocados Love Wool Socks

To ripen an avocado, just place it in a wool sock in the back of a dark closet for 2 days. Avocados should never be stored in the refrigerator if they are not fully ripe. When they are ripe they should be stored in the vegetable drawer in the refrigerator and should stay fresh for 10-14 days. Avocados may be frozen only if puréed, and will keep for three to six months.

Monkey's Favorite Food

As soon as a banana ripens at room temperature it should be stored in the refrigerator to slow down the ripening process. The skin will turn black but this does not affect the flesh for a number of days. Bananas will freeze well for a short period of time; however, they will be a bit mushy when thawed and are better used in dishes. Frozen banana treats are eaten while the banana is still frozen solid, which does not give them the thawing time to make them mushy.

Mushrooms Need Room To Breathe

Fresh mushrooms have a very short shelf life of only 2-3 days and need to be stored in an open container in the refrigerator. Plastic containers should never be used since they tend to retain moisture. It is best to use the original container or a paper product to store them in. Never clean them before storing them or they will retain moisture and become soggy. If you need to keep them stored for a few days, place a piece of single-layer cheesecloth on top of the container. If they do become shriveled, they can be sliced and used in dishes. When freezing mushrooms, just wipe them off with a piece of damp paper towel, slice them, sauté them in a small amount of butter until they are almost done, allow them to cool, then place them in an airtight plastic bag and freeze. They should keep for 1 year.

New Storage Bags: A Must For Every Kitchen

A new plastic storage bag for fruits and vegetables is now on the market. The bag contains hundreds of microscopic holes that allow air to circulate around the produce. The bag is also impregnated with "oya," a natural substance that will absorb the ethylene gas that is released by the produce as it ripens and helps the produce ripen. Unfortunately, the more ethylene gas the produce expels around the food, the faster the food ripens and spoils. The bags are tinted green to reduce the effects of light reducing the potency of the vitamins. The bag is marketed under the name "Evert-Fresh." Produce stored in these bags will last 10 times longer than produce stored in standard plastic storage bags. In tests over a 12 day period, 50% more of the vitamin C was retained. If you are unable to locate them call (800) 822-8141 to order your supply.

Storing Margarine

Margarine very readily will absorb odors from foods that are stored nearby. It should be sealed as tightly as possible and should store for 4-6 months in the refrigerator. Margarine freezes well and will keep for 1 year if the temperature is kept at 0° F.

Storing Onions

Ideally, onions should be stored in hanging bags which will allow the air to circulate around them. Never purchase an onion if it has the slightest hint of decay since it will spread rapidly to the other healthy onions if stored with them. The location should be cool and dry. If the weather is hot and humid it will cut the storage time in half; otherwise they should last about 2-3 weeks. If you refrigerate onions they will last for about 2 months but may pass their aroma on to other foods in the refrigerator, even eggs. Sprouted onions are still good to use, as well as the sprouts. To freeze onions just slice them (do not blanch them) and seal them in plastic bag. They will hold well for about 1 year.

Garlic, The Pungent Cousin Of The Onion

Storing garlic is relatively simple. All you have to do is place the garlic in a cool, dry location as close to 50° F. as possible or even at room temperature It will easily last for about 1-2 months. Garlic will retain its flavor better if it not stored in the refrigerator; however, there is no harm in storing it there. Storing garlic in a small jar of olive oil is the chef's way of keeping the flavor in the garlic for 2-3 months. Garlic should never be frozen, as it will lose its flavor.

Should You Buy A Frosted Package Of Vegetables?

No! This usually means that the food has thawed either partly or completely and a percentage of moisture has already been lost. If one package of that product is damaged, the chances are very good that the balance of the shipment may also have deteriorated.

Why Should Meats Be Wrapped Tightly When Freezing?

As foods are frozen, evaporation continues and the meat fluids are lost. The entire surface area of the meat needs to be protected from the loss of moisture with a moisture-resistant wrap. The best wrap for freezing meats is plastic wrap with a protective freezer paper over the wrap. This still does not entirely protect the meat from a percentage of evaporation in which water vapor causes freezer burn. A good tight wrap will also reduce the risk of oxidation and rancidity.

Refrigerated Storage Times For Vegetables

VEGETABLE	DAYS IN REFRIGERATOR
Artichoke	6-7
Arugula	3
Asparagus	4-6
Bamboo Shoots	7
Beans, Lima	2-3
Beans, Green	3-5
Beets	7-10
Bitter Melon	5
Black-eyed Peas	2-3
Bok Choy	3-4
Broccoli	4-5
Brussels Sprouts	3-5
Cabbage	8-14
Carrots	7-14
Cauliflower	4-7
Celery	7-14
Celery Root	2-3
Chickpeas	2-3
Chicory	3-5
Chinese Cabbage	4-5
Cooked Fresh Vegetables	3-5
Corn	1
Cucumbers	4-5
Eggplant	3-4
Escarole	3-5
Fennel	7-14
Ginger	7-14
Green Onions	7-14
Greens (Dandelion, Mustard)	1-2
Horseradish	10-20
Jicama	7-14
Kale	2-3
Kohlrabi	4-5
Leeks	7-14
Lettuce, Iceberg	7-14
Lettuce, All Others	6-10
Mushrooms	4-5
Okra	2-3
Onions	7-14
Peas	7-10
Peppers, Green & Chili	4-6
Peppers, Sweet Red & Yellow	2-3
Radishes	2-3
Rutabagas	7-14
Salsify	7-14
Sauerkraut, Fresh	6-7
Soybeans	2-3

Spinach	2-3
Sprouts	2-3
Squash, Summer	4-5
Swiss Chard	2-3
Tomatoes	3-5
Tofu	3-10
Turnips	5-7
Water Chestnuts	6-7
Watercress	2-3

Note: Unless otherwise noted in this chapter, all vegetables should be stored in perforated plastic bags.

Storage Times For Fresh Fruit

FRUIT	RIPEN AFTER HARVESTING	REFRIGERATOR STORAGE TIME
Apples	Yes	2-4 Weeks
Apricots	Yes	2-3 Days
Avocados	Yes	10-14 Days
Bananas	Yes	1 Week
Berries	No	3-7 Days
Melons	Yes	7-10 Days
Cherries	No	2-4 Days
Cranberries	No	1 Month
Currants	No	1-2 Days
Dates	No	1-2 Months
Figs, fresh	No	1-2 Days
Grapefruit	No	10-14 Days
Grapes	No	3-5 Days
Guava	Yes	2 Weeks
Kiwi Fruit	Yes	1 Week
Kumquats	No	3 Weeks
Lemons	No	2-3 Weeks
Limes	No	3-4 Weeks
Lychees	No	1 Week
Mangoes	Yes	2-3 Days
Nectarines	Yes	3-5 Days
Oranges	No	10-14 Days
Papayas	Yes	2 Weeks
Peaches	Yes	3-5 Days
Pears	Yes	3-5 Days
Persimmons	Yes	1-2 Days
Pineapple	Yes	3-5 Days
Plums	Yes	3-5 Days
Pomegranates	No	2-3 Weeks
Prunes	Yes	3-5 Days
Rhubarb	No	4-6 Days
Star Fruit	Yes	5-7 Days
Uglifruit	No	10-14 Days

| Watermelons | No | 1 Week |

Storage Times For Nuts In The Shell

NUT	CUPBOARD	REFRIGERATOR	FREEZER
Almonds	1 Year	1 Year	1 Year
Brazil Nut	9 Months	9 Months	
Canned Nuts	1 Year	1 Year	1 Year
Cashews		6 Months	9 Months
Chestnuts		6 Months	9 Months
Coconuts		1 Month	
Filberts	3 Months	9 Months	1 Year
Macadamia Nuts		6 Months	1 Year
Mixed Nuts		9 Months	1 Year
Peanuts, Raw	2 Months	6 Months	1 Year
Peanuts, Roasted	1 Month	3 Months	9 Months
Pecans	2-3 Months	6 Months	1 Year
Pine Nuts		1 Month	6 Months
Pistachios		3 Months	1 Year
Pumpkin Seeds	2-3 Months	1 Year	1 Year
Sunflower Seeds	2-3 Months	1 Year	1 Year
Walnuts	2-3 Months	1 Year	1 Year

Storage Times For Refrigerated Dairy Products

PRODUCT	DAYS UNDER REFRIGERATION	MONTHS IN FREEZER 0° F.
Butter	45-90	7-8
Butter, Clarified	60-90	7-8
Buttermilk	7-14	3
Cream	3-5	3
Cream, Whipped		
Commercial	30	Do Not Freeze
Homemade	1	2
Eggnog	3-5	6
Half & Half	3-4	4
Ice Cream, Commercial		2-3
Frozen Desserts		1-2
Margarine		
Regular and Soft	120	12
Diet	90	
Milk	3-7	3
Non-dairy Creamer	21	12
Non-dairy Toppings		
Container	7	12
Aerosol Can	90	Do Not Freeze
Sour Cream	14	

Yogurt 14 2

Storage Times For Cheeses

CHEESE	WEEKS UNDER REFRIGERATION
Appenzellar	4
Bel Paese	4
Blue Cheese	2-4
Brick	4-8
Brie	3-5 Days
Camembert	3-5 Days
Cheddar	5-8
Cheshire	5-8
Colby	4-8
Cold Pack Cheese	2-3
Cottage Cheese, All Curds	1
Cream Cheese	1-2
Derby	4-8
Edam	4-8
Farmer's	1-2
Firm-Type Cheeses	4-8
Feta	8-12
Fontina	4
Goat	2-4
Gorgonzola	2-4
Gouda	4-8
Gruyêre	2-4
Havarti	3-4
Herkimer	4-8
Jarlsberg	4
Liederkranz	3-5 Days
Limburger	1-2
Mascarpone	1
Monastery Type	2-4
Monterey Jack	2-4
Muenster	1-3
Mozzarella, Fresh	2-3 Days
Mozzarella, Dry	2-4
Neufchâtel	1-2
Parmesan	10-12
Port du Salut	2-4
Pot Cheese	1
Processed Cheese, Opened	3-4
Provolone	8-12
Ricotta	1
Roquefort	2-4
Semi-Soft Type	2-4
Stilton	2-4
Swiss	4-5

Tillamook 4-8
Tilsiter 2-4

Note: The unprocessed natural cheeses will freeze for 4-6 months and retain most of their flavor.

Storage Times For Meats

MEAT	DAYS UNDER REFRIGERATION	MONTHS IN FREEZER
BEEF		
Roasts, Steaks	3-5	9
Ground, Stew	1-2	2-4
Organs	1-2	2-4
VEAL		
Roasts, Chops, Ribs	3-5	6-9
Ground, Cutlet, Stew	1-2	3-4
Organs	1-2	1-2
PORK		
Roasts, Chops, Ribs	2-4	3-6
Ground, Sausage	1-2	1-2
Organs	1-2	1-2
LAMB		
Roasts, Chops, Ribs	2-4	6-9
Ground, Stew	1-2	3-4
Organs	1-2	1-2

Storage Times For Baking Staples

PRODUCT	SHELF LIFE
Arrowroot	1 Year
Baking Powder	3-6 Months
Baking Soda	18 Months
Cornstarch	1 Year
Cream of Tartar	1 Year
Extracts	1 Year
Gelatin, Boxed	1 Year
Salt	Forever If Kept Dry
Tapioca	1 Year
Vinegar	1 Year
Yeast	Date on Package

Never Freeze Foods In Aluminum Foil

Aluminum foil is so efficient at maintaining a food's temperature that it retards the transfer of heat to its surrounding area. This simply means that the foods wrapped in foil will not freeze as fast as you would prefer them to and may start the growth of bacteria which will stay dormant until the food is thawed. The best use for foil is to keep hot foods hot longer and cold foods cold longer.

Can Herbs Be Refrigerated?

When a jar or package of herbs is opened at room-temperature, moisture and air are allowed to enter the container. The cold air in the refrigerator then causes the condensation to remain in the jar. Herbs are very susceptible to loss of flavor and should be stored in a cool, dry location for maximum freshness over a long period of time.

Which Is Better, A Thermal Bottle Or A Vacuum Bottle?

When a hot beverage is placed in a container for storage, the heat is lost to the colder air through conduction. A cold beverage will lose the cold and gain heat from its surroundings. Both a thermal and a vacuum bottle slow the transfer of heat and cold between the beverage and its surroundings by placing a barrier between the food and the environment. A vacuum bottle places the food in a space within a vacuum surrounding the food. The unit is hermetically sealed between the bottle's inner and outer glass lining. In the thermal bottle, the exterior is solid and a poor conductor of heat, but nowhere as poor as a vacuum bottle. Thermal bottles will not break as easily since they do not have the glass interior.

The Dangers In Raw Food

The bacterium *Salmonella* comes from the intestines of humans and animals and is often found in raw meats and eggs. *Salmonella* can be present after foods are dried, processed, or frozen for long periods. The bacteria can also be transferred to food by insects or human hands, especially infants and people with poor cleanliness habits. *Salmonella* is easily killed with high heat, which is why raw meats need to be cooked thoroughly. Food preparation surfaces that are not cleaned adequately after preparing raw meats and egg dishes are the cause of most cases of *Salmonella* illness.

CHAPTER 5
CONDIMENTS, SAUCES AND THICKENERS

How Foods Become Emulsified

Emulsification is the process of combining two liquids that do not normally wish to come together. A good example of this is oil and water. Oil and vinegar is another example, and if they are used to make salad dressing you know that it takes a bit of shaking to bring them together before you can pour the dressing out of the bottle. When the oil and vinegar solution is shaken the oil is broken into small droplets for a short period of time. There are a number of emulsifying agents that will help keep the liquids in suspension. One of the best emulsifiers for oil and vinegar is lecithin. This can be obtained at a health food store in ampoules. One or two of the ampoules emptied into the mixture will place the ingredients into suspension. Lecithin is found naturally in egg white, which is why egg whites are used in many sauces to keep the ingredients in suspension.

Gelatin: The Great Thickener

Gelatin can be acquired from a number of different sources. The most common source is animal bones and connective tissue. Other sources include seaweed from which agar-agar is produced and Irish moss from which carrageenan is made. Both of these are popular commercial thickeners. Carrageenan is especially useful for thickening ice cream products. Gelatin granules have the capability of trapping water molecules and then expanding to ten times their original size. The firmness of a product will depend on the gelatin to water ratio. If the product becomes too firm, a small amount of heat is all that is needed to change the firmness closer to a liquid. If you chill the product it will become firm again. A number of ingredients will inhibit the gelatin from setting up. These include excessive amounts of sugar and fresh pineapple because of the enzyme bromelain. The enzyme bromelain can, however, be neutralized by simmering the pineapple for a few minutes.

When using gelatin for a dish, be sure to moisten the gelatin first with a small amount of cold water, then use the hot water to completely dissolve the gelatin. When hot water is poured into the dry gelatin a number of the granules will lump and some will not totally dissolve which may cause your dish to be somewhat grainy. The hot water should never be over 180° F. for the best results. If your recipe calls for an equal amount of sugar and gelatin, the cold-water step is not required since the sugar will stop the clumping. Never pour the hot water into the gelatin. Pour the gelatin into the water instead.

Who Really Invented Ketchup, Or Is It Catsup?

Ketsiap, the first name for this sauce, was invented in China in the 17th century. It was mainly used on fish dishes and was made from fish entrails, vinegar, and hot spices. The Chinese imported the sauce to Malaya and it was renamed "kechap." The Malays sold the kechap to the English sailors during the 18th century. The sailors brought it back to England, where mushrooms were substituted for the fish entrails. In 1792 a cookbook by Richard Briggs, *The New Art Of Cookery*, named the sauce "catsup" and included tomatoes as one of the main ingredients. Ketchup became popular in the United States in 1830 when Colonel Robert Gibbon Johnson ate a tomato on the courthouse steps in Salem, New Jersey, and didn't die. (At the time, tomatoes were thought to be poisonous.) H.J. Heinz started producing ketchup in the early 1870's. The company today is a $6.6 billion ompany.

How Did Heinz Become The Number One Ketchup?

In the 1940's Hunt's was the number-one selling ketchup in the United States, mainly because it poured more easily and this was viewed as a real asset since you didn't have to fight with the bottle to get the ketchup out. Heinz was also selling ketchup but sales were lagging far behind the Hunt's product. In the 1950's Heinz placed simple TV ads that stated, "Heinz, slowest ketchup in the West....East....North....South." The public then started viewing the quality of ketchup as a measure of the viscosity and Heinz, with the thickest product, took the market away from Hunt's. Hunt's has never regained it, even though all ketchups are now slow. Quality ketchups now flow at 4-6.5 centimeters in 30 seconds. Government standards (USDA) for ketchup flow is 3-7 centimeters in 30 seconds. Ketchup is a $600 million industry; annually, 7 bottles, at 14 oz apiece, are sold per person in the United States.

All About Vinegar

Vinegar can be found in a number of varieties, depending on the food that is used to produce it. It is a mild acid called acetic acid. The actual amount of acid that is in the vinegar varies from 4-7% with the average being 5%. Common types include apple cider vinegar, plain white distilled, red and white wine, barley, malt, rice, and balsamic. The acetic acid content of vinegar is measured by "grains." A "5% acetic acid" content is known as a 50 grain vinegar. The "50 grain" means that the product is 50% water and 50% vinegar. A 6-7% vinegar will keep foods fresher longer because of the higher acid content. Vinegar will have a shelf life and retain its effectiveness for about 18 months.

The Jelly Thickener

Pectin, a carbohydrate, is the most common thickener for jellies. If your jelly doesn't set, it will probably be the result of too little pectin or the wrong proportions of other ingredients. For certain types of fruit jellies only a small amount of pectin may be needed, since the fruits are relatively high in pectin. Some of the higher pectin fruits include all citrus fruits, apples, and cranberries. The lower ones include, peaches, cherries, raspberries, apricots, and strawberries. To get the most out of the pectin that is found in the fruit, the fruit should be very fresh. The fresher the fruit, the more active pectin will be available for processing the jelly. Jelly requires a number of ingredients to set properly; pectin is only one of them. The acid and sugar content will both affect the properties of the product in regard to setting up. Cooking the jelly at too high a temperature will also destroy the pectin.

How Was Worcestershire Sauce Invented?

Actually, Worcestershire sauce was produced by accident by John Lea and William Perrins. In 1835, Lea and Perrins were running a small drug store in Worcester, England, when Lord Marcus Sandys came in and asked if they could produce his favorite Indian sauce that he had liked while in Bengal. They mixed up a batch of sauce prepared from vegetables and fish, didn't like the smell or flavor, and placed the mixture in their cellar for 2 years. While cleaning the cellar they accidentally found the sauce, tried it and were surprised at the taste. Lea & Perrin's Worcestershire Sauce is now one of the most popular steak sauces in the world.

The recipe has hardly changed from the original in 1835, which used anchovies layered in brine, tamarinds in molasses, garlic in vinegar, chilies, cloves, shallots, and sugar as a sweetener. The mixture must still age for 2 years; before it is sold, the solids are filtered out and preservatives and citric acid are added.

CHAPTER 6
FATS

Shortening vs. Oil

Shortening is just a solid form of fat that is always a solid at room temperature. It can be made from either an animal or vegetable source or a combination of the two. Shortenings that are made from vegetable sources are hydrogenated, which is the addition of water to a liquid fat until it becomes the consistency that is desired by the manufacturer. The term "pure shortening" means that the product can contain either vegetable or animal sources or a combination of both. If the product is labeled "pure vegetable shortening," it has to be made from only vegetables sources. If the product does not have the word "pure" on the label, a number of additives were added to increase the shelf life. When this is done it does lower the smoke point and is not as good a product. One of the best shortenings is Crisco, which has a balanced proportion of saturated fat to unsaturated fat of 1:1.

Oils are always liquid at room temperature and are always from vegetable sources. The ones to avoid (high in saturated fat) are coconut and palm kernel oils which may now be called "tropical oils."

Why Frying Oil Lands On The Inside of Lenses

If you wear eyeglasses and fry foods, you may have noticed that the oil droplets collect on the inner surface of the lens rather than the outer surface. This is the reason: when you are frying, the minute droplets become airborne and then fall back toward the floor. When you are bending over your cooking task the oil droplets fall on the inner lens.

Why Oil Can't Be Used For Baking

Because of their liquid nature, oils tend to collect instead of evenly distributing through the dough. This may cause the baked goods to become grainy. When a solid fat is used, baked items tend to be more fluffy and retain their moisture better. Especially bad are the "all-purpose" oils, which are not up to the standards that most cooks desire, even though the label may say that they can be used for baking and frying. A number a additives used to produce these oils may affect the flavor and taste of the food.

The Floating Fat

Fat that floats to the top of gravy, soups, or stews is easily removed by placing a slice of fresh white bread on top of the fat for a few seconds. The fat will be quickly absorbed and the bread can be disposed of. Be sure to not leave the bread on too long or it will deteriorate and fall apart in your food.

Frying At Too Low Or Too High A Temperature

It is never wise to fry at too low a temperature, especially if the food is breaded. The oil will not be hot enough to seal the breading or outer surface of the food and too much of the oil will enter the food before the sealing takes place. When the oil is too hot, the food may end up being burned on the outside and not cooked through. Most breaded foods that are fried are normally fried at 375° F. It is best to check the recipe for the particular food you are frying for the correct frying temperature.

Who Invented Margarine?

Margarine was invented by a French chemist in the late 1800's upon a request from Napoleon III who wanted a low-cost fat. Originally, it was produced from animal fat. Today it is made from vegetable oil (mainly soy), milk solids, salt, air, and water.

Eliminating Fats From Soup And Stews

Fats can be eliminated through the use of certain foods and ice without refrigerating the food and taking the time for the fat to rise to the top. A good percentage of fat can be eliminated by either placing 4-5 ice cubes in a piece of ordinary cheesecloth and swirling it around in the soup or stew, or placing a few lettuce leaves in the food and stirring them for a few minutes. Then remove them and throw them away. Fat is attracted to the cold and tends to have an affinity for lettuce leaves. Another method is to gently place a piece of paper towel on the top to absorb the fat (this works great on pizzas).

Some Canola Oil Is Now Being Ruined By Biotechnology

Canola oil is now being altered through genetic engineering so that it contains high levels of the saturated fat laurate. Laurate is not normally found in canola oil but by producing a high saturated fat product it may now be used in the baking industry to replace palm and coconut (tropical oils) which are more expensive to import. Since the public has recently become aware that canola oil is high in mono-unsaturated oil (which is good for the body in moderation) they may view the product containing canola oil as a product that contains a "good oil." The new canola oil will be used initially in non-dairy products such as coffee creamers and whipped toppings.

Stop Gravy From Separating

One of the more frequent problems when cooking gravy is when the gravy decides to separate into fat globules. To solve the problem, all you have to do is add a pinch or two of baking soda. This will emulsify the fat globules in a matter of seconds.

CHAPTER 7
FOWL, MEAT, FISH

Like Dark Meat? Eat Wild Fowl!

People tend to choose dark meat over white the majority of the time. When you ask them why, they explain that the dark meat is juicier and more tender. The

reason the dark meat is the way it is, is because we raise fowl for table food and do not allow them to use their breast muscles. Therefore they have a poor blood supply and underdeveloped muscles. Wild fowl have stronger muscles and good blood supply.

They also have more fat since they are in the wild and subject to many temperature changes.

How Much Chicken To Buy For Each Person?

Type of Chicken	Amount Per Person
Broiler/Fryer	½ lb.
Capon	¾ lb.
Cornish Game Hen	1 bird
Whole Chicken with bones	1 lb.
Breast	½ breast
Drumstick	2 drumsticks
Thighs	2 thighs

5 pounds of chicken will provide about 3 cups of meat.

Is Barbecued Bitter Chicken A Problem?

If you are going to use a barbecue sauce you need to know when to apply it. Otherwise the chicken will have an acid taste. Barbecue sauces contain sugar, and high heat tends to burn sugar very easily as well as some of the spices. The barbecue sauce should never be placed on the bird until about 15 minutes before the bird is fully cooked. Another secret to the perfect barbecued bird is to use lower heat and leave the bird on for a longer period of time. Never place the bird too close to the coals.

Why The Difference In Meat Color?

The dark meat on fowl is the result of their using these muscles more. The muscles have more of a blood supply. The breast muscles are rarely used in a production bird since they are cooped up most of their lives. The breast meat on wild fowl is always dark, since these fowl must fly for long journeys and use the muscles extensively.

Never Cook A Stew At A Full Boil

Stew should be cooked at a medium heat and not allowed to boil. The turbulence causes all the ingredients to be blended with each other and flavors intermingle instead of picking up the flavor of the base. Stew meat should not be too lean or the taste will suffer, since the taste for the most part comes from the fat. Fish stew, on the other hand, is made with some olive oil and needs to be boiled somewhat vigorously to blend the oil in with the ingredients. Bouillabaisse is a good example.

Skin Color vs. Quality

Since the public would prefer to see a nice yellowish-colored chicken skin instead of a bluish-white sickly, looking skin, farmers are now placing marigold petals into the chicken feed to make their skin yellow. Production chickens are never allowed to run free and soak up the sunlight to make their skins yellow, and their skins are actually a sickly bluish color. Since the marigold petals are "all-natural" they do not have to be listed anywhere on the packaging. Free-range chickens always have yellowish skins as well as being more flavorful.

Quail: A Dangerous Bird?

Over the years a number of people have become ill with symptoms of nausea, vomiting, shivers, and even a type of slow-spreading paralysis, from eating quail. The problem may be the result of their diet in certain parts of the country. Occasionally a quail may consume hemlock, which is be toxic to humans, as part of their feeding pattern. The green quail of Algeria has caused a number of illnesses. If you do experience illness after eating quail, it would be best to contact the local health authorities.

It's Best Not To Eat Ready-To-Eat Hot Dogs

The bacteria *Listeria monocytogenes* may be lurking in a number of foods, such as hot dogs, sausage, raw milk, chicken, and deli-prepared salads and sandwiches. *Listeria* first became noticed 1985 when 48 people died from eating a Mexican-style cheese. The number one food-related risk in the United States is from bacterial food contamination, not pesticides or fertilizers. The *Listeria* organism can survive refrigeration or freezing and over 1,700 cases of food poisoning are reported annually. People with weak immune systems are more at risk. To avoid the problem the following should be adhered to:

- Be sure to cook all ready-to eat hot dogs, sausage, and leftovers until good and hot.

- Chicken should be cooked until the juices run clear.

- Never drink raw milk, only pasteurized milk.

- Foods should always be kept hot (above 140° F.) until they are ready to eat.

- Be aware of "sell by" and "use by" dates on all processed food products.

Fowl Antibiotics

Because of the way chickens are cooped up and the questionable sanitary conditions they must endure, diseases are common occurrences. Almost all poultry, approximately 85% of all pigs, and 60% of all beef in the United States is fed either penicillin or tetracycline. Almost 50% of all antibiotics manufactured are used on animals. The fear now is that the animals will develop antibiotic-resistant bacteria. In Europe many countries will not allow the indiscriminate use of antibiotics for this reason.

A Chicken By Any Other Name

Free-range chickens: These chickens are allowed to forage for food and consume a well-balanced diet. According to USDA rules, the cage doors must be kept open and the chickens are usually sold whole.

Organic chickens: May be raised only on land that has not had any chemical fertilizer or pesticide used on it for at least 3 years. They must also be fed chemical-free grains and are for the most part free-range chickens.

Mass-produced chickens: Commercially raised in crowded coops and never allowed to run free. They are marketed in exact sizes in the same number of months.

Kosher chickens: Chickens which have been slaughtered and cleaned in compliance with Jewish dietary laws.

Broilers/Fryers: These are 7 week old birds that weigh from 3-4 pounds.

Roasting chickens: These are usually hens that weigh 5-8 pounds, with more fat than broilers.

Stewing hens: Usually weigh 4-8 pounds and are a year old. Basically, these are retired laying hens. They are tough old birds and need to be slow-cooked but are flavorful.

Capons: These are castrated roosters which average 10 weeks old and weigh 8-10 pounds. They usually have large white-meat breasts.

Poussins: These are baby chicks only 1 month old and weighing about one pound. They lack flavor and are only used for grilling.

Cornish hens: These are baby chicks that are 5-6 weeks old and weigh about 2 pounds. They are best grilled or roasted.

You're In A Muddle If There's A Puddle

When choosing meats or fowl, make sure that there is no liquid residue, either wet or frozen, on the bottom of the tray. If there is, it means that the food has been frozen and the cells have released a percentage of their fluids. When cooked, the bones will be noticeably darker than a fresher product.

Which Came First, The Chicken Or The Turkey?

According to the history books, the chicken was forced to come to the Western Hemisphere by Spanish explorers who weren't sure what kind of meat they would find when they arrived and wanted a meat they were familiar with. The turkey, however, is a native American and was introduced to Europe by the same explorers. The Europeans didn't know what to call the turkey and the Spanish were not sure where they landed. Thinking they were in India, they called the turkey bird of India or Calcutta hen.

Sticky Chicken Skin

When cooking chicken on a barbecue rack, always grease the rack well first. The collagen in the skin will turn into a sticky gelatin which causes it to stick to the rack. To really solve the problem, try first baking the chicken for 15-20 minutes in a preheated oven, breast side up. This gives the gelatin time to infuse into the fat and meat, or to be released into the pan.

How Fast Do Bacteria On Chicken Multiply?

If a piece of chicken has 10,000 bacteria on a 1-square-centimeter area, when it is processed and reaches the supermarket that will increase to 10,000 times that figure if the chicken is left in the refrigerator at about 40° F. for 6 days. The Centers for Disease Control in Atlanta estimates that 9,000 people die each year from food-borne illness. Thousands of others become ill from bacterial, chemical, fertilizer, and pesticide residues left on foods and poultry. According to the USDA, 40% of all chickens are contaminated with *Salmonella*. Even if contaminated they can still pass the USDA inspection. Almost 50% of all animal feed may contain *Salmonella*.

Mini-Pigeon?

If you ever wondered what a squab is, it is just a "mini-pigeon" that is no more than 1 month old. They are specially bred to be plump and are raised to be marketed. They are usually sold frozen and will not weigh over 1 pound. Look for birds with pale skin, the plumper the better. Squab will store frozen for about 6 months at 0° F.

Best Method Of Cleaning A Chicken

Chickens need to be cleaned thoroughly inside and out before cooking them to remove any residues that are left from the slaughtering process. While it is impossible to completely clean the bird, you should do the best you can. The preferred method is to place 1 tablespoon of baking soda in the water that you will use to clean the chicken and rinse the bird several times with the water and then rinse with clean water several times. The mild acidic action and abrasiveness of the baking soda will do the job.

Are We Losing Our Forests For A Hamburger?

Presently, in the continental United States we are cutting down our forests at the rate of 12 acres every minute. The land is needed to produce feed for livestock or for them to graze. The deforestation is seriously reducing land that is the habitat for thousands of species of wildlife. Animals are actually being slaughtered during this process. The same problem on an even larger scale is happening in Central and South America to produce more feed and livestock.

Like A Juicy Steak, Don't Sear It

There's an old wives' tale that has been handed down from generation to generation regarding searing a steak to keep the juices in. This really didn't seem to have a good ring to it so I put it to the test. The results are in, and it turns out that searing a piece of steak does not help in any way to retain the juices. In fact, the steak dried out faster because of the more rapid, higher-temperature cooking. The investigation found that if the steak is cooked at a lower heat and more slowly, it will be more tender and retain more of its juices.

How Is Veal Produced?

Veal is from a calf that has been fed a special diet from the day it completes its weaning to the time of slaughtering, which is usually at about 3 months old. Their diet lacks iron which would turn the meat a reddish color undesirable for veal. The animal is placed into a stall and not allowed to even lick a pail or anything else which might contain the slightest amount of iron. They are not allowed to exercise and are fed a formula of either special milk (milk-fed veal) or a formula consisting of water, milk solids, fats, and special nutrients for growth. When the calf is about 3-4 months old the texture of the meat is perfect for tender veal. The most desirable is the milk-fed at 3 months old. However, the second formula is being used more since the calf will be larger at 4 months, meaning more meat.

The Color Of Cooked Ham

After ham is cured it contains nitrite salt. This chemical reacts with the myoglobin in the meat and changes it into nitrosomyoglobin. This biochemical alteration forces the meat to remain reddish even if cooked to a high temperature.

Ham Slices Salty? Give Them A Drink Of Milk

If your ham slices are too salty, try placing them in a dish of low-fat milk for 20 minutes, then rinse them off in cold water and dry with paper towels before you cook them. The ham will not pick up the taste of the milk.

Is There A Black Market In Drugs To Livestock Producers?

The FDA cracked down in the 1980's on illegal drug traffic to livestock producers. However, the problem may still exist. The FDA tries to control it with only minimal success. FDA testing of beef has shown that a number of drugs are still being used. One common unapproved drug is the antibiotic chloramphenicol, which can cause aplastic anemia and a number of nervous disorders if it shows up in your beef in sufficient amounts. A number of other illegal livestock drugs that are still showing up and are still a problem are carbadox, nitrofuazone, dimetridazole, and ipronidazole, all known to be carcinogens.

Is A Rare Steak Really Bloody?

No! The blood in meats is drained at the slaughterhouses and hardly any ever remains in the meat. There is a pigment called myoglobin in all meat that contributes to the reddish color of the meat. Myoglobin is found in the muscles but not the arteries. Blood obtains its color from hemoglobin. Those red juices are, for the most part, colored by myoglobin and not hemoglobin. Beef will have a more reddish color than pork since the meat contains more myoglobin.

Testing For Doneness

The experienced chef rarely uses a thermometer when cooking a steak. Meat has a certain resiliency. After testing thousands of steaks, a chef can just place his finger on the steak and, by putting a small amount of pressure on the meat, can tell if it is rare, medium, or well done. When meat cooks it tends to lose water and loses some of the flabbiness. The more it cooks the firmer it becomes.

Why Is The Fell Left On Larger Cuts Of Lamb?

The "fell" is a thin parchment-like membrane or thin piece of tissue that covers the fat on the lamb. It is usually removed from certain cuts (such as lamb chops) before they are marketed. However, it is usually left on the larger cuts to help retain the shape of a roast and to retain the juice, thus producing moister roasts.

Is A Fatty, Marbled Steak The Best?

Those white streaks running through the meat are fat. They are a storage depot for energy. For the meat to be well-marbled, the animal must be fed a diet high in rich grains such as corn, which is the source of the old saying that corn-fed beef was the best. The fat imparts a flavor to the meat and provides a level of moisture which helps tenderize the meat. The presence of fat means that the animal did not exercise a lot and the meat will be more tender.

Best Way To Thaw Meat

When thawing meat there are two considerations to be aware of. First, you want to reduce any damage from the freezing process. Second, you need to be cautious of bacterial contamination. Rapid thawing may cause excessive juices to be lost since some of the flavor is in the juices which are now combined with water and ice crystals. To thaw the meat and avoid excessive loss of flavor and reduce the risk of bacterial contamination, it is best to thaw the meat in the refrigerator once it is removed from the freezer. This means that you will have to plan ahead. Placing the meat in the microwave to quick-defrost will cause a loss of flavor and possibly a dried-out piece of meat after it is cooked.

Which Came First, The Hot Dogs Or The Sausage?

Actually, the sausage was first on the scene in 900 B.C. Hot dogs were first called a number of names such as frankfurters and wieners in Germany and Austria and even dachshund sausages in the United States. Hot dogs as we know them were first sold at Coney Island in Brooklyn, New York, in 1880 by a German immigrant by the name of Charles Feltman. They were called frankfurters. The actual name "hot dog" was coined at a New York Giants baseball game in 1901 by concessionaire Harry Stevens. When the weather was too cold to sell his normal ice cream treats he started selling dachshund sausages and instructed his sales team to yell out, "Get 'em while they're hot." A newspaper cartoonist seeing this drew a cartoon showing the salespeople selling the sausage, but since he didn't know how to spell "dachshund" he called the food a "hot dog." Hot dogs were sold at Coney Island from carts owned by Nathan Handwerker (Nathan's Hot Dogs). His employees who sold the dogs dressed in white coats and wore stethoscopes to denote cleanliness. The year 1913 was a dark one for hot dogs. They were banned at Coney Island when a rumor was started that they were made from ground dog meat. It was cleared up and they were allowed to be sold a few months afterwards.

How Many Names Are There For Sausage?

The following are a few of the names for sausage: blood sausage, bologna, bratwurst, cervelat, chorizo, cotto salami, wieners, Genoa, kielbasa, knockwurst, liver sausage, pepperoni, bockwurst, mettwurst, braunschweiger, kiszka, liver loaf, yachtwurst, mortadella, Krakow, prasky, smoked Thuringer, teawurst, Vienna sausage, frizzes, Kosher sausage, Lebanon bologna, Lyons, medwurst, metz, Milano, and Thuringer.

The Wahoo Wiener, One Of The Last Hand-Made Hot Dogs

The finest homemade hot dogs are made by the O.K. Market in Wahoo, Nebraska. The hot dogs have no preservatives or fillers and the ground hamburger and pork are placed in Australian sheep casings. The casings are expensive and imported but make the finest hot dog, providing just the right texture and flexibility. The market has been in business since 1926 and if you want to taste a hot dog without nitrites call Harold Horak at (402) 443-3015.

Spam, Hawaiians' Favorite Canned Meat

In 1937, Spam, a canned spiced ham product, was introduced by Geo. A. Hormel & Company. Spam was extremely popular with the troops during World War II as a military ration. It is actually scraps of shredded pork, with added fat, salt, water, sugar, and a dose of sodium nitrite as a preservative and bacterial retardant. The consumption of Spam in the United States is about 114 million cans annually. Hawaii outdoes itself, with an annual consumption of 12 cans per person. Alaska come in second with 6 cans per person, with Texas, Alabama, and Arkansas all tying for third with an average of 3 cans per person.

Buying The Best Hamburger Meat

Hamburger meat really depends on your taste. The news is full of information telling you to purchase only the leanest hamburger meat you can find, and over the years I have been telling my patients the same thing. However, after reading of experiments that were conducted on hamburger meat relating to fat content and flavor, I have decided to change my mind and start purchasing the ground chuck instead of ground round. For the most part the extra fat content tends to be released from the meat during cooking if the meat is cooked on a small platform or grate that allows the fat to drip below the cooking surface. The flavor of the hamburger is far superior to the ground round since the chuck cut is from an area of the animal that is more exercised. Do, however, make sure that the ground meat is very fresh, to avoid bacterial contamination.

How Many Hamburgers Do Americans Order In 1 Second?

In 1996, estimates were that 240 hamburgers are ordered every second, 24 hours a day, in the United States at more than 150,000 fast-food outlets. These hamburgers are ordered by about 47 million people.

What Is Wool On A Stick?

If you are a Texan you will know this phrase. It refers to lamb, and in Texas that's a nasty word. However, there are 100,000 sheep farms in the United States producing 340 million pounds of lamb. New Zealand and Australia, always thought of as big producers, export only 40 million pounds per year. Colorado sheep ranchers are using llamas to protect the sheep, which is more effective than dogs.

Fried Rattlesnake

Rattlesnake is actually a good eating meat. To prepare it, just cut off the head and make sure you bury it in a hole at least 12-18 inches deep. Slit the skin near the head and peel it back an inch or so, then tie a cord around the peeled back area and hang the snake on a tree limb. This will allow you to have both hands free to peel the skin off using a sharp knife. Loosen the skin from the flesh from the balance of the snake, then slit the belly open to remove the intestines. Rinse the snake in cold, salted water several times, then cut into bite-sized pieces. Flour and fry as you would chicken or add to soups or stews.

The Room-Temperature Roast

When a roast is brought to room temperature or near room temperature, it will cook more quickly than one that is placed into the oven directly from the refrigerator. This will also prevent the outside of the roast from over-cooking and becoming too dry before the insides are cooked. The only caution is that if the roast is very thick (over 6 inches in diameter) there may be a problem with bacterial contamination from spores in the air. Leaving a refrigerated roast out for about 1 hour should be sufficient to warm it without risking contamination. However, this should not be done in a warm, humid climate.

Why Is Liver Recommended Only Once A Week Or Less?

The liver acts as a filtration plant for the body and may concentrate toxins in its cells. These may include pesticides and heavy metals, depending what the animal's ate. The liver is also extremely high in cholesterol, more than any beef product the average person consumes. A 3.5 ounce serving of beef liver contains 390 mg of cholesterol, compared to 95 mg in 3.5 ounces of grilled hamburger.

When Should Soup Bones Be Added To Soup?

A frequent mistake made by people when they are preparing soup is to place the animal bone into the boiling water. In most instances this tends to seal the bone to some degree and not allow all the flavor and nutrients to be released. The soup bone should be added to the cold water when the pot is first placed on the range. This will allow the maximum release of the flavors, nutrients, and especially the gelatinous thickening agents.

Resting Your Roast

A roast should never be carved until it has had a chance to rest and allow the juices to dissipate evenly throughout the meat. When you cook a roast the juices tend to be forced to the center as the juices near the surface evaporate from the heat. A roast should be left to stand for about 15 minutes before carving. This will also allow the meat to firm up a bit, making it easier to carve thin slices.

Determining How Well Cooked A Steak Is Without Cutting It

You should never cut into a steak to tell how well cooked it is since this will release juices. Just press on the meat lightly with your finger. If it is soft, it is rare. If the meat resists just a little and then easily springs back it is medium, and if it is relatively firm it will be well done.

Should You Eat More Wild Game?

Restaurants, mail-order food catalogues and gourmet stores nationwide are now selling more wild game than ever before. The most popular are buffalo, venison, wild boar, and pheasant. The majority of the wild game sold is farm-raised not hunted, since the supply would be too limited. Venison hamburger is selling for $4.00 per pound while a steak sells for $14.00 a pound. Most game has a high price tag; however, it seems to be selling and gaining in popularity. Most wild animals don't get fat and the meat, therefore, is lower in fat, calories and cholesterol than our conventional meat fare. The lower fat content may relate to the cuts of meat being less tender than we are used to. Marinating may be needed. To remove the "gamy flavor" just add some ginger ale to the marinade or soak the meat in the ginger ale for 1 hour before cooking. Beware of over-cooking because this will cause many of the cuts to become tougher.

Room Temperature Ham

Many times you will see hams placed on the shelves in the market and not under refrigeration. These hams are actually sterilized to retard bacterial growth for longer periods of time. This sterilization, however, tends to detract from the flavor, texture, and nutritional values of the ham. It is best to purchase one that is under refrigeration.

Porkers Like To Play With Pigskins

In England pigs are now given footballs to play with, which is keeping them from chewing on each other's ears and tails. Pigs do like being penned up and pester each other all day. The pigs are more content and are gaining weight at a faster rate.

Why Is Ham So Popular At Easter?

Serving ham for a special festival predates Christianity. When fresh meats were not available in the early spring months, pagans buried fresh pork butts in the sand close to the ocean during the early winter months. The pork was cured by the "marinating" action of the salt water which killed the harmful microbes. When spring arrived, the salt-preserved meat was dug up and cooked over wood fires.

The Iridescent Ham

I'm sure at one time or another you have purchased a ham that has shown some signs of a multicolored sheen that glistens and is somewhat greenish. This occasionally occurs when a ham is sliced and the surface exposed to the effects of oxidation. It is not a sign of spoilage, but is caused by the nitrite-modification of the iron content of the meat which tends to undergo a biochemical change in the meat's pigmentation.

The Colors Of Fat

The color of fat that surrounds a steak can give you an idea of what the cow ate and the quality of the beef. If the fat has a yellowish tint it indicates that the cow was grass-fed. If the fat is white the cow was fed a corn and cereal grain diet. The white fat meat should be more tender and will probably be more expensive.

Why Is The Beef Industry Forced To Hormonize Cows?

If the beef industry did not use growth hormones the price of beef would increase about 27 cents per pound. With the use of hormones, cows increase in size at a faster rate and have more body mass that is converted to usable meat. This will reduce the cost of raising cattle by about $70 per steer. Over 90% of all cattle raised for beef in the United States are given hormones. The hormone capsule is implanted in the skin on the back of the animal's ear.

Cooking vs. Meat Color

As beef cooks, we can see that the color of the meat changes depending on how long we cook it. The red pigment of the myoglobin changes from a bright red in a rare steak to brown in a well done one. The internal temperature in a rare steak is 135° F., medium-rare is 145° F., medium is 155° F., and well done is 160° F.

Is The Source Of Meat Being Treated?

In many instances when we purchase meats the outside is a nice red color and the insides are darker with almost a brownish tint. Butchers have been accused of dying or spraying the meats but it is really not their fault. Actually, when the animal is slaughtered and the oxygen-rich blood is not pumped to the muscles, the myoglobin tends to lose some of its reddish color and may turn a brownish color. Then, when the meat is further exposed to the air through the plastic wrap, oxidation tends to turn the myoglobin a red color. Butchers call this process the "bloom" of the meat. If you would like to see the insides a bright red color, just slice the insides open and leave the meat in the refrigerator for a short period of time. The air will turn the meat a reddish color. Remember, however, that if the meat is exposed for too long a period the oxygen will eventually turn the meat brown.

The Splattering Bacon

If bacon were still produced the old fashioned way by curing it slowly and using a dry salt, it would not be splattering all over the place. Today's bacon is cured using a brine which speeds up the process. The brine tends to saturate the bacon more, causing the grease to be released and splatter more. To reduce splattering, use a lower heat setting. This will also reduce the number of nitrites you will convert into a carcinogen since the higher heat tends to convert the nitrites faster.

Pound Per Pound Better Than Beef

Over 2,000 years ago, Chinese farmers knew that pork was one of the most efficient forms of livestock in providing meat. The pig's efficiency at converting fodder into edible meat far surpasses the cow. For every 100 pounds of food a pig consumes, it produces 20 pounds of edible meat. For every 300 pounds of food a cow consumes, it produces 20 pounds of edible meat. More of the pig is also edible than any other animal. Fish farmers can produce a pound of fish for every pound of feed and chickens only need 2 pounds of feed to produce a pound of meat.

Does Pork Need To Be Fully Cooked?

The latest information regarding our old pork enemy, trichinosis, is that the parasitic problem has been almost eliminated in the United States. Only 1 in 1,000 hogs are found to be infected. Pork should still be cooked to an internal temperature of at least 160° F. to be on the safe side, which is about medium. At 137° F. the parasite is killed and the meat is safe.

How To Ruin Wild Game

How many times have you seen a deer strapped to a bumper of a car and being transported home with the proud hunter grinning all the way? Well, he may have enjoyed the macho feeling but what he has done to the kill is to destroy it before he got it home. The heat from the car engine can increase the level of bacterial growth ten fold and render the meat worthless by the time he gets it home. The animal should be bled in the field, cleanly gutted, cooled if possible and placed, covered, on top of the car on a rack.

Why Bad Meat Smells Bad

Bacteria, spores, and mold may all be either airborne or already on the surface of the meat because of poor sanitary conditions when the animal was slaughtered and processed. These contaminants break down the surface of the meat, liquefying the carbohydrates and proteins and producing a putrid film on the meat. This film produces carbon dioxide and ammonia gases which results in a noxious, offensive odor. The meat may also be discolored by this action on the myoglobin (red coloring pigment) in the meat, converting the myoglobin into yellow and green bile pigments. The more the reaction is allowed to take place, the farther the breakdown occurs. Protein is converted into "mercaptans," chemicals that contain a substance related to skunk spray, as well as hydrogen sulfide, which has the rotten egg smell. Meats must be kept refrigerated and not allowed to remain at room temperature for more than a short period of time.

What Is Meat Composed Of?

Meat	% Water	% Protein	% Fat
Beef	60	18	22
Pork	42	14	45
Lamb	56	16	28
Turkey	58	20	20
Chicken	65	30	6
Fish	70	20	9

Marinade Facts

If you ever wondered why meats turn brown too quickly when they are cooked on a shish kebab or similar method of cooking, it's the marinade. Marinade has a high acid content that tends to react with the myoglobin and turn it brown very quickly.

The lower the temperature, the slower the marinade will react to tenderize the meat. If you marinate at room temperature it will take less time than if you do it in the refrigerator. Large pieces of meat should be placed into a large, tightly sealed plastic bag to conserve the amount of marinade needed.

The acid in most marinades may reduce the moisture-retaining properties of the meat and the meat may not be as moist as you would expect. This problem is usually countered by the fact that the meat will have a better flavor and may contain some of the marinade.

The Cooler The Meat, The Tougher

When meat cools on your plate it will get tougher because the collagen, which has turned to a tender gelatin, thickens. The best way to counter this problem is to be sure you are served a steak on a warmed or metal plate. After carving a roast, it would be best to keep it in a warmer or back in the oven with the door ajar.

Bacteria Risks of Ham Compared To Chicken

Recent studies have shown that a typical piece of pork found in a supermarket may only have a few hundred bacteria per square centimeter, compared to over 100,000 bacteria in the same area of a piece of chicken. This is one of the reasons it is so important to clean up well after handling poultry.

I Wonder Where The Flavor Went

When cooked beef is refrigerated, the flavor changes noticeably. After only a few hours fat, which is the main source of the flavor, tends to produce an off-flavor within the meat. This off-flavor is caused by the heating process which tends to release reactive substances from the muscle tissue and produces oxidation of the fats, especially the phospholipids and the polyunsaturated fats in the muscle itself. One of the reasons this occurs is that the iron in the muscles is broken down and released from the hemoglobin and myoglobin. This encourages the oxidation reaction. To slow the process down and fight the off-flavor problem, try to avoid using iron or aluminum pots and pans, and try not to salt meats until you are ready to eat them. Pepper and onions, however, seem to slow the process down and even inhibit them.

Can A Cow Be Tenderized Before Slaughtering?

A number of slaughterhouses in the United States are injecting animals with a papain solution shortly before they are slaughtered. The solution is carried to the muscles via the bloodstream and then remains in the meat since it does not have time to be broken down before the animal is killed. When the meat is cooked, the enzyme is activated at 150° F. There is a drawback, however, since the flesh occasionally becomes mushy and lacks the firmness we are used to.

Should A Steak Be Salted Or Peppered Before Cooking?

The rule is never to use a seasoning that contains salt before cooking. The salt tends to draw liquid from the meat. The liquid then boils in the pan and the surface of the meat may not have the desired texture or brown color. The salt does not work its way into the meat to flavor it unless you puncture the meat, which is not recommended. If you wish the flavor of a seasoned salt, the best method is to season both sides of the meat just before serving. Ground pepper should never be placed on any meat that is cooked in a pan using dry heat. Pepper tends to becomes bitter when scorched.

When Were Animals Domesticated?

ANIMAL	APPROXIMATE DATE B.C.	COUNTRY
Sheep	9000	Middle East
Dog	8400	North America
Goat	7500	Middle East
Pig	7000	Middle East
Cattle	6500	Middle East
Horse	3000	Russia
Chicken	2000	India

The Difference In Freezer Life Between Chicken And Beef

Chicken has a shorter freezer life due to its higher relationship of polyunsaturated fat to saturated fat. Polyunsaturates are more prone to destruction by oxidation and subsequent rancidity. There are more hydrogen sites in a polyunsaturated fat for oxygen to attach to. Beef is higher in saturated fat and has hardly any open sites.

Why Are Certain Cuts Of Beef More Tender?

There are a number of factors that relate to the tenderness of a piece of meat. They are the actual part from which the meat is cut; the activity level of the animal; and how old the animal is. The areas of the animal that are the least exercised are the areas that will be the most tender. However, even if a steak is labeled sirloin and expected to be tender, it will still depend on which end it is cut from. If it is cut from the short loin end it will be more tender than if cut from the area near where the round steaks are cut from. Activity level in most beef is kept to a minimum so that they will develop only minimum levels of connective tissue. Kobe beef from Japan actually are massaged to relax them, since stress and tension may cause muscles to flex, resulting in exercise that would increase the level of connective tissue.

To Age Or Not To Age?

Aging meat causes the enzymes in the meat to soften the connective tissue and the meat to become more tender. When aging beef, the temperature is very important, and must be kept between 34° and 38° F. The meat should not be frozen since the enzymes will be inactivated. Too high a temperature will cause bacterial growth.

How Much Beef To Buy For Each Person

Type of beef	Per Serving
Chuck roast/rib roast	½ lb
Filet mignon	5 oz
Hamburger	¼ lb
Pot roast with bone	¼ lb
Ribs	1 lb
Round beef roast with bone	¼ lb
Round steak	½ lb
Sliced lunch meats	¼ lb
Steaks without bones	7 oz
Steaks with bones	12 oz
Stew meat	¼ lb
Tenderloin of beef	½ lb

Relax The Animal Before Slaughtering

The mental state of the animal hours before it is slaughtered is important to the storage life of the meat. When you slaughter an animal that is stressed-out, tense, or afraid, its body gears up for the flight-or-fight reflex and starts to convert glycogen (carbohydrate) into glucose for quick energy needs. This will provide the animal with greater strength but when it is slaughtered the excess glucose shortens the storage life of the meat. The glycogen needs to remain in the muscles to convert to lactic acid and help retard bacterial growth. When you are hunting, the meat will be better if the animal is killed instantly instead of being wounded it and allowed to live and convert the glycogen. Most slaughterhouses are aware of this problem and see to it that the animal is relaxed, most of the time by playing soothing music, before they kill it.

Rigor Mortis And Tenderness

The process of rigor mortis occurs in all animals and is characterized by the stiffening of the meat that occurs a few hours after slaughtering. If meat is not consumed immediately after it is slaughtered then you should wait at least 15-36 hours, which gives the enzymes a chance to soften the connective tissue.

Will Freezing Raw Meat Make It Safe To Eat Rare?

Unfortunately, freezing will not kill all the bacteria in meat or chicken and you will still have a risk if the meat is consumed without fully cooking it. Some microbes will survive the freezing and will multiply very quickly as the meat is thawed. If you desire a rare hamburger, just purchase a steak, sear it well on both sides, grind it in your meat grinder and cook it immediately.

Tenderizing Meats

Since the main problem with tough cuts of beef is the level of collagen (protein substance) in the connective tissue, it is necessary to use a moist heat to break down the collagen and soften the connective tissue. A slow, moist heat will solve the problem. However, if you cook the meat too long it will actually cause the meat to get tough again due to another constituent in the connective tissue called elastin which does not soften and become tender. The best method of slow cooking meat is to cook it at 180° F. for about 2-3 hours using a moist heat. Boiling is not effective nor is slow cooking at 140° F. for an extended period. Meat tenderizers that actually break down the protein are papain and bromelein. Baking soda is the easiest product to use when tenderizing beef, since all you have to do is rub it on the meat and allow it to stand for 3-5 hours before you rinse and cook it.

What Is A Chitlin?

Chitlins, chitlings, or chitterlings are all the same Southern delicacy made from pigs' intestines. One 3-ounce serving of simmered chitlings contain 260 calories, 222 of which come from fat.

Should A Roast Be Cooked In A Covered Pan?

When cooking a roast there are two methods that are normally used, either dry heat (without liquid) or moist heat (with liquid). When the meat is covered it is cooked with steam that is trapped in the pan. Many cooks use this method to prevent the roast from drying out. Dry heat with the lid off will keep the outside of the roast crisp instead of mushy and, if you wish, the roast can be basted every 15 minutes to provide the desired moisture. This is the method preferred by most chefs. However, if you do roast with a lid on and in liquid, you must lower the temperature by 25° F. Roasts should always be cooked on a rack or stalks of celery and never allowed to sit in the liquid on the bottom of the pan, which gives them mushy bottoms.

What Is The Favorite Pizza Topping?

Pepperoni is at the top of the list. Americans consume 300 million pounds on pizza every year. If you placed all the pepperoni pizzas eaten in the United States next to each other they would take up an area the size of 13,000 football fields.

There's A Catch To This Fish Story

You probably think that if you purchase tuna in water it will have fewer calories than the type that is packed in oil. Well, the truth is that albacore tuna may have a fat content that will vary by as much as 500%. Tuna processors always try to use low-fat tuna in their product (about 1 gram of fat per serving). However, when the demand for the product gets extremely high, they have to resort to packaging the higher fat albacore which contains 4-5 grams of fat per serving. It's best to check the label.

Clamming Up

The shells of a healthy clam should be closed when being cooked; they should relax and open after they are boiled. If you keep the clams on ice they will probably relax and open their shells. To test their condition just tap the shells and they should close. If they don't close then they are sick or dying and should not be used. If the shells do not open after they are cooked they should be discarded and the shell not forced open.

What Are Angels On Horseback?

Angels on Horseback are appetizers made by wrapping bacon around a shucked oyster and then cooking it. They are served on toast and accompanied by a lemon wedge or Hollandaise sauce.

This Clam Will Really Fill You Up

In 1956, the largest clam on record was caught in Manila. It weighed in at 750 pounds. Clams are all males unless they decide to change to female later in life. Luckily, many do.

Fishercise

River fishes have more flavor since they must swim against the currents and thus exercise more than lake fish. For this reason trout is one of the best fish to eat. Cooler water fishes also have a higher fat content which imparts more flavor.

Red Spots Are Not Measles

If you see red spots on fish filets it means that the fish has been bruised and has been handled roughly. This may occur if the fish was roughly thrown around when caught, or if it was poorly filleted. Too many bruises may affect the flavor of the fillet by causing deterioration of the surrounding flesh.

Can 45,000 Men Be Wrong?

Researchers at Harvard University tracked 45,000 men and their dietary habits in relation to eating fish. They found that the heart attack rates for men who ate fish six times per week was the same as those who ate fish approximately twice per month.

How Did Celery Turn Into A Swizzle Stick?

Placing a stalk of celery into a Bloody Mary and using it as a swizzle stick came about in the 1960's when a celebrity (who wishes to remain anonymous) needed something to stir his drink and grabbed a stalk of celery from a nearby relish tray in a restaurant at the Ambassador East Hotel in Chicago. Celery was first grown in the United States in Kalamazoo, Michigan, in 1874 and to popularize them were given to train passengers free. Presently 2 billion pounds are grown annually.

Is Canned Tuna Safe To Eat?

A study performed in 1992 and reported in *Consumer Reports* stated that tuna, for the most part, is safe to eat. Only a few insect parts were found and the level of mercury was too low to be a health threat. Americans consume 3.7 pounds of canned tuna annually.

Tender Fish

Fish and shellfish do not have the extensive connective tissue that is found in land animals. Since the amount is small it doesn't take a lot of cooking to gelatinize the connective tissue with moist heat. If you over-cook fish it will toughen the muscle fibers. A fish will be more tender when cooked if you leave the head and tail on. If they are removed, the juices tend to be released when the fish is cooked. When the flesh turns from translucent to opaque, the fish will be fully cooked.

Since Raw Fish May Contain Parasites, What About Lox?

Smoked salmon, lox, or Nova that are commercially preserved should pose no health threat. When processed, lox is heavily salted and not smoked. Nova is salmon that originally came from Nova Scotia and is not as heavily salted. According to researchers at the Centers for Disease Control and the FDA, no cases of parasitic contamination have ever been reported in lox or Nova. Occasionally parasites are found in wild salmon but almost all the lox sold in the United States is aqua-cultured. Cold-smoked salmon is always kept frozen, which will kill any parasites.

Robot Sushi Chef

The Japanese have developed a robotic sushi chef that is capable of producing 1,200 pieces of sushi in one hour. The record of 200 pieces in one hour is held by a Japanese sushi chef under ideal conditions. The sushi chef robot will cost about $65,000 to produce in quantity.

How Sweet It Is

Have you ever wondered why shellfish tastes so sweet? Shellfish contain a high percentage of glycogen which is a complex sugar that readily turns into the simple sugar glucose. Lobster will have the sweetest flavor, with crab following close behind. However, if shellfish is stored for more than 2 days the sweetness will disappear.

Is A Prawn A Shrimp Or Is A Shrimp A Prawn?

Biologically, a prawn is different from a shrimp in that it has pincer claws similar to a lobster. A relative of the prawn is scampi, both of which are considerably larger than the average shrimp. Restaurants in the United States rarely serve real prawns, just large shrimp. Jumbo shrimp cost less than the giant prawns and are not as tasty. If you do eat a "real" prawn you will know the difference. The head of a shrimp or prawn contains almost all of its organs, even most of the intestinal tract.

Cut Off Their Beard And They Die

Mussels are a common shellfish enclosed in a bluish shell and are for the most part raised on aquafarms. They should always be purchased live and should be cleaned with a stiff brush under cold water. The visible "beard" needs to be removed and once they are debearded they will die.

Staying Alive, Staying Alive

Lobsters and crabs have very potent digestive enzymes that will immediately start to decompose their flesh when they die. Both should be kept alive until they are to be cooked. The complexity and location of their digestive organs make it too difficult to remove them. If you are uncertain as to whether a lobster is alive or dead, just pick it up; if the tail curls under the lobster its alive. Lobsters should never be placed into boiling water as a method of killing them. The best way is to sever the spinal cord at the base of the neck with the end of a knife, then place them into the water. In some restaurants the lobster will be placed into a pot filled with beer for a few minutes to get them drunk before placing them into the boiling water.

What Fish Are Aquacultured In The United States?

Aquaculture or fish farming originated in 2000 B.C. in China. The first fish to be farmed was carp. China and Japan lead the world's production, with the United States coming in fifth. At present almost 90% of all trout sold in supermarkets and fish markets is aquacultured. In 1996 farmed fish totaled over 1 billion pounds, about 15% of the nation's seafood. There are 3,400 fish farms in 23 states raising catfish, salmon, striped bass, sturgeon, tilapia, and trout. Over 450 million pounds of catfish are marketed annually and 10 million pounds of salmon.

Claw Renewal

Crabs and lobsters have the capability to regenerate a new claw when one is broken off. The crab industry in many areas now catch crabs and break off one of the claws, then release the crab to grow another one. The crab is able to protect itself and forage for food as long as it has one claw.

The Secret To Removing The Meat From Crayfish

To begin with, crayfish are always cooked live, similar to lobsters and crabs. They have a much sweeter flavor and may be called crawdads. All the meat is found in the tail of the crayfish. To easily remove the meat, gently twist off the tail away from the body, then unwrap the first three sections of the shell to expose the meat. Next you need to pinch the end of the meat while holding the tail in the other hand and pulling the meat out in one piece. If you wish, you can also suck out the flavorful juices from the head.

White Lox

More and more salmon are being farm-raised which may mean that the color of salmon may someday be white instead of salmon-colored. The farm-raised salmon are not exposed to the same food supply in a pen that they are in the wild. Fish farmers are now adding synthetic pigments to the farm-raised salmon's food supply to make the color salmon.

You'll Never See Scallops On The Half Shell

There is a major difference between this bivalve and clams, lobsters, and mussels: it cannot close its shell to protect itself in a closed liquid environment. The scallop does have two shells but these shells never close tightly. Because of this they are unable to protect their juices when they are caught, which allows the juices to be released.

When this occurs the process of deterioration and enzymatic breakdown begins very quickly and therefore once they are caught they must be shucked on the boat, the viscera thrown away and the muscle preserved.

What Does Newburg Mean In Lobster Newburg?

The "Newburg" in any seafood dish means that the recipe contains a special cream sauce that includes sherry. The name refers to a Scottish fishing village called Newburg. The dish was first introduced in the United States in the early 1900's.

Can A Lobster Be Microwaved?

Microwaving a lobster is actually the preferred method in many of the better restaurants. The taste and texture are far superior to boiled or steamed lobster. Microwaving allows all the natural juices to be retained. The color of the lobster is better as well. The problem some restaurants have is that it takes too many microwave ovens to handle a large volume of business. To microwave a lobster you need to place the lobster in a large microwave plastic bag and knot it loosely. A 1½ pound lobster should take about 5-6 minutes on high power, providing you have a 600- to 700-watt oven. Allow about 8 minutes if you have a lower-wattage oven. To be sure that the lobster is fully cooked, just separate the tail from the body; if the tomalley (mushy stuff in the cavity) has turned green, the lobster is fully cooked. The lobster must still be cooked live due to the bacterial problem which occurs immediately upon their death. If you are bothered by the lobster's movements, (which are just reflex) place the lobster in the freezer for 10 minutes to dull its senses. It will have a reflex reaction for only about 20 seconds.

Porcupine Fish: A Japanese Delicacy Or A Potent Poison?

This fish may go by a number of names, including fugu fish or balloon fish. It may contain a very potent poison, tetradotoxin, which is concentrated in the liver, ovaries, and testes. If the poison is eaten, the person may experience numbness of the lips, tongue, and fingertips, with death following in a few hours. Japanese chefs who prepare the fish must be licensed by the government and are trained to discard the poisonous organs.

Sizing Up Shrimp

Shrimp are classified by the number of shrimp per pound. Jumbo shrimp should average 16-25, large shrimp 20-32, medium shrimp 28-40, and the tiny bay shrimp 65-70 per pound.

Pollution And Shellfish Still A Problem

Presently, about 34% of all shellfish beds in the United States have been officially closed because of pollution. All coastal waters worldwide are also in jeopardy of being closed to fishing. One of the world's best-known seaports, Boston Harbor, is so polluted that fisherman are advised not to fish there anymore. Mutant fish infected with tumors and bacteria are being caught in Boston Harbor. The sewage problem is so bad in the Gulf states of Louisiana and Florida that 67% of the oyster beds have been closed to fishing. In Europe about 90% of the sewage is still dumped into coastal waters.

Are Oysters Safe To Eat In The Months Without An "R"?

This may have been true decades ago before refrigeration. However, there is really no medical evidence that shows it to be dangerous to eat oysters in any month of the year. However, oysters tend to be less flavorful and less meaty during the summer months (which do not have an ''R'') because it is the time of the year that they spawn.

A Left-Handed Lobster?

Believe it or not, Maine lobsters may be either right- or left-handed. They are not symmetrical with identical sides. The two claws are different and are used differently. One is larger with very coarse teeth for crushing, and the other has fine teeth for ripping or tearing. Which side the larger, coarse-toothed claw is on will determine whether the lobster is right- or left-handed. The flesh found in the smaller fine-toothed claw is sweeter and more tender.

What Is The Black Tube On A Shrimp's Back?

The dark-colored tube is actually the intestinal tract of the shrimp. It should be removed since it does harbor bacteria but is safe to eat if the shrimp is cooked (which kills the bacteria). If you do eat it and you notice that the shrimp is somewhat gritty, it is because the intestinal tube remained. De-veining the shrimp is relatively simple. All you have to do is run a small ice pick down the back and the tube will fall out.

What Is Imitation Crab?

Hundreds of years ago the Japanese invented a process called ''surimi'' to make imitation shellfish. In recent years it has become a booming industry in the United States. Presently, we are producing imitation crab meat, lobster, shrimp, and scallops. Most of this is made from the deep-ocean fish whitefish or pollack. Surimi contains less cholesterol than the average shellfish and contains high quality proteins and very little fat. Unfortunately, most surimi does contain high levels of salt (sometimes 10 times that of the real shellfish) and in some products MSG is used to bring out the flavor. The processing also lowers the level of other nutrients that would ordinarily be found in the fresh pollack.

Why Lobsters Turn Red When Boiled

The red coloring is always there but is not visible until the lobster is boiled. The lobster, along with other shellfish and some insects, has an external skeleton which is made up of ''chitin.'' Chitin contains a bright red pigment called astaxanthin which is bonded to several proteins. While the chitin is bonded it remains a brownish-red color; however, when the protein is heated by the boiling water the bonds are broken, which releases the astaxanthin. Then the exo-skeleton turns a bright red color.

Lobster Liver A Delicacy?

Shellfish lovers seem to think that a special treat is to consume the green tomalley or liver found in lobsters or the ''mustard'' found in crabs. These organs are similar to our livers and are involved in detoxifying and filtering toxins out of the shellfish. Many of these organs do retain a percentage of the toxins and possibly even some PCB's or heavy metal contaminants. Since, in most instances, you do not know where these crustaceans were found, you should never eat these organs. However, the roe (coral) found in female lobsters is safe to eat.

Should Fresh Fish Be De-Gilled?

If the fish is caught fresh and prepared shortly afterwards, then it not necessary to remove the gills. However, if the fish is more than 24 hours old the gills should be removed. The gills tend to spoil faster than the rest of the fish and the flavor may be affected.

Seafood Poisoning

Seafood is becoming more and more of a problem. The consumer hardly ever knows the source of the seafood or whether it is contaminated. Two types of poisoning are the most prevalent. Mytilotoxism is found in mollusks, clams, and oysters. These filter feeders may feed on microorganisms that are toxic. Ciguatera may be found in any type of seafood. Both types are serious enough to either make you very ill or kill you. Commercial fisherman have a better idea where the safe fishing beds are. A person who is just out fishing in a river or lake and not aware of any contamination that may be present is at high risk in many areas of the United States.

Fish Spoilage And Storage

The sooner a fish is gutted the better. The enzymes in a fish's gut tend to break down the meat very quickly if allowed to remain for too long a period. They are very aggressive and very powerful, which is one reason why fish is easier to digest than any other form of meat. When storing fish you need to remember that the muscle tissue in fish is high in glycogen, which is their energy source. When the fish is killed, this carbohydrate is converted into lactic acid, which is usually an excellent preservative. However, the fish tends to use up too much of its energy source thrashing around and trying to escape when it is caught. Another problem with lengthy storage is that certain bacteria tend to be located outside of the digestive tract (unlike beef) and will remain active even below the freezing point.

Never Flip Your Fillet

Fillets are so thin that they cook through in a very short period of time. The meat of the fillet is also so delicate that it has the tendency to flake apart when over-cooked or even if it is turned. To prevent the fillet from sticking to the pan, use a liquid oil spray.

Adding An Acid: A Must When Poaching Fish

When poaching fish, the contents of the pot are usually somewhat on the alkaline side and may react with a pigment in the flesh of the fish known as "flavone." If this is allowed to occur, the flesh may become yellow instead of the desired white color. If you add a small amount of wine, lemon juice, or other acid to the pot it will neutralize the alkalinity and render the flavone harmless. If the mixture turns slightly acidic it will actually whiten the meat more than it would normally be.

How Can You Tell If A Fish Is Fully Cooked?

The flesh of a fish is normally translucent. When it turns opaque and a solid white color, the protein has coagulated and the fish is fully cooked. If you wish to be really sure, you will have to cut into the center at the thickest part with a fork. If the flesh flakes it means that there was sufficient heat to gelatinize the collagen in the myocommata (fish connective tissue). Fish flesh contains very thin, parallel rows of muscle fibers that are held together by the connective tissue. It is these separate sheets of muscle fibers that flake.

Oysters A Shellfish Game?

Be cautious of oysters that are harvested from the Gulf of Mexico during June, July, and August. These summer months are months when the oysters may be contaminated with bacteria called *Vibro vulnificus*. Cooking the oysters will kill the bacteria but raw oysters can be deadly to people who suffer from diabetes, liver disease, cancer, and some gastrointestinal disorders. The bacteria kill about 20 people a year. The FDA may require that all Gulf Coast oysters caught in the summer months be shucked and bottled with a warning not to consume them raw.

Why You Should Never Fish From A Bridge

One of the more popular locations for people to fish is a bridge near the highway. Fishermen in the know will never fish from a highway bridge because of the auto exhaust pollution and the garbage that is thrown off the bridge by the passersby. Waters near bridges are polluted to such a degree that many are already posted with "No Fishing" signs. Fishermen think that the signs are posted to protect the fishermen from the passing cars, when it is actually to save them from becoming ill.

Does Food Need To Be Chewed And Chewed And Chewed?

Over the centuries a number of medical professionals have investigated digestion and how food is utilized more efficiently. Chewing your food seems to top most lists as one of the most effective methods of gaining more nutrition out of less food. In the early 1900's, Horace Fletcher was one of the most outspoken advocates of chewing your food. He called the mouth "Nature's Food Filter." He felt that the sense of taste and the desire to swallow were a poor guide to proper nutrition practices. He felt that food should be chewed until there is no taste left, which he calculated at about 50 chews per mouthful. He once said that he had to chew 722 times to eliminate the taste of onions before swallowing. In fact, "Fletcherism" was very popular at Dr. Kellog's Battle Creek sanitarium. In England they actually held "munching parties" to honor him. All this hard work, he explained, would also make people eat less and thus reduce their overall caloric intake.

How Many People Get Sick From Food In The U.S.?

Food-borne illnesses will make over 6 million Americans ill in 1997, according to the Centers for Disease Control. However, a more accurate total is probably closer to 86 million. Approximately 10,000 people will die from food-borne illnesses in 1997.

CHAPTER 8
SUGAR AND SUGAR
SUBSTITUTES

How Sweet It Is

In a recent study by Dr. Andrew Waterhouse at the University of California at Davis, chocolate was found to contain an antioxidant called "phenols." This is the same compound found in red wine that was thought to lower the risk of heart disease in France. The study found that cocoa powder prevented the oxidation or breakdown of LDL's (bad cholesterol). When LDL's are broken down, they tend to convert into fatty plaque-forming particles that may contribute to the clogging of healthy arteries, thus becoming a risk factor for heart disease. A 1½-ounce chocolate bar has the same amount of phenols as a 5 oz glass of red wine.

The Greatest Chocolate-Covered Marshmallow

This is by far one of the finest candies you will ever taste. The Schwartz family has been making the candy since 1939, keeping its original logo and box all through the years. The marshmallow is light and airy and no comparison to the ones you buy at the store. They are covered with dark semi-sweet chocolate and if you really want a delicacy, try the ones with a caramel bottom. All ingredients are the finest possible and they can be ordered by calling (800) 358-0940.

Certain Honey Can Be Dangerous

Honey that is produced from certain geological areas may contain substances that are harmful to the human body. Farmers call this honey "mad honey." Bees that obtain nectar from flowers such as the rhododendron, azalea, and laurel family may cause symptoms of numbness in the extremities, vomiting, and muscle weakness. These are rarely fatal but will cause a bit of discomfort for a few days. Honey should never be given to babies since their digestive system is too immature to handle the botulism bacillus if it is present and they tend to develop a form of infant botulism.

The Birth Of The Lollypop

In 1909 an employee named George Smith made a new confection on a stick while employed by a Connecticut candy maker. He was an avid race fan and named the confection after one of the most popular race horses of that time, Lolly Pop.

Can Babies Detect Sweet Tastes?

Babies that are only 1 day old can detect the taste of sweet; however, it will take them 6 weeks to respond to the taste of salt. Taste buds are able to detect sweetness in a food if the food has only 1 part sweetness in 200. Saltiness can be detected if the food only has 1 part in 400.

What Is A Goo-Goo Cluster?

This has been one of the favorite candies of the South since 1912, when Howell H. Campbell went into the candy business. He prepared the candy from chocolate, marshmallow, caramel, and peanuts. The candy is occasionally found in some of the better stores in major cities around the country. The candy was named by a Nashville woman who suggested that Campbell name the bar after the only two words his infant son could utter, "goo-goo." The Goo-Goo Cluster was the first combination candy bar produced in the United States. To order some of the bars call (615)889-6360.

Eliminate A Sweet Craving

There are two ways to eliminate the craving for sweets. First, place a small amount of salt on your tongue. Second, dissolve about 1 teaspoon of baking soda in a glass of warm tap water and just rinse your mouth out (don't swallow the water). The salt or baking soda tends to stimulate the hypothalamus gland, causing the papillae to become active and secrete saliva, this will eliminate the craving for sweets.

Gourmet Chocolate

For years wine has been labeled from a particular vineyard or region and many connoisseurs will drink wines only from that particular vintage or region. Wine tasters can tell you by sipping a wine the complete history of that wine and its level of quality. Well, chocolate has finally come of age and the latest craze is to purchase chocolates from a particular Epicurean grower and from a particular variety of the cocoa bean.

What Is Chocolate Plastic?

This actually is a pliable decorating paste prepared from a mixture of chocolate and corn syrup and has a texture similar to marzipan. It is used to wrap around the outside of cakes to make a ribbon, ruffles, decorative flowers, or any other complex design. It can be rolled out to make a thin layer with a rolling pin.

Was The Baby Ruth Candy Bar Named After Babe Ruth?

Many people think that the Baby Ruth candy bar was named after the famous baseball player, especially since he did wish to produce a candy bar with his name on it. The candy bar was actually named after the daughter of then-President Grover Cleveland, to honor her after she was born in the White House. Ruth did take the matter to court and lost.

The Remarkable Honey Story

Bees gather honey by drawing the flower nectar into their proboscis (tube extending from their head). The nectar then passes through their esophagus into a honey sac (storage pod) located just before the intestine. The nectar is stored until the bee arrives back at the hive. While the nectar is in the sac, enzymes are secreted that begin to break down the starch into simple sugars and fructose. The hive contains one mature queen, about 100 male drones, and 20,000 male workers. The bees utilize 8 pounds of honey for daily activities for every 1 pound that reaches the market. Bees must forage an equivalent of 3 times around the earth to provide sufficient nectar to make 1 pound of honey. For every gallon of honey the bees consume, they travel 7 million miles, or 7 million miles to the gallon if you prefer. When the workers reach the hive, they pump the nectar in and out of their proboscis until the carbohydrate concentration is about 50-60%. Then it is deposited into the honeycomb.

Honey storage is very important and honey should be stored in as airtight a container as possible since the sugars are "moisture attracting" and will absorb water from the air very easily, especially if the humidity is over 60%. If the water content of honey goes above 17%, the honey yeast will activate, the honey will ferment and the sugars will change to alcohol and carbon dioxide. Honey tends to crystallize easily, which causes the glucose to be released from the sugars. Heating the honey slightly will force the glucose back into the sugar molecule and return the honey to a liquid.

Does Your Chocolate Stiffen Too Soon?

When you are melting chocolate, water droplets, excess condensation, and high temperatures may cause the chocolate to stiffen prematurely. To alleviate this problem, add a teaspoon of corn oil to the pan and stir. More oil can be added if needed to assure the proper consistency.

It's Just Divinity

Divinity fudge cannot be made on humid days. The air must be relatively dry, since the ingredients used and the type of preparation tend to attract moisture and will ruin the fudge.

The Candy Man Can

Hershey's Candy Company produces 2.2 million Kisses every day but the Dutch outdo us when it comes to candy consumption. They consume 64 pounds of candy per person annually. Americans only consume 21 pounds of candy each year.

Origin Of Chewing Gum

A variety of gums, resins, and plant latexes have been chewed for thousands of years. The first recorded history of mixing a gum with sugar can be traced to the Arab sugar traders who mixed the sugar with acacia, known as "gum Arabic." A number of gums were even used in early days as carriers for a variety of medications which allowed the medicine to be released gradually. Commercially, chewing gum as we know it today was produced in Bangor, Maine, in 1850, by the Curtis family, with only mediocre results. However, in 1859 a New Yorker by the name of Thomas Adams used "chicle," the dried latex material of the sapodilla tree of Central America. In 1871 a patent was issued to Adams for "chicle gum." Then in 1885 William J. White of Cleveland further refined and improved the gum by adding corn syrup and flavoring the gum with peppermint, which was very successful. In 1893 William Wrigley invented Juicy Fruit and Spearmint gums and in 1900 Frank Fleer of Philadelphia placed a hard shell on the gum and called it Chiclets. Fleer invented Bubble gum in 1928.

The gums of today are produced from synthetic polymers, mostly styrene-butadiene rubbers and polyvinyl acetate. The final product is composed of 60% sugar, 20% corn syrup, and only 20% actual gum material.

A Trick To Stop Syrup From Crystallizing

When boiling syrup, one of the more frequent and annoying problems is that the syrup may crystallize when you are cooking it. The easiest way to avoid this problem is to put a pinch of baking soda in the syrup while it is cooking. This will prevent the syrup from crystallizing by adding just a small amount of acidity.

The Jelly Bean Rule

Jelly beans have zero fat, no cholesterol, and no nutritive value at all. The FDA has a new rule for advertisers of worthless foods to follow so that they will not be able to label a food such as jelly beans a "healthy" food. This rule is actually called the "jelly bean rule." For a food to be labeled "healthy," it must contain a minimum of 10% of the Daily Values for any one of several key nutrients. The food must also be low-fat, low-saturated fat, and low in sodium and cholesterol.

The Difference In Cane, Beet, White And Brown Sugar

Basically, all table sugar is sucrose, a simple carbohydrate that breaks down in the body to glucose in a short period of time. Cane and beet sugars are not noticeably different in appearance or taste. Brown sugar still contains traces of molasses, which is a by-product of the sugar refining process. The nutritional difference between white and brown sugar is so insignificant it is not worth purchasing brown over white unless it is called for in a recipe.

What Is Sorghum?

Sorghum is usually thought of as just another type of molasses. However, there is a difference and it is really a unique product. While molasses is produced from the juice of the sugar cane stalk, sorghum is made from the juice of a different breed of sugar cane stalk called the sweet-sorghum cane, which is normally grown for animal feed.

Molasses is usually darker and may be somewhat bitter since much of the sugar is refined out. Sorghum retains its sugar and is sweeter as well as containing more nutritional value. Sorghum has more calcium, iron, and potassium than honey, molasses, or any other commercial syrup. The finest sorghum in the United States is made by Golden Mill Sorghum, (316) 226-3368.

What Is Chocolate Liquor?

Real chocolate is made from chocolate liquor, which is produced from cocoa pods. It is not really liquor in the sense that most of us think of liquor, but the name is given to the processed product obtained from the fruit of the cocoa tree. The cocoa tree is a member of the evergreen family and can be found only in equatorial climates. The tree grows to about 20 feet and the pods that contain the cocoa bean are about 8-10 inches long, with each pod averaging 30 beans. In 1995 the cocoa bean crop was about 1.5 million tons, most of which came from

West Africa. The first step in the processing is actually in the field, with the pods being opened and the beans allowed to sit in the sun.

This exposure causes a number of microbes to multiply, killing the seeds' embryos as well as producing changes in the structure of the cells. The cell walls deteriorate, releasing substances that mix together and result in the bitter phenolic compounds binding to each other and reducing the degree of bitter taste. The beans are cleaned and dried, then shipped to other countries.

The beans now must be processed into the chocolate liquor. They are roasted for about 1 hour at 250° F. which finally gives them the chocolate flavor. This involves approximately 300 different chemicals and results in the "browning reaction" and the color of chocolate. After they are browned, they are cracked open and the nibs (kernels) are separated from the shells. The nibs are then ground up to release the cocoa butter, carbohydrates and proteins which are all in the thick liquid oil called chocolate liquor. The refining process continues until the mixture ends up as a coarse chocolate or a powder.

Why Does Carob Powder Burn Instead Of Melting?

When you heat cocoa powder used in "real" chocolate, it contains fat which allows it to melt. Carob does not contain any fat and will therefore not melt but only burn. When carob flour is heated with water, the starch granules absorb moisture and rupture. This releases a gum that is used as a stabilizer and thickener in processed foods. If you use carob flour in a cake recipe it will act like any other flour.

The Real Sap: Maple Syrup

The "sap run" is one of the more interesting mysteries that nature has recently shared with us. Pure maple syrup is the product of the rock maple tree, which is the only tree that produces a high quality syrup. The sap is collected only in the spring, providing ideal conditions exist. The amount of sugar available is dependent on the leaves converting the right proportions of sunlight, water, and carbon dioxide into sugar. Sap is collected only from the first major spring thaw until the leaf buds begin to burst. If the sap collection is not discontinued at this point the syrup will have a bitter flavor.

Conditions must be near-perfect to have a good "sap run." The winter must be severe enough to freeze the tree's roots; the snow cover must extend to the spring to keep the roots very cold; the temperature must be extreme from day to night; and the tree must have excellent exposure to adequate sunlight. To produce sap, the tree must have stored sugar from the previous season in the trunk, especially in specialized cells known as xylem cells. Transport tubes are formed in the tree (from both live and dead cells) in which the xylem normally carries water and nutrients from the tree's root system to the leaves and trunk.

In early spring when the rock maple tree thaws, the xylem cells tend to pump sugar into specialized xylem vessels, the transport tubes are activated and the increase in sugar content in the xylem vessels creates a pressure that draws water into the vessels, increasing the water pressure. As the pressure increases, the xylem cells become more active and start to release waste products and carbon dioxide. The carbon dioxide gas level in the water tends to decrease with the rise in spring temperature and the trunk of the tree warms, causing the gas pressure and water to build up in the xylem tissues and forcing the sap to run and be collected.

Maple tree sap is about 3% sucrose, with one tree averaging about 10-12 gallons of sap per spring season. To produce one gallon of "pure maple syrup" requires 35 gallons of sap. The final syrup is composed of 62% sucrose, 35% water, 1% glucose and fructose, and 1% malic acid. The more the syrup is boiled during processing, the darker the syrup becomes due to a reaction between the sugars and proteins.

What Is Blown Sugar?

This is sugar that has been cooked to a point just below the hard crack stage and then poured onto an oiled marble slab and worked with a metal spatula until it has cooled enough to be worked by hand. The sugar is "satinized" by pulling it back and forth until it has a glossy, smooth sheen. It is then formed into a ball and an air hose attached to a pump is inserted into the ball of sugar and air is gently blown in. As it expands, the sugar is gently formed into sugar animals or other shapes. It is similar to glass blowing. The finished objects are then painted with a food coloring and used for display or consumed. They will last for months at room temperature if stored in an airtight container.

Why All The XXXXXXX'S On Sugar Bags?

The "X" symbol on sugar bags pertains to the fineness of the sugar. The more X's, the finer the grade of sugar you are purchasing. It actually indicates the number of holes per inch in the screening material used to form the size of the sugar crystals. If the package has four X's, there were four holes per inch in the screen. A ten-X sugar is usually a confectioners' sugar.

Carob: No Better Than Chocolate

Carob in its pure form does contain less fat than chocolate. Carob powder that is used to make carob confections is less than 1% fat, but has up to 48% sugar. Cocoa powder used in the manufacture of chocolate bars is 23% fat and only 5% sugar. However, when either one is processed into candy or chocolate bars the differences are, for the most part, erased. In fact, some carob bars contain a higher level of saturated fat than a Hershey bar and more sugar than a scoop of regular ice cream. Carob does not, however, contain the caffeine that is found in chocolate.

Sugarless Gum: Friend Or Foe?

Sugarless products that contain sorbitol or mannitol as the artificial sweetening agent may now be suspected of causing tooth decay just as much as regular gum. Neither one of these sweeteners actually causes tooth decay; however, they tend to provide nourishment for bacteria that are influential in causing tooth decay. The bacteria in question are called *Streptococcus mutans,* which have the tendency to stick to your teeth. They are is relatively harmless until they obtain sweets. The bacteria thrive on sorbitol and mannitol, as they do on real sugars. This was reported by Dr. Paul Keyes, the founder of the International Dental Health Foundation.

Is The New Sweetener Stevia Safe To Use?

This sweetener is new to the United States but has been used in South America and Japan for a number of years as a calorie-free sweetener. Stevia is an herbal extract from a member of the chrysanthemum family that is being sold in health food stores as a "dietary supplement." Since it is a natural herbal product, the Dietary Supplement Act of 1994 applies and the product was allowed into the country. However, the FDA is still not sure of any potential problems that might arise since testing is not conclusive at present. Research from Japan says it is safe and may even prevent yeast infections and act to boost energy levels. The Japanese research also reports that it does not promote tooth decay. The extract is concentrated and is 200-300 times sweeter than table sugar. It is being used for cooking and may leave a licorice-flavored aftertaste.

Coke Buys More Sugar Than Any Company Worldwide

Coca Cola is consumed over 190 million times every 24 hours in more than 35 countries speaking 80 languages. Colas have a higher physiological dependency than smoking and alcohol and are harder to give up. The Coca Cola company is the world's largest purchaser of sugar and vanilla. The vanilla is mainly supplied by Madagascar which was placed into a panic situation when the company switched to the "New Coke" which had no vanilla. Luckily for Madagascar the New Coke was rejected and the company had to put the vanilla back into the product. Americans consume 500 bottles /cans (48 gallons) of soft drinks annually per person.

M&M's Investigates Candy Colors?

The Mars company actually does continuing research to determine the colors and the number of each color that will be found in their packages of M&M's. The following is the current breakdown, which changes as their research is updated at regular intervals:

COLOR	PLAIN	PEANUT
Brown	30	30
Yellow	20	20
Red	20	20
Green	20	20
Orange	10	10
Tan	10	

The different colors have nothing to do with a flavor. All M&M's are the same chocolate inside.

How Many Pounds Of Candy Are You Eating?

In 1980 Americans were consuming 16.1 pounds of candy per person annually and by 1993 the figure was up to 20 pounds. The candy industry had set their sights on a goal of "25 by '95." They were hoping that they could reach that goal but failed. The current estimates are that they will reach their goal by 1999. For the companies to reach their goal, you will have to eat the equivalent of 195 candy bars per year. The candy companies are trying to have the government set one day in May ("Candy Carnival Day") as a national holiday.

Aging vs. Taste Buds

The tongue contains a number of clusters of specialized cells that form "taste buds." Each taste bud contains about 50 of these cells attached to a small projection which adheres to the upper surface of the tongue. Most adults have a few thousand of these taste buds but some adults have only a few hundred. Most of our taste buds are concentrated on the back of the tongue; however, the taste of sweet and salt are located in the front of the tongue and sour on either side. Children have considerably more taste buds than adults, with locations on the back of the throat, the tongue, and even the inner surfaces of the cheeks. Taste buds gradually decrease with age, especially after the age of 50. The cells that compose the taste bud have a life of only about 10 days, which is just as well if we burn our tongue regularly.

CHAPTER 9
HERBS AND SEASONINGS

How Should Herbs Be Added To A Dish?

Herbs are noted for their aroma more than for their taste in most instances. Chefs know how to appeal to your sense of smell when preparing a dish and will add either some or all of the herbs just before the dish is served, since many herbs lose some of their flavor during the cooking process.

60 Varieties Of Basil

There are more than 60 varieties of basil found worldwide. Basil is one of the most popular herbs used in the United States and is a member of the mint family. It can be used in almost any dish. The most common varieties are sweet and dwarf basil.

Can The Oil Of The Same Herb Be Substituted For That Herb?

This is never a good idea, although it is tried all the time. Oils are so concentrated that it is almost impossible to calculate the amount that you will need to replace the herb to acquire the same taste. A good example is cinnamon, where the oil is 50 times stronger than the ground cinnamon. If you did want to substitute the oil to replace the cinnamon extract, you would need to use only 1-2 drops of the oil to replace ½ teaspoon of the extract in candy or frostings.

The Color Of Pesto

Pesto sauce tends to turns brown in a very short period of time instead of remaining the pleasant medium green we are used to seeing. The browning, which is almost black at times, is caused by enzymes in one of the herbal ingredients, basil. Both the stems and the leaves of basil will cause the pasta to quickly be discolored with brown spots, as well as turning the sauce brown. When nuts such as walnuts, sunflower seed or pine nuts are added, the sauce will turn almost black. There is little to be done unless the pesto and pasta are prepared and served as soon as possible. One method of keeping the pasta yellow is to add ¼ cup of lemon juice or 1⅓ tablespoons of cream of tartar to each quart of cooking water. You may have to stir your noodles more frequently and keep the water boiling rapidly to keep the noodles from sticking together since the acid tends to cause excess attraction between the noodles.

Vanilla Bean Rustlers

The vanilla pod is the only food produced by a plant member of the orchid family. The reason "real" vanilla is so expensive is that is hand-pollinated when grown commercially. In the wild it is pollinated by only one species of hummingbird. They are expensive to grow. Over 75% of the beans are grown in Madagascar where the pods are actually branded with the grower's brand because "vanilla bean rustlers" are stealing the crop. Pure vanilla extract can be made by only percolating the bean, similar to making coffee. Imitation vanilla is produced from the chemical vanillin which is a by-product of the wood pulp industry.

Licorice: Sweeter Than Sugar

The word "licorice" actually means sweet root. The plant is a member of the legume family and was used by the Egyptians over 4,000 years ago as a medicine. The most common form found today is in candy and tobacco. The licorice extract is produced by boiling the yellow roots of the plant in water and then extracting the solid through evaporation. The black solid mass has 2 components: the oil anethole which contributes the flavor, and glycerrhetic acid which is the sweet component. Glycerrhetic acid is derived from glycerrhizin, found in the raw root and 50 times sweeter than table sugar (sucrose). The Egyptians used to chew the raw root for its sugary flavor.

Green, Black, And White Peppercorns

Basically, these are all the same. The only differences are that they are harvested at different times of maturity, and the method of processing. The green peppercorns are picked before they are fully ripe and are preserved and used mainly in the pickling industry and in dishes that do not require a strong pepper flavor. Black peppercorns are picked when they are just slightly immature and are the wrinkled peppercorns we use in our household pepper shakers or in the fresh pepper grinders. The white peppercorns are harvested when fully ripe and have a smooth surface. These are used in dishes where the color of the black peppercorns would detract from the color of the dish, such as a white cream sauce.

Sea Salt, Table Salt, Kosher Salt

The majority of the salt used in the United States is mined from salt deposits that were laid down thousands of years ago and are readily accessible. Sea salt, as its name implies, is acquired by allowing salt water to accumulate in pools and having the sun evaporate off the water, which leaves a more strongly flavored salt with a few more trace minerals than table salt. Actually, the difference does not justify the higher price for sea salt. Kosher salt has larger salt crystals and a more jagged shape which means that it will cling to food better. Because of its characteristics, kosher salt has the ability to draw more blood from meats, since kosher meats must be as free from blood as possible to meet the strict Jewish dietary laws.

Garlic: More Than A Remedy For Vampires

Garlic has been under investigation for a number of years in relation to heart disease, with studies published in *The American Journal of Clinical Nutrition*. Most studies were done using garlic oil in which the active ingredients were retained. Studies showed that garlic inhibited the coagulation of blood, reduced the level of LDL (bad cholesterol), and raised the level of HDL (good cholesterol). When the subjects consumed the equivalent of 10 cloves of garlic daily, blood levels of cholesterol dropped 14% and the HDL levels were raised by 41%. Most garlic products in health food stores, it was stated, had most of their active ingredients removed by processing.

Heavy-Handed With The Garlic

If you have used too much garlic in your soup or stew, just simmer a sprig or small quantity of parsley in it for about 10 minutes. To remove the garlic odor from your hands, try rubbing your hands with salt on a slice of lemon.

Is It Really Cinnamon?

The bark of two different trees is used to make cinnamon. The trees are evergreen trees in the laurel family and are the cinnamon and cassia varieties. However, these two trees are often confused and some stores are selling cinnamon from the cassia variety which is really not cinnamon. The color is the giveaway: true cinnamon is actually a light tan color, while cassia is a dark reddish-brown. Cassia is a product of Vietnam.

It's Turkey Time

Poultry seasoning is the one ingredient that really makes stuffing, stuffing. All poultry seasonings are not alike. There is a big difference in the freshness of the herbs and the methods of blending and storage before shipping. The finest poultry seasoning is produced by Brady Enterprises of East Weymouth, Massachusetts. The poultry seasoning was created around 1864 by William Bell. Bell's poultry seasoning is more potent than what you may be used to, so if you do use it remember that a little goes a long way. If you can't find it in a specialty market call (617) 337-5000.

Peppermint: An Herb And More

Peppermint is related to the spearmint family and contains the active oil menthol. Menthol is used in cigarettes, candies, liquors, toothpaste, mouthwash, etc. Menthol in low concentrations can also be used to raise the temperature of our skin, making a warm area feel cool. It has also been used as an anesthetic or as an irritant. Menthol is the active ingredient that will also chase the rodent population from your house or property. A small amount of oil of peppermint on a cotton ball placed anywhere you have a problem will solve it instantly. It works great on underground rodents, too.

Garlic Or Herbs Stored In Oil May Be Harmful

Many chefs and cooks have been known for years to store garlic or other herbs in oil for longer shelf life and to flavor their olive oil. The latest studies are showing some possible health hazards from this practice that may become serious. The mixture may contain the rare and deadly *Clostridium botulinum* bacteria which are present in the environment and may be present on herbs. The bacteria do not like an oxygen environment but love a closed environment such as in the oil. Oil gives the bacteria a perfect oxygen-free place to multiply. A microbiologist at the FDA has warned that a number of people have become ill due to placing store-bought chopped garlic in an oil medium. This type of mixture should be refrigerated and used within ten days to be on the safe side. When purchasing an herb and olive oil mixture from the market, it should be labeled to be refrigerated and will contain a preservative, probably phosphoric acid or citric acid.

The Top 10 Selling Herbs/Botanicals

1. Chamomile
2. Echinacea
3. Ephedra
4. Feverfew
5. Garlic

6. Ginger
7. Gingko
8. Ginseng
9. Peppermint
10. Valerian

What Is Chinese Five-Spice Powder?

This a common, fragrant spice mixture used in a number of Chinese dishes. It is a combination of cinnamon, anise seed, fennel, black pepper, and cloves. The formula is 3 tablespoons of ground cinnamon; 2 teaspoons of aniseed; 1½ teaspoons of fennel seed; 1½ teaspoons of black pepper; and ¾ teaspoons of ground cloves. Combine all the ingredients in a blender until they are powdered.

The Royal Breath Cleanser

In the year 300 B.C. the Chinese emperor had a breath problem and was given cloves to sweeten his breath. Cloves contain the chemical eugenol which is the same chemical that is used in a number of mouthwashes. Eugenol (oil of cloves) is also used to stop the pain of a toothache.

Some Herbs Need To Be Roasted Before Being Used

Allspice berries and peppercorns should be roasted before being used, to intensify their flavor. Roast them in a 325° F. oven on a small cookie sheet for 10-15 minutes before using them and you will be surprised at the difference in their flavor and aroma. They can also be pan-roasted, if you prefer over a medium-high heat for about 5 minutes with the same result.

CHAPTER 10
NUTS AND GRAINS

Plan Or Self-Rising Flour: The Taste Test

Have you ever wondered how to tell the difference in your flours after they have been placed in a flour bin? The plain flour has no taste and the self-rising has a salty taste due to the baking powder.

Competing With The Squirrels

According to Greek legend, acorns were a popular food during the Golden Age. Their high carbohydrate content made them an excellent cereal food for the North American Indians. The nut does contain a high level of tannin which can be removed by soaking in hot water and changing the water several times. The acorn pulp is then mashed and flat cakes made, similar to tortillas.

Is There A Fungus Among Us?

Rye is one grain that needs to be carefully inspected before processing. It is very susceptible to the fungus ergot. In Europe 300 years ago ergot was responsible for spreading disease over a widespread area. It is even believed that ergot was responsible for causing the disease among peasants that led to the French Revolution. Ergot looks like purplish-black masses in the rye and should be removed or the entire batch discarded. Rye grain that contains more than .03 % ergot is presently discarded and present day rye products should be perfectly safe.

The Brazil Nut

The Brazil nut can be grown only in the Amazon. Attempts to grow the tree in different parts of the world have all failed. The majority of the producing trees are still in the wild since commercial plantations have difficulty raising the trees. The tree grows to about 150 feet with a diameter of about 6 feet. The Brazil nut is actually the seed and is found in a pod that resembles a coconut and is about 6 inches across, with 12-20 seeds per pod. The pod weighs about 5 pounds and harvesters must wear hard hats or risk being killed. They have a high oil content and 2 nuts have the same number of calories as one egg.

Peanut Butter: By Prescription?

In 1890 Dr. Ambrose Straub of St Louis, Missouri made a batch of peanut butter for elderly patients who needed a source of protein and were not able to chew well. Dr. Straub also patented a peanut grinding mill on February 14, 1903. Peanut butter was first introduced to the public in the United States in 1904 at the St. Louis World's Fair. The first recorded history of "peanut paste" being consumed was by the Peruvian Indians and African tribes hundreds of years ago. The fat separation was a problem with the early peanut butters, but when hydrogenation came along, keeping the oil in suspension, it became one of the most popular foods in America. Peanut butter must be at least 90% peanuts to use the term "peanut butter." Almost 50% of the peanut crop in the United States goes for peanut butter production.

Cashews Related To Poison Ivy

Cashews and almonds are the two most popular nuts that are traded worldwide. The cashew is a relative of the poison ivy family, which is why we never see the cashew in its shell. The shell contains an oil which is irritating and must be driven off by heat processing before the cashew nut can be extracted without the nut becoming contaminated. The extraction process is a delicate operation, since no residue can be associated with the nut. The oil that is liberated is then used in paints and as a rocket lubricant base. The cashew is the seed of a fruit that resembles an apple, with the cashew seed sitting on top. In some countries the cashew is discarded because of the extreme difficulty of obtaining the seed in favor of consuming the apple or, better yet, fermenting it and using it to produce an alcoholic beverage.

Flaxseed: A Real Disease-Fighter

Flaxseed is now being processed so that it no longer has any toxicity and will store longer. It is being studied by the National Cancer Institute because it is an important source of lignins, which are plant compounds that provide a specific fiber that may contain anti-cancer properties. It is being studied in relation to breast, colon, and prostate cancers. Flaxseed is also rich in omega-3 fatty acids and is the richest plant source of alpha-linolenic acid, an essential fatty-acid. In a recent study, men who ate six slices of bread containing 30% flaxseed reduced their cholesterol levels by 7% and LDL's (bad cholesterol) by 19% without lowering the good cholesterol.

What Happens When You Toast Bread?

The browning reaction of toast was first discovered by a French chemist by the name of Maillard. He discovered that when bread is heated, a chemical process takes place that caramelizes the surface sugars and proteins, turning the surface brown. The sugar then becomes an indigestible fiber and the protein (amino acids) loses its nutritional value. The toast then has more fiber and less protein than a piece of bread that is not toasted.

Can Poppy Seeds Give You A Positive Drug Test?

Poppy seeds are commonly used in the baking industry in bagels, muffins, and cakes. However, since poppy seeds are derived from poppies, from which morphine and codeine are made, it will cause a positive urine test for opiates. Even 5 hours afterwards your test will still be positive. In one incident in Michigan a woman ate a lemon poppy seed muffin and gave a positive urine test. She was in trouble until the authorities and the University of Michigan solved the problem.

What Is The Ancestor Of Wheat?

There are over 30,000 varieties of wheat. They have all developed from just one common ancestor, known as "wild einkorn." Genetically, all the wheats grown today are from a different strain; however, two of the ancient strains are occasionally available in health food stores. The two that you may find are called kamut and spelt, which are produced as flour and pasta. These wild wheats can be traced back thousands of years.

Why Is Barley A Common Thickener For Soups And Stews?

Barley contain the starch molecules (complex carbohydrates) amylose and amylopectin packed into a granule. When barley is cooked in water, the starch granules absorb the water molecules, swell and become soft. At 140° F., the amylose and the amylopectin relax and some of their internal bonds come apart and form new bonds. This new network is capable of trapping and holding water molecules. As the starch granules swell, the barley becomes soft and provides bulk. If the barley is cooked farther the granules will rupture, releasing some of the amylose and amylopectin which are able to absorb more water, making the soup or stew thicker. To retain a large percentage of the B vitamins in barley, you will need to consume the liquid as well as the barley.

Debugging Your Flour

It is almost impossible to purchase flour of any kind without some sort of bug infestation. In fact, the FDA allows an average of 50 insect fragments per 50 grams (about 2 ounces) of grain. It is not a danger to your health at this level and is unavoidable. Insects and their eggs may set up residence when the grain is warehoused, during transit, or even in your home. To reduce the risk of infestation, just store your grains and flour in the freezer to prevent any eggs from hatching.

Wild Rice Is Really A Grass Seed

Wild rice is not a member of the grain family but is actually a grass seed that is cultivated only in paddies in Minnesota. It has twice the protein of rice and was a staple food of the Chippewa and Dakota Native American tribes. The only difference in the preparation is that the wild rice needs to be washed first, since dust seems to adhere easily to the surface.

How Do They Make Puffed Cereals?

Puffed cereals were invented in the early 1900's by Alexander P. Anderson. He was interested in the nature of starch granules and some of his experiments exploded into large puffy masses of starch. Making puffed cereals was somewhat like making popcorn. The starch or dough is compressed and cooked to gelatinize the starch and is then placed under high pressure until the water vapor expands, puffing out each small morsel. The final product is produced from "oven puffing." Quaker Oats was the first to produce puffed cereal. It was introduced to the public in 1904 at the St. Louis World's Fair and sold as a snack, like popcorn. In 1905 it was sold as a breakfast cereal.

Soybeans: Getting Popular

Soybeans are now the single largest cash crop in the United States, producing more protein products and oil than any other source. The soybean originated in China and was popularized by the Buddhists, who were vegetarians. The beans became popular in the United States after Commodore Matthew Perry's 1854 expeditions brought back two varieties from the Far East. The bean has a high protein content of 40% and an oil content of 20% and was originally used in paints, soaps, and varnishes. It was not used in foods due to an off-flavor until the process of hydrogenation was invented, which placed water into the soybean and made it more acceptable as a food product. The first use in the food industry was in margarine to replace butter, during World War II.

Is The Green Really Spinach In Spinach Pasta?

Actually, spinach pasta contains hardly any real spinach. In a cup of cooked spinach pasta there is less than one tablespoon of spinach. The nutritional value is almost identical to regular pasta and that is true with the other vegetable-colored pastas.

Does Peanut Butter Contain A Carcinogen?

Yes. Aflatoxin has been found in almost all peanut butters on the market. A study that was performed by Consumers Union showed that the major brands such as Jif, Peter Pan, and Skippy had less of the aflatoxin than store brands. The biggest offender turned out to be the freshly-ground peanut butter in health food stores, which had ten times the levels of the major brands. The U.S. government allows no more than 20 parts per billion (ppb) of aflatoxin, which members of the health field feel is too high. According to Consumers Union, eating levels that contain an average of 2 ppb of aflatoxin every 10 days will result in a cancer risk of 7 in a million. This is a higher risk that exists from most pesticides in foods. It is best to purchase a major brand or one that states on the label "aflatoxin-free."

Can Too Much Popcorn Jam Up Your Intestinal Tract?

Popcorn is composed of a complex carbohydrate (starch), and includes insoluble fiber (cellulose), which may help prevent constipation. It is always best, however, to drink plenty of fluids when consuming any large amount of insoluble fiber. Insoluble fiber tends to absorb water from the intestinal tract and will add bulk. The only risk would be if you ate 1-2 large tubs of popcorn without drinking any liquids. Then you may have a major traffic jam.

Almond Paste And Marzipan: Is There A Difference?

There is a difference, although both are initially made from blanched almonds. Marzipan contains more sugar and is stiffer and lighter in color. Almond paste contains more blanched almonds. Therefore it costs more. In California, almond orchards are second only to grapes in orchard space. Almonds are California's major food export.

What Is Masa Harina?

Masa harina is a special corn flour that is made by boiling the corn in a 5% lime solution for 1 hour to increase the amount of available calcium. The corn is then washed, drained, and ground into a corn flour that will be mainly be used to make tortillas and other Mexican dishes.

What Are Ginkgo Nuts?

A ginkgo nut is actually the pit of the ginkgo fruit and has a sweet flavor. It can be found in most Oriental markets. However, if you find it with the skin still on, be cautious, since the skin contains a skin irritant and you will need to wear gloves to handle the fruit until the skin is removed.

What Is The Oldest Tree Food In The World?

The oldest tree food that is known to man is the walnut, which dates back in Persia to 7000 B.C. The first walnuts were planted in the United States in 1867 by Franciscan missionaries. The Central Valley of California produces 98% of the total U.S. crop and 33% of the world's commercial crop.

Is Beanut Butter Better Than Peanut Butter?

A new substitute for peanut butter called Beanut Butter is now being marketed in the United States by Dixie USA. It provides a high quality protein and is made from soybeans. The product contains sufficient quantities of an estrogen-like substance called isoflavones to perhaps be effective in reducing the symptoms of menopause and lowering the risk of heart disease and osteoporosis. It is being studied in relation to reducing the risk of certain cancers. The fat content is 11 grams per 2 tablespoons compared to 16 grams in regular peanut butter and has half the saturated fat. The fat tends to separate like natural peanut butter and can be poured off to reduce the fat content even farther. For additional information call (800) 347-3494.

The Secret To Softening Beans

The nature of beans is such that some beans tend to soften more easily than others, even when placed in a liquid. To avoid the problem of hard beans, try adding ½ teaspoon of baking soda to the water in which the beans are soaking. Also, add ½ teaspoon of baking soda to the beans when they are boiling.

CHAPTER 11
FOOD ADDITIVES

The following additives and chemicals are some of the more common ones that may be recognized by the general public or that will easily be found on labels. The information contained in this chapter pertains only to the more pertinent facts regarding these substances and will not be overly technical. In 1995 over 800 million pounds of additives were used in the manufacture of foods. The USDA and FDA have classified food additives into 32 different categories.

1. Anti-caking and free-flowing agents: These are usually added to foods that are finely powdered or in a crystalline form to prevent them from caking or becoming lumpy.

2. Anti-microbial agents which are substances used in food preservation to prevent the growth of bacteria which might cause spoilage.

3. Antioxidants which are used to preserve foods by limiting their deterioration, rancidity, or discoloration caused by oxidation. Oxygen is one of food's worst enemies.

4. Coloring agents are mainly used to enhance the color of foods and are classified as color stabilizers, color fixatives, or color retention agents.

5. Curing and pickling agents are used to provide flavor and retard bacterial growth as well as increasing shelf life.

6. Dough strengtheners are used to modify starch and gluten to produce a stable dough.

7. Drying agents are substances that have a moisture-absorbing ability which keeps the humidity in the product at a standard moisture level.

8. Emulsifiers keep oil and water in suspension so that they do not separate after being mixed.

9. Enzymes are used to assist in food processing by helping the chemical reactions take place in an orderly fashion.

10. Firming agents are added to assist in the precipitation of residual pectins, strengthening the tissue that supports the food. This prevents the food from collapsing during processing and storage.

11. Flavor enhancers are added to either enhance or change the original taste or aroma of the food. The substance must not change the normal taste or aroma, just improve it.

12. Flavoring agents are added to add a specific flavor to a food.

13. Flour-treating agents are added to flour that has been milled to improve its color or baking qualities.

14. Formulation aids are used to bring about a desired physical characteristic or special texture in the food. These include carriers, binders, fillers, plasticizers, film-formers, and tableting aids.

15. Fumigants are more volatile substances that are used for pest and insect control.

16. Humectants are substances added to foods to assist the food in retaining moisture.

17. Leavening agents are used to either produce or stimulate the production of carbon dioxide gas in baked goods. This helps give the food a light texture. A number of yeasts or salts are used.

18. Lubricants and release agents are added to surfaces that come into contact with foods to stop the foods from sticking to them.

19. Non-nutritive sweeteners are sweeteners that contain less than 2% of the caloric value of sucrose (table sugar) per equivalent of sweetening capacity.

20. Nutrient supplementation are substances that are necessary for a person's metabolic and nutritional needs.

21. Nutritive sweeteners must have more than 2% of the caloric value of sucrose per equivalent unit of sweetening capacity.

22. Oxidizing and reducing agents chemically oxidize or reduce specific food ingredients to produce a more stable food.

23. pH control agents are added to assist in the maintenance of acid/base balance in the food. These include buffers, acids, alkalis, and neutralizing agents.

24. Processing aids are used to enhance the appeal or the utility of a food or ingredient of a food and include clarifying agents, clouding agents, catalysts, flocculents, filter aids, and crystalline inhibitors.

25. Propellants, aerating agents, and gases are used to add force in expelling a product or used to limit the amount of oxygen that will come into contact with the food during packaging.

26. Sequestrants are substances that combine with certain metal ions, which changes them into a metal complex that will blend into water or other liquid to improve the stability of that product.

27. Solvents are used to extract or dissolve substances placing them into solution.

28. Stabilizers and thickeners are used to produce a blended solution or disperse substances to give foods more body, to improve the consistency, stabilize an emulsion, and assist in the setting of jellies.

29. Surface-active agents are used to change the surface of liquid foods, other than emulsifiers. These include stabilizing agents, dispersants, detergents, wetting agents, rehydration enhancers, whipping agents, foaming agents, and defoaming agents.

30. Surface-finishing agents are used to increase the palatability of foods, preserve their natural gleam, and inhibit discoloration. Also included are glazes, polishes, waxes, and protective coatings.

31. Synergists are substances that will react with other food ingredients, causing them to be more effective when incorporated into a food product.

32. Texturizers affect the appearance or "mouth feel" of the food.

Acetic Acid	Acetic acid is known as the acid that makes vinegar acidic. Vinegar is about 4-6% acetic acid. It is used as a solvent for resins, gums, and volatile oils, can stop bleeding and has been used to stimulate the scalp circulation. Commercially it has been used in freckle-bleaching products, hand lotions, and hair dyes. In nature it occurs in apples, cheeses, cocoa, coffee, oranges, pineapples, skim milk, and a number of other fruits and plants. A solution of about 14% is used in the pickling industry and as a flavor enhancer for cheese.
Acid-Modified Starches	These starches are produced by mixing an acid (usually hydrochloric or sulfuric) with water and starch at temperatures that are too low for the starch to gelatinize. After the starch has been reduced to the desired consistency, the acid is neutralized and the starch is filtered and dried. The modification produces a starch that can be cooked and used at higher concentrations than the standard unmodified starches. The acid-modified starch is mainly used to thicken salad dressings and puddings.
Alum	Alum may go under a number of different names, such as potash alum, aluminum ammonium, aluminum sulfate, or potassium sulfate. Aluminum sulfate (cake alum) is used in the food industry to produce sweet and dill pickles and as a modifier for starch. The other chemicals are used in astringent lotions such as after-shave lotions to remove phosphates from waste water, harden gelatin, and waterproof fabrics.
Ammonium Bicarbonate	An alkaline leavening agent used in the production of baked goods, candies, and chocolate products, this is prepared by forcing carbon dioxide gas through concentrated ammonia water. Is is also used commercially in products that will break up intestinal gas.
Ammonium Chloride	Has a mild salt taste and does not blend well with alkalis. It is mainly used in yeast foods, rolls, buns, and as a dough conditioner. Commercially, it is used in permanent wave solution, eye lotions, batteries, safety explosives, and medically as a diuretic.
Amylase	An enzyme that breaks down starch into sugar, commercially derived from the pancreas of hogs. It is used in flour and as a texturizer in cosmetics. Sometimes used medically to fight inflammations, it is completely non-toxic.
BHA and BHT:	Both of these chemicals substances are frequently found in foods and are potent antioxidants. They are used in beverages, ice creams, chewing gum, potato flakes, baked goods, dry breakfast cereals, gelatin desserts, and soup bases. They are used as a preservative, antioxidant to retard rancidity, and as a stabilizer. Some animal studies have shown that abnormal

behavior patterns and brain abnormalities appeared in offspring after ingestion of these substances by the adults. The percentages of BHA that are allowed in foods are 1,000 ppm in dry yeast, 200 ppm in shortenings, 50 ppm in potato flakes, and 50 ppm when BHA is combined with BHT. The percentages of BHT allowed are 200 ppm in shortenings, and 50 ppm in breakfast cereals and potato flakes.

Caffeine

This is the number one psychoactive drug in the United States. It is used as a flavor in some root beers and found naturally in coffee, tea, and chocolate. It affects the central nervous system, heart, and is a respiratory stimulant. It is capable of altering the blood sugar release system in the body and easily crosses the placental barrier. Other side affects are extreme nervousness, insomnia, irregular heart rhythm, ringing in the ears, and even convulsions in high doses. Soft drinks that are labeled "cola" or "pepper" that are not artificially sweetened must contain caffeine. The soft drink industry is trying to have this changed.

Calcium Carbonate

The main chemical compound constituent in common chalk, limestone, marble, and coral. Commonly used as an alkali to reduce acidity in foods. Also used as a neutralizer in ice cream and cream syrups. Commercially, used as a carrier for a variety of bleaches. Its use as a white dye in foods was withdrawn by the FDA in 1988. Medically, is used to reduce stomach acid and as an anti-diarrhea medicine. Animal studies show that over-consumption may affect mineral absorption, especially iron.

Calcium Hypochlorite

Used as a germicide and sterilizing agent. Used in washing the curd on cottage cheese. Kills algae. A potent bactericide and fungicide. When used in a 50% solution is valuable in sterilizing fruits and vegetables. Dilute hypochlorite is commonly found in household laundry bleach. Can cause serious damage to all mucosal membranes if ingested. Should never be mixed with other household chemicals as it may produce deadly chlorine gas.

Calcium Lactate

A white, odorless powder which is commonly used as a bread dough conditioner and oxidizing agent. Nutritionally, it is used as a source of calcium for calcium deficient patients; however, it may cause intestinal and heart disturbances.

Calcium Propionate

A preservative that is used to reduce the prevalence of certain bacteria and molds. May also be used as sodium propionate, depending on the food.

Calcium Sulfate

Also known as "Plaster of Paris." A powder that is used as a firming agent and as a yeast dough conditioner. Commonly used in the brewing industry as well as other alcoholic products that need fermentation. Commercially, it is used in jellies, cereal flours, breads, rolls, blue cheese, and canned potatoes and tomatoes. Reduces the acidity in cottage cheese and tooth pastes. Industrially, it is used in cement, wall plaster, and insecticides. Because it tends to absorb moisture and harden quickly, some known problems have been related to intestinal obstruction. When it is mixed with flour it is an excellent rodent killer.

Carrageenan	Also known as Irish Moss. A common stabilizer used in oils, cosmetics, and foods. Used as an emulsifier in chocolate products, chocolate milk, cheese spreads, ice cream, sherbets, French dressing, and gassed cream products. It is completely soluble in hot water and is not coagulated by acids. It is under further study by the FDA since it has caused cancerous tumors in laboratory animals. In the present levels in food, however, it should be harmless.
Chlorine Gas	A common flour-bleaching agent and oxidizing agent. May be found naturally in the earth's crust and is a greenish-yellow gas that is a powerful lung irritant. It can be dangerous to inhale; only 30 ppm will cause coughing. The chlorine in drinking water may contain carcinogenic carbon tetrachloride which is formed during the production process. Chlorination may not be the safest chemical to use in water.
Chlorophyll	This is the green color found in plants that plays the essential role in photosynthesis. It is used in deodorants, antiperspirants, dentifrices, and mouthwashes. Also, it is used to give a green color to soybean and olive oil.
Diacetyl	A naturally occurring substance found in cheese, cocoa, pears, berries, cooked chicken, and coffee beans. It appears as a yellowish-green liquid and tends to assist in retaining the aroma of butter, vinegar, and coffee. Also used in chocolate, ginger ale, baked goods, and flavoring in ice creams, candy, and chewing gum. Certain diacetyl compounds have been found to cause cancer in laboratory studies.
Disodium Phosphate	Used to trap mineral ions in foods that would cause the food to spoil and affect their colors. Mainly used in the processing of evaporated milk, pork products, and in sauces, and commonly used as an emulsifying agent in cheeses spreads.
Ethyl Acetate	This is a colorless liquid that has a pleasant fruit odor and occurs naturally in a number of fruits and berries. It is extracted and made into a synthetic flavoring agent and used in berry products, butter, a number of fruit products, rum, mint products, ice creams, baked goods, chewing gum, puddings, and certain liquors. Also used in nail enamels and nail polish remover. The

	vapors are an irritant to the central nervous system, with prolonged inhalation leading to possible liver damage.
Ethyl Vanillin	Has a stronger flavor than natural vanilla and is used as a synthetic flavoring agent in berries, butter, caramel, coconut, macaroons, cola, rum, sodas, chocolate, honey, butterscotch, imitation vanilla extract, and baked goods. Has caused mild skin irritations in humans and injuries to a number of organs in animals.
Eucalyptus Oil	Has a camphor-like odor and is used in mint, root beer, ginger ale flavoring, ice creams, candy, baked goods, chewing gum, and some liquors. Medically, it has been used as a local antiseptic, expectorant, and vermifuge. Deaths have occurred from people consuming as little as 1 teaspoon and there are reports of coma from consuming 1 milliliter.
Gluten	A combination of the two proteins gliadin and glutelin. It is obtained from wheat flour, is extremely sticky, and is produced by washing out the starch in the flour. Responsible for the porous and spongy structure of breads.
Gelatin	Gelatin is used as a thickener in many foods and commercial products. When gelatin is mixed with water, the protein molecules will create a new network of molecules and stiffen into a more solid gel mass. As additional moisture is evaporated, the mass becomes more solid. Since gelatin is high in protein you can never use fresh figs, papaya, or pineapple in the product since it will break the protein down and ruin the product.
Guar Gum	Derived from the seeds of a plant found in India. It has 5-8 times the thickening power of starch and is used as a stabilizer in fruit drinks, icings and glazes. Frequently used as a binder in cream cheese, ice creams, baked goods, French dressing, etc. Has been very useful in keeping vitamin tablets from disintegrating. Also used as an appetite suppressant and to treat peptic ulcers.
Gum Arabic	This also called acacia and is the odorless, colorless, and tasteless sap from the stem of the acacia tree which grows in Africa and parts of the southern United States. It is considered a natural gum and has the ability to dissolve very quickly in water. It is mainly used to stop sugar crystallization, as a thickening agent in the candy-making industry, and to make chewing gum. Gum acacia is used in the soft drink and beer industry to retard foam.
Hydrogenated Oil	An oil that has been partly converted from a liquid polyunsaturated oil into a more solid saturated one. This process

adds hydrogen molecules from water to increase the solidity of the fat. Basically, it turns a relatively good fat into a bad fat which is more easily used in products.

Invert Sugar	Composed of a mixture of 50% glucose and 50% fructose. It is much sweeter than sucrose (ordinary table sugar). Honey is mostly invert sugar. Invert sugar is mainly used in candies and the brewing industry. It tends to hold moisture well and prevents products from drying out. Medically, it is used in some intravenous solutions.
Lecithin	It is a natural antioxidant and emollient composed of choline, phosphoric acid, fatty acids, and glycerin. It is normally produced from soybeans and egg yolk. Used in breakfast cereals, candies, chocolate, baked goods, and margarine.
Malic Acid	Has a strong acid taste and occurs naturally in many fruits, including apples and cherries. Used to age wines, and in frozen dairy products, candies, preserves, and baked goods. Commercially, used in cosmetics and hair lacquers. Skin irritant.
Mannitol	Usually produced from seaweed and is sweet tasting. Used as a texturizer in chewing gum and candies. Commonly used as a sweetener in "sugar-free" products although it still contains calories and carbohydrates. Studies are under way and may show that mannitol is a significant factor leading to cancer in rats. It may also worsen kidney disorders and cause gastrointestinal upsets.
Modified Starch	Modified starch is ordinary starch that has been altered chemically and used in jellies as a thickening agent. Since babies have difficulty digesting regular starch, modified starch is easier to digest since it is partly broken down. Chemicals that are used to modify the starch include propylase oxide, succinic anhydride, aluminum sulfate, and sodium hydroxide.
Monosodium Glutamate (MSG)	This actually the salt of glutamic acid, one of the amino acids. It occurs naturally in seaweed, soybeans, and sugar beets. Its main purpose in foods is to intensify existing flavors, especially in soups, condiments, candies, meats, and baked goods. A number of symptoms have been reported after ingesting MSG which include headaches, facial tingling, depression, mood changes, light flashes, and rapid pulse rate. A study released by the Federation of American Societies for Experimental Biology in 1995 stated that MSG was declared safe for most people. However, other reports indicate that people with asthma may be affected by as little as 0.5 grams, which is the minimum amount that would be absorbed through most foods. Should be consumed in moderation if at all.

Nitrate   Potassium and sodium nitrate is also known as saltpeter. It is mainly used as a color fixative for processed meat products. They tend to combine with saliva and food substances (amines) to form nitrosamine, a known carcinogen (cancer-causing agent). Animal studies have proved that mice developed cancer after being given nitrosamines. This chemical reaction may be neutralized in most instances by ingesting one 500mg chewable vitamin C tablet 5-10 minutes before eating a processed meat product such as a hot dog, strip of bacon, lunch meat, or sausage.

Nitrite   Potassium and sodium nitrite are used as a color preservative in meats as well as providing a chemical that will assist the meat product in resisting certain bacteria. Sodium nitrite will actually react with the myoglobin in meat and protect the red color for a long period of time. It is used in all processed meat products, Vienna sausage, and smoke-cured fish products. Similar reactions take place as with the nitrates and there is the same risk of the chemical converting to a carcinogenic substance. Vitamin E as well as vitamin C will block the conversion of nitrites. The author's personal recommendation is not to consume any product with either nitrites or nitrates added as a preservative.

Papain   An enzyme that will break down meats. It is prepared from papaya and is an ingredient in a number of meat tenderizers or marinades. It is also used for clearing beverages and added to farina to reduce the cooking time. Medically, it is used to prevent adhesions. It is, however, deactivated by cooking temperatures.

Pectin   An integral part of many plants, it is found in their roots, stems, and fruits. The best sources are derived from lemon or orange rind which contains 30% of the complex carbohydrate. It is used as a stabilizer and thickener for beverages, syrups, ice creams, candies, French dressing, fruit jellies, and frozen puddings. Mainly used in foods as a "cementing or binding agent."

Peroxide   Three forms of peroxide are used commercially: benzoyl, calcium, and hydrogen. Benzoyl peroxide is mainly used as a bleaching agent for flours, oils, and cheeses as well as medically made into a paste and used on poison ivy and burns. Should not be heated as it may explode. Calcium peroxide is used as a dough conditioner and oxidizing agent for baked goods. Has been used as an antiseptic. Hydrogen peroxide is used as a bleaching agent, a modifier for food starch, a preservative, and to reduce the bacterial count in milk products. It is a strong oxidant that is capable of injuring skin and eyes. Commercially, it is used in hair bleaches. Rubber gloves should always be worn at all times when using this product.

Potassium Chloride	A crystalline, odorless powder that has a somewhat salty taste. It is used in the brewing industry to improve fermentation and to assist in the jelling process with jellies and jams. It is also used with sodium chloride as a salt substitute. Should be used in moderation as testing is being done relating to gastrointestinal irritation and ulcers.
Sodium Benzoate	Used in acidic foods to reduce the microorganism count. Has been used to retard bacterial growth and act as a preservative in carbonated beverages, jams and jellies, margarine, and salad dressings. Sodium benzoate may be found naturally in cranberries and prunes.
Sodium Bisulfate	Used as an anti-browning agent and a preservative in beverages, corn syrup, dehydrated potatoes, dried fruits, sauces, soups, and some wines. Tends to destroy vitamin B1 (thiamine) when added to foods.
Sodium Carbonate	An odorless crystal or powder that is found in certain ores, in lake brine, and seaweed. Has the tendency to absorb water from the air and is used as a neutralizer for butter, milk products, and in the processing of olives. Commercially, it is used in antacids, soaps, mouthwashes, shampoos, and foot preparations. If ingested may cause gastrointestinal problems, nausea, and diarrhea.
Sodium Caseinate	A protein used as a thickener and to alter the color of foods. Usually found in coffee creamers, frozen custards, and ice cream products.
Sodium Chloride	This is the chemical name for common table salt. It is used in numerous food products as both a preservative and taste enhancer. Readily absorbs water. Many breakfast cereals are high in salt, such as Wheaties with 370 mg. of sodium per oounce. Most potato chips have 190 mg per ounce. Your daily intake should not exceed 1200 mg.
Sodium Citrate	Used as an emulsifier in ice cream, processed cheeses, and evaporated milk. Also used as a buffer to control acidity and to retain carbonation in soft drinks. Has the ability to attach itself to trace metals that are present in water and prevent them from entering live cells.
Tannic Acid	May be found in the bark of oak and sumac trees and the fruit of plants as well as in coffee, cherries, and tea. It is used as a flavoring agent and to clarify beer and wine. It has been used medically as a mild astringent. Commercially, it is also used in antiperspirants, eye lotions, and sunscreens.

CHAPTER 12
DAIRY PRODUCTS
AND SAUCES

Is Low-Fat Milk Really Low-Fat?

Some is and some isn't. If that sounds confusing, it is meant to be, by the milk producers. A good example of this is 2% low-fat milk, which most people think is really low-fat. Actually, when the water weight is removed from the milk it is approximately 34% fat (not a low-fat product). Whole milk is actually 3.3% fat or about 50% fat, while 1% low-fat milk is about 18% fat. There is a new milk ready to hit the supermarkets which is .5% fat and that will contain about 9% fat. It is best to use skim, non-fat, or buttermilk which is now made from a culture of skim milk. All are about 4% fat or less.

Reduced-Fat Ice Cream a.k.a. Ice Milk

Reduced-fat ice cream used to be called ice milk. All products now have the new name, provided they contain at least 25% less fat than the same brand of the regular ice cream product. However, you will need to read the label. Since the 25% refers to the corresponding brand, the amount of fat will vary from brand to brand. So don't be fooled into thinking that all "reduced-fat ice cream" has the same level of fat per serving.

Aerated Ice Cream A Must

Air must be whipped into all commercial ice cream. It is a step in the manufacture called "overrun." If the air were not added, the ice cream would be as solid as a brick and you would be unable to scoop it out. The air improves the texture and is not listed on the list of ingredients. However, ice cream must weigh at least 2¼ ounces per ½ cup serving.

How Perishable Is Milk?

Every half gallon of Grade A pasteurized milk contains over 50 million bacteria and if not refrigerated will sour in a matter of hours. Milk should really be stored at 34° F. instead of the average refrigerator temperature of 40° F. Milk should never be stored in light as the flavor and vitamin A are affected in 4 hours by a process known as "autoxidation." The light actually energizes an oxygen atom that invades the carbon and hydrogen atoms in the fat.

Why Is Milk Homogenized?

Homogenization is the process where fresh milk is forced through a very small nozzle at a high pressure onto a hard surface. This is done to break up the fat globules into more uniform very tiny particles. The process is done so that the cream which is high in fat will not rise to the top and form a layer. The fat particles become so small that they are mixed in the milk and are evenly dispersed. Fresh milk cannot be homogenized until it is pasteurized because it will go rancid in a matter of minutes. If the fat is broken down before pasteurization, the protective coating on the fat is exposed to enzymes that will cause the milk to become rancid.

What Are Condensed Milk And Evaporated Milk?

Condensed milk is milk that is not sterilized due to its high sugar content, which is usually 40-45%. The sugar acts as a preservative, retarding bacterial growth. However, the milk is not a very appetizing food. Evaporated milk is milk that is heated in the can to over 200° F., which sterilizes it.The milk tends to end up with a burnt flavor as well as picking up additional flavor from the metal if stored for a long period.

Why Does A Skin Form On The Top Of Milk?

The skin that forms on the top of milk is composed of the milk protein casein (which is the result of the protein coagulating) and calcium (which is released from the evaporation of the water.) The skin contains a number of valuable nutrients and should be minimized by covering the pan or rapidly stirring the mixture for a few seconds to cause a small amount of foam to form. Both of these actions will slow the evaporation and reduce the amount of skin formation.

Is It True That Dairy Products May Cause Mucus?

As far back as I can remember, I was told that I should never drink milk when I am sick because it will increase mucus production. In the last several years the "mucus-milk" connection has been studied and some interesting results surfaced. In Australia 125 people were given chocolate-peppermint-flavored cow's milk or an identically flavored non-dairy soy milk so that they could not tell the difference by taste. The people who believed in the theory that milk produced mucus reported that both milks (even though one was a non-dairy product) did produce a coating on their tongue and in their mouth. They also reported that they had trouble swallowing because of a thickened, harder to swallow saliva.

In another study, the same researchers infected a group of healthy people with a cold virus and tracked their dietary habits and cold symptoms and found that there was no difference in the amount of mucus secreted. It was concluded that milk did not produce any excess mucus, and the feeling of mucus production was due to the consistency and texture of the milk.

What Is Acidophilus Milk?

It is milk that is produced from low-fat or skim milk with a bacterial culture added to it. As the milk is digested, the bacteria are released and become active at body temperature, helping to maintain the balance of beneficial microorganisms in the intestinal tract. It is especially useful when taking antibiotics to replenish the bacteria that are destroyed, especially the ones that produce the B vitamins.

Spinning Off The Cream

Cream is produced by spinning milk in a centrifuge which causes the fat globules to release from the watery substance and become more concentrated. They are then removed. Supermarkets carry three grades of cream: light cream which is between 20-30% butterfat; light whipping cream which is between 30-36% butterfat; and heavy whipping cream which is between 36-40% butterfat (as compared to whole milk which is only 3.3-4% butterfat.)

Stick Butter vs. Whipped Butter

All recipes that call for butter always calculate the measurements for standard butter. Whipped butter has a higher air content due to the whipping. If you do wish to use it, you need to increase the volume of butter used by about 33%. Whipped butter is 25% air and better to use on toast since it will spread more easily.

What's In The New Imitation Butter Spray?

The product "I Can't Believe It's Not Butter" spray is made from water, a small amount of soybean oil, salt, sweet cream buttermilk, gums and flavoring. The average 4-spray serving only contains 15 mg of salt. It will not make your popcorn soggy and 20 squirts will only give you just over 2 grams of polyunsaturated fat.

It's Best To Use Unsalted Butter In Recipes

Depending on the area you live in and the particular supermarket,s butter product, the salt content of salted butter will vary from 1.5% to 3%. This can play havoc with certain recipes unless you are aware of the actual salt content of a particular butter and how the level of salt in that butter will react with your recipe. It is best in almost all instances to use unsalted butter and just add the salt.

Butter Easily Scorched? Use Clarified Butter

When butter is heated, the protein goes through a change and causes the butter to burn and scorch easily. A small amount of canola oil added to the butter will slow this process down. If you use clarified butter (butter from which the protein has been removed) you can fry with it for a longer period and it will also store longer than standard butter. Clarified butter, though, will not give your foods the rich real butter flavor you may desire.

Salmonella In Your Hollandaise

Recently some eggs have been found to contain *Salmonella* bacteria even if they are in perfect condition. You may therefore have cause for concern when making sauces that call for raw eggs, if the sauce is not cooked thoroughly. When preparing a Hollandaise or Bearnaise sauce it might be best to microwave the eggs before using them in your sauce. This can be accomplished without damaging the eggs too badly and still allowing them to react properly in your sauce. This should be done with no more than 2 large Grade A egg yolks at a time and in a 600-watt microwave oven.

First you need to separate the egg yolks completely from the white and the complete cord. Second, place the yolks in a small glass bowl and beat them until they are well mixed. Third, add 2 teaspoons of lemon juice and mix thoroughly again. Fourth, cover the bowl and place into the microwave on high and observe the mixture until the surface begins to move. Allow it to cook for 10 seconds past this point, remove the bowl and beat the mixture with a clean whisk until it appears smooth. Return the bowl to the microwave and allow to cook again until the surface starts to move. Allow it to remain another 10 seconds. Then remove and whisk again until it is smooth. Finally, allow the bowl to stand for about 1 minute. The yolks should now be free of any *salmonella* and still usable in your sauce.

How About Some Donkey Butter?

While almost all butter sold in the United States is produced from cow's milk, butter may be produced from the milk of many other animals. When cow's milk is not available, butter can be made from the milk of donkeys, horses, goats, sheep, buffalo, camels, and even yaks.

Why Does Whipped Cream Whip?

Fat globules in cream allow the cream to be whipped. Whipping cream causes the fat globules to be encompassed by air bubbles. This makes the foam and produces a solid reinforcement to the mixture. The fat globules actually cluster together in the bubble walls. The higher the temperature of the ingredients and the utensils, the more difficult it will be to whip the cream. Fat globules are more active and tend to cluster more rapidly at low temperatures. The cream should actually be placed in the freezer for 10-15 minutes before it is whipped. Adding a small amount of gelatin to the mixture will help stabilize the bubble walls and the mixture will hold up better. Sugar should never be added in the beginning as it will decrease the total volume by interfering with the proteins that will also clump on the bubble. Always stop beating whipped cream at the point when it becomes the stiffest, so that it won't turn soft. If small lumps appear in your whipping cream, this is a sign of butter formation and there is nothing that can be done to alter the situation. You will never obtain a good volume once this occurs.

Is A Low Cholesterol Milk On The Horizon?

Whole milk contains about 530mg of cholesterol per gallon. A new process being developed by researchers at Cornell University may reduce the cholesterol level to just 40 mg per gallon. The process involves injecting carbon dioxide into butterfat at high pressures. The butterfat is then removed from the milk, the cholesterol extracted, and the butterfat returned to the milk. The result is a milk with only 2% butterfat, low cholesterol, and a taste close to that of 2% milk.

Why Does A Recipe Call For Scalded Milk?

When a recipe calls for scalded milk, it is concerned with destroying certain enzymes that might keep emulsifying agents from performing their thickening task, and to kill certain bacteria that might be present. However, any recipe that still calls for scalding the milk has been reproduced in its original form since scalding is no longer necessary. All milk is pasteurized now, which accomplishes the same thing.

Is Buttermilk Made From Butter?

While it is still possible to find the "old fashioned" buttermilk that was drawn off butter, the majority of buttermilk is produced from skim milk cultures. The milk is incubated for 12-14 hours (longer than yogurt) and kept at least 40° cooler while it is fermenting. The buttery flavor is the result of a by-product of the fermentation process and is derived from diacetyl.

Why Is There Water In My Yogurt?

To begin with, it really isn't water that collects on the top of the yogurt but a substance called whey. Whey is a protein that tends to liquefy easily and may either be discarded or stirred back in. If you place a piece of cheesecloth directly on top of the yogurt it will absorb the whey. Discard the cheesecloth. If you do this for 2-3 days in a row it will stop weeping the protein and the yogurt will become much thicker, more like sour cream (which will also leak whey).

The Secret To Saving A Curdled Hollandaise Sauce

The secret to saving the Hollandaise sauce is to catch the problem and nip it in the bud. As soon as the sauce starts to curdle, add 1-2 tablespoons of hot water to about ¾ of a cup of the sauce and beat it vigorously until it is smooth. Repeat this for the balance of the sauce.

Can Butter Go Rancid?

Oxidation will take its toll on butter just like any other fat. It tends to react with the unsaturated fats and causes rancidity. This reaction can be slowed down if the butter is either under refrigeration or placed into the freezer. Butter should always be kept tightly wrapped.

Microwaving Butter

We all have the experience of microwaving butter too long and ending up with a runny mess. Butter is somewhat softer on the inside than the outside. When butter is microwaved the inside melts first. This causes a rupture in the outer surface and butter leaks out. It is best to microwave it for a few seconds and then allow the butter to stand for 2-3 minutes before using it. This allows the inner heat to warm and soften the outside.

What Is Margarine Made From?

Regular margarine must contain no less than 80% fat along with water, milk solids, salt, preservatives, emulsifiers, artificial colors, and flavorings. The fat may be tropical oils which are high in saturated fat or any of the polyunsaturated oils. The higher quality margarines will use corn or safflower oils. Soft margarines are produced from vegetable oils and do not have the milk solids added. They still contain salt and the artificial flavorings and preservatives. Liquid margarines are all polyunsaturated fat and will not harden in the refrigerator. Light/diet margarines vary from 40-60% fat content and have more air and water added along with the preservatives, salt, and flavorings.

Saving The Cream From Souring

When you need to use cream that has a somewhat off-odor, try mixing in ⅛ teaspoon of baking soda. The baking soda will neutralize the lactic acid in the cream that is causing the souring. Before you use the cream, make sure the flavor is within normal boundaries.

Up, Up, And Away, Super Egg

A new egg, called EggsPlus, is appearing in supermarkets. The hens are being fed a diet rich in flaxseed. These "super eggs" will be higher in vitamin E and omega 3 and omega 6 fatty acids. These fatty acids have been shown in studies to lower triglyceride (blood fat) levels about 6% as well as increasing the HDL (good cholesterol) levels by 20%. However, the cholesterol content is about the same as a regular egg (about 200 mg). A dozen eggs will sell for approximately $2.89.

What Happens To Egg Protein When It Is Cooked?

When egg white protein is cooked, the bonds that hold the proteins together unravel and a new protein network is created. The molecules of water in the egg are trapped in this new network and as the protein continues to cook, the network squeezes the water out. As more heat is applied, more water is released and the white becomes more opaque . If you over-cook the egg it will release all its moisture and will have a rubbery texture. The nutritional value of dried-out eggs is the same as fresh eggs.

The Secret To A Fluffy Omelet

To make the greatest omelet in the world, just make sure that the eggs are at room temperature. Leave them out of the refrigerator for 30 minutes before using them. Cold eggs are too stiff for an omelet. If you always add a little milk to your omelet, try adding a small amount of water instead. The water will increase the volume at least 3 times more than the milk. The water molecules surround the egg's protein, which results in more heat being required to cook the protein and make it coagulate. Another great addition is ½ teaspoon of baking soda for every 3 eggs. If you try all these tips you will have the greatest looking omelet and your guests will be impressed.

A True Separation

The albumen or egg white portion will be easier to separate from the yolk if the egg is at room temperature for 30 minutes. The protein tends to relax at room temperature and tense up under refrigeration. The yolk will also be less likely to break when the egg is moved back and forth during the separation process. A small funnel is the easiest way to separate an egg yolk from the white.

Where Did The First Chicken Come From?

We are still not sure whether the egg or the chicken came first. We do know, however, that eggs are millions of years old. The chicken that we are familiar with today is only 5,000 years old and not one of the first domesticated animals. The ancestors of the chicken were jungle fowl that were native to Southeast Asia or India. Chickens were probably domesticated for their eggs. By removing the eggs at regular intervals the chicken feels that it must lay more eggs, which it keeps doing. Some fowl will only lay one or two eggs and no matter what you do, will not lay any more.

How The Chicken Makes An Egg

The making of a chicken egg is really a remarkable feat. The trouble a chicken goes through to make sure we have our eggs for breakfast is the result of her daily reproductive efforts. A chicken is born with thousands of egg cells (ova) and only one ovary. As soon as the hen is old enough to lay eggs, the ova will start to mature, usually only one at a time. If more than one matures then the egg will be a double-yolker. Since chickens do not produce any more ova, as soon as their supply is depleted they stop laying eggs and end up in the pot. The liver continually synthesizes fats and proteins to be used to be used in the egg and provides enough nutrients for the embryo to survive the incubation period of 21 days. The egg shell is 4% protein and 95% calcium carbonate. The shell is porous. It allows oxygen in and expels carbon dioxide.

It's A Yolk

The chicken egg yolk consists of 50% water, 34% fat, and 16% protein, as well as traces of glucose and a number of minerals, of which sulfur is one. The yellow color is produced from pigments known as xanthophylls, which is a distant relatives of the carotene family.

Who Invented Mayonnaise?

Mayonnaise was invented by a German immigrant named Nina Hellman in New York City in 1910. Her husband, Richard Hellman, operated a deli in the city where he sold sandwiches and salads. He soon realized that the secret to his success was based on Nina's recipe for the dressing she put on the sandwiches and salads. He started selling the spread he called "Blue Ribbon" for ten cents a dollop and did so well that he started a distribution business, purchased a fleet of trucks and in 1912 built a manufacturing plant. The rest is mayo history with Hellman's Mayonnaise becoming one of the best selling spreads in history. At present, we consume 3 pounds of mayonnaise per person annually. To date Hellman's has sold 3.5 billion pounds of mayonnaise without changing the original recipe.

Counting Chickens And Eggs

In 1996 the chicken population in the United States totaled about 260 million, which means that there were more chickens than people. In 1800, chickens were only laying 15-20 eggs each year while they strolled around the barnyard pecking and scratching here and there and living a pretty normal chicken lifestyle. Presently, the poor fowl are cooped up in a controlled-temperature warehouse, fed a special diet, not allowed to move about and forced to lay egg after egg to about 300 per year. Each "breeder house" holds 9,000 chickens and 900 roosters to keep them happy. The record for a cooped up chicken is 371 eggs in one year at the University of Missouri College of Agriculture. The larger chicken farms produce 250,000 eggs per day. Americans are consuming about 250 eggs per person, which is down from 332 eggs per person in 1944 due to all the cholesterol scares by the medical community.

Whipping Egg Whites? Use A Copper Bowl

For some unknown reason, a copper bowl tends to stabilize egg whites when they are whipped. Next best is stainless steel but you will need to add a pinch of cream of tartar to accomplish the stabilization. Make sure either bowl has a rounded bottom to allow the mixture to fall easily to the bottom and come into equal contact with the mixing blades. Also, be sure that there is not even a trace of egg yolk in your mixture. The slightest hint of fat has a negative effect on the final product. Remove any yolk with a piece of the egg shell.

Why Place A Drop Of Vinegar In Poached Eggs?

Add vinegar to the water in which you are poaching your eggs and it will create a slightly acidic medium. This allows the eggs to set and retain a more desirable shape as well as helping the whites to retain their bright white color. The proper amount of vinegar is 1 teaspoon to 1 quart of water. Lemon juice will also work at ½ teaspoon to 1 quart of water. To repair a cracked egg, remove it from the boiling water and pour a generous amount of salt on the crack while it is still wet. Allow it to stand for 20 seconds, then wrap it in aluminum foil and continue cooking it.

Why Eggs Crack When Boiled

When an egg is laid it is very warm and tends to cool down. As it does, the yolk and white cool and shrink. This cooling and shrinkage results in an air space at the egg's large (non-tapered) end. This air pocket (trapped gas) tends to expand as the egg is heated in the boiling water. The gas has no place to go except out of the shell, which results in a crack. The albumen escapes and solidifies in the boiling water almost immediately. To prevent the problem all you have to do is make a small hole in the large end with a pushpin, the type with a small plastic end and a small short pin point. It is easy to handle and will not damage the egg nor release the white.

How Are Chickens Slaughtered And Inspected?

When the chicken is approximately six weeks old it is ready for harvesting. The live chickens are packed into cases of 22 birds per case and sent to the slaughterhouse where the cages are dumped onto a conveyer belt and workers grab the birds and hang them upside down with their feet hooked into a type of locking device. Workers can grab a bird and lock them up in about one second. They are then dampened with a spray and sent past an electrically charged grid that they cannot avoid. The charge is only 18 volts and is just enough to stun them so that they won't put up a fight. As the limp chicken moves on the conveyer, it passes a mechanical knife that slits its throat and allows it to bleed freely. After a minute the blood has drained and the conveyer reaches a scalding water bath where they are literally dragged through the 135° F.-water, which loosens their feathers.

Next they pass the de-feathering machine which consists of six-inch spinning rubber projections which literally flog all the feathers off the bird. The bird now arrives at the point where a machine or a worker cuts off its head, cuts open the cavity and removes the entrails. The USDA inspector will inspect the bird at this point for diseases, tumors, or infections. The inspector is given a whole 2 seconds to accomplish this task that should take at least 20 seconds or more. If the bird has 1 tumor it is removed and the bird is passed. If it has two or more it is rejected. Cleaning is then done, with 5,000 chickens to a bath of chilled water. One billion pounds of chicken are shipped in the United States every week. Americans' average consumption of chicken is 24 birds per year.

Can Cows Be Milked Too Soon After They Eat?

If you have ever purchased a quart of milk that had a cooked flavor, the milk was poorly pasteurized, which does happen occasionally. If the milk has a grassy or garlicky taste it was because the cows were milked too soon after their recent meal.

Can Baby Formula Be Re-Heated After The Baby Drank From It?

It is best to dispose of the unused portion since bacteria from the baby's mouth will enter the formula through the nipple. The bacteria will multiply to high levels. Even if the formula is refrigerated and re-heated, there may still be enough bacteria left to cause illness. Formula bottles should be filled with enough formula for a single feeding and the leftover discarded.

Breast Milk And Exercise Don't Mix

Studies show that if you are nursing your baby you should breast-feed the baby before you exercise. Lactic acid builds up during exercise and will give the breast milk a sour taste. The lactic acid level in milk will remain elevated for about 90 minutes after exercise before it can be cleared by the blood. If you need to feed during the recovery period, it would be best to collect milk for that feeding.

Grade B Eggs For Baking

The only significant difference among Grade AA, Grade A, and Grade B eggs is that the yolk will be plumper and the egg white somewhat thicker in the higher grades. The nutritive value of the egg is the same. When a recipe calls for a beaten egg you might just as well save the money and use Grade B eggs.

Blood Spots: Are They Harmful?

When the yolk membrane travels down the reproductive tract before it is surrounded by the albumen, it is possible for a small drop of blood to attach itself to the yolk. The blood may be the result of a small arterial rupture or from some other source of bleeding. It does not indicate that fertilization has taken place and if the egg is properly cooked is not harmful. If you feel uncomfortable with the blood spot, you can remove it with a piece of the shell.

The Green Egg

When eggs are overheated or cooked for a prolonged period of time, chemical change takes place. This change tends to combine the sulfur in the egg with the iron in the yolk which form the harmless chemical ferrous sulfide. This reaction is more prevalent in older eggs since the elements are more easily released. Eggs should never be cooked for more than 12-15 minutes to avoid this problem.

Telling The Age Of An Egg

Fill a large bowl ¾ full with cold water. Drop an egg in. If the egg goes to the bottom and lies on its side it is fresh. If it stays on the bottom at a 45° angle it is about 3-5 days old. If it stays on the bottom and stands up at a 90° angle it is about 10-12 days old. If it floats to the top it is bad and should not be opened in the house. When an egg ages it develops a degree of buoyancy as the yolk and the white lose moisture and the air pocket gets larger. Egg shells are porous and moisture will go through the shell

The Upside Down Egg

Eggs should be stored with the tapered end down. The larger end should be upright to reduce spoilage since it maximizes the distance between the yolk and the air pocket which may contain bacteria. The yolk is more perishable than the albumen. Even though the yolk is somewhat centered it does have some movement, and will move away from any possible contamination.

The Breathing Egg

When eggs are laid they begin to change in a number of ways. The most significant to the cook is that the pH (acid/base balance) of both the yolk and the white changes. Eggs "breathe" and release low levels of carbon dioxide even after they are laid. The carbon dioxide is dissolved in the internal liquids and causes changes in the pH of the egg. The older the egg, the more change occurs. The yolk and the white tend to increase in alkalinity with time, the yolk going from a slightly acidic 6.0 to an almost neutral 6.6, and the white going from 7.7 to about 9.2. Because of the changes in the alkaline nature of the white, the white tends to change from a strong white color to a very weak, almost clear, color. Coating the shell of a fresh egg with a vegetable oil will slow this process down. The older egg tends to be runnier which may make it more difficult for the chef to work with. The yolk is more easily broken as well.

Why Cheese May Refuse To Melt

One of the more frequent problems with melting cheeses is that the cheese is heated at too high a temperature for too long a period of time. The protein then separates from the fat and the cheese becomes tough and rubbery. Once this occurs it cannot be reversed and the cheese is ruined. Remember to keep the heat on low and use a double boiler if possible. If you are going to melt cheese don't try to melt large pieces. Cut the large piece into a number of small chunks before you attempt to melt it. Cheese should be added last to most recipes. Grating the cheese will also make it easier to melt and this method is best for sauces.

Maytag Is A Cheese, Not A Washing Machine

The Maytag blue cheese is one of the finest in the world and is produced from the freshest unpasteurized milk obtainable from only two Holstein herds located near Newton, Iowa. The moisture content is higher than that of most other blue cheeses, making it very spreadable and creamy. The cheese is aged in a special man-made cave that was dug into the side of a hill. The cheese is a somewhat sharp, yet mellow to the taste. It can be ordered by calling (515) 792-1133.

How Many Organisms Can A Cheese Culture Culture?

One teaspoon of a cheese-starter culture can contain 5 trillion living organisms. In the past, cheese producers were never sure of the activity of their culture which came from milk-souring lactic acid. Today there are companies that specialize in producing cultures of bacteria in whey (a protein) which actually separate the curd in the cheese-making process. These companies use lactobacillus and lactococcus to ferment milk sugar IO (lactose) into lactic acid. The acid is necessary in preventing unwanted microbes from growing in the cheese.

Cheetos Made Mostly Of Cornmeal?

Cheese is not the main ingredient in Cheetos. It is actually fourth on the list of ingredients, after cornmeal, vegetable oil, and whey. It was invented in 1948 by Frito-Lay who uses stone-ground cornmeal and adds moisture to turn it into a doughy mass. The dough is forced through small holes of an extruder (round wheel with holes). As the hot dough moves out of the extruder it comes into contact with the cooler air and "explodes" similar to popcorn. A knife then slices the long pieces into the bite-sized pieces we are used to seeing.

How To Buy Soft Cheeses

Two very popular soft cheeses are Brie and Camembert and both are sprayed with special mold to form a very thin, white, flexible rind. These cheeses ripen from the outside in and turn creamier with a more intense flavor as time passes. These cheeses are normally found in boxes which when opened may smell a little musty but should never have an ammonia smell. Ideally, the cheese should be somewhat springy when prodded and never have a hard core. These cheeses will continue to ripen when refrigerated for 1-2 days and should be consumed in 3-5 days after purchase for the best taste. If the cheese appears runny then it is over-aged and may be bitter. Other cheeses in this category include Limburger, Coulommiers, and Liederkranz.

Velveeta: A Cheese With A College Degree?

A bacteriologist working at Cornell University was hired by the Phenix Cheese Company and developed the product in 1915. The emphasis was to try to duplicate the consistency of Gerber's Swiss Gruyère cheese, which was a processed Swiss cheese. Eldridge separated the whey (the liquid protein) from the cheese and, after removing the protein, used the protein mixed with real cheese and a small amount of sodium citrate as an emulsifier to help the product stay in solution and stabilize. The original name was Phen-ett Cheese, named after the Phenix Company. Eldridge also developed another product at the same time for Kraft called NuKraft which eventually became Velveeta. Velveeta is presently labeled "cheese spread" and contains about 60% water and not less than 20% butterfat, plus a few gums to hold it together and, of course, sweeteners. Velveeta was marketed to stores in 1921 when Kraft patented a new method of packaging the cheese spread in a tinfoil-lined wooden box. The trick was to make the foil stick to the cheese and not the box. This created a hermetic seal and kept the cheese fresh for longer periods.

Choosing A Good Cheddar

One of the first things to look for when purchasing cheddar cheese is uniform color. If the cheese has white spots or streaks it has not ripened evenly or is starting to develop mold. The texture should always be relatively smooth although it is not uncommon to purchase cheddars that are grainy and crumbly. If the cheddar has a rind, be sure that the rind is not cracked or bulging which may mean that the cheese will be bitter due to poor manufacturing practices. Cheddar will continue to age in the refrigerator for months and should be stored in a container with a vinegar-dampened paper towel.

How Did Swiss Cheese Get Its Holes?

When Swiss cheese is curing, special microorganisms produce a gas that cause pockets of air to form and remain after the cheese ripens. The holes, however, should be relatively the same size and there should not be oversized irregular holes, especially large ones. The borders of the holes should also have a moist, shiny look about them. If the rind is grayish-looking it should not be purchased. The flavor of Swiss cheese will become stronger when wrapped in plastic wrap and refrigerated. Cut wedges should last for about 1-2 months.

Why Do Ice Crystals Form In Ice Cream?

The problem is that ice cream is removed from the freezer so often that it tends to freeze and thaw too many times. Water is released from the fat in the ice cream and the result is the formation of ice crystals. Home freezers rarely freeze ice cream solid, since most will not go down to 0° F. and hold that temperature for any length of time.

Who Invented The Ice Cream Cone?

The "waffle cone" was invented at the 1904 St. Louis World's Fair. A concession vendor by the name of Ernest Hamwi was selling waffle pastries called "zalibia." The vendor in a neighboring booth was selling ice cream in cups, ran out of cups, and was panicking. The waffle vendor came to his rescue by making a cone-shaped waffle that would hold the ice cream. The cone was called the "World's Fair Cornucopia" and was the food sensation of the fair.

The Secrets Of Making Ice Cream

The following tips should be adhered to if you wish the best results when using an ice cream maker:

- Before you start the freezing process, chill the mixture in the refrigerator for 4-5 hours. This will reduce the freezing time and the ice cream will be smoother and have more volume.

- The canister should be only ⅔ full. Under-filling it will allow more room for the ice cream to expand as the air is beaten into it. The result will be ice cream that is creamier and fluffier.

Eating Your Curds And Whey

Curds and whey are two proteins found in milk and milk products. The curd is actually casein and tends to form into a solid. The whey may be composed of several proteins, the most predominant being lactoglobulin. All are suspended in liquid. The liquid that you see on the top of yogurt or sour cream and other natural dairy products is the protein whey, not water, and should be stirred back into the product.

Storing Dairy Products

All dairy products are very perishable and contain tens of millions of bacteria. The optimal refrigeration is actually just over 32° F. Few refrigerators are ever set that low or will hold that low a temperature. Most home refrigerators remain around 40° F., which increases every time the door is opened.

The Limburger Story

Once one of the most popular cheeses in America, Limburger is eaten by few people now. It is a smooth, creamy, semi-soft aged cheese. It is a stronger smelling cheese than we have become used to and is now produced by only one plant in the United States, the Chalet Cheese Company of Monroe, Wisconsin. This company produces about a million pounds per year, using 32 cows. Limburger is "real" cheese, while most of the processed cheeses in the market are only 45% real cheese, fortified with whey powder and lactose. Limburger will continue to age after it is purchased and will actually develop more flavor. It will last for 5-6 months. It should be stored in a sealed glass container.

Deciphering The Secret Code On Egg Cartons

Before eggs are graded they are "candled." This means that the egg is viewed by passing it in front of an intense light that allows a person to see the contents. If the yolk is obscured by a cloud of white, the egg is very fresh. If the air pocket at the base of the egg is about the size of a dime, this is also an indication of a fresh egg. Grade AA eggs are the freshest, Grade A are just a bit older, Grade B goes to restaurants and bakeries. If your state requires a sell date, that will also help determine the freshness. If not, there may be a 3-digit code that was placed there the day the egg was packaged. The code pertains to the day of the year that the egg was packaged. January 1 would have a code of 001, meaning that it is the first day of the year. February 1 would be coded 032 since there are 31 days in January.

What Is Egg Wash?

Egg wash is a mixture composed of a whole egg or egg white that is combined with milk, cream, or water and beaten well. The egg wash is then brushed on the top of baked goods before they are baked to help the tops brown more evenly and give them a shiny, crisp surface. It also is used as a sort of glue, to hold poppy seed or similar toppings on rolls.

What Is The Chinese 1,000-Year-Old Egg?

This a Chinese delicacy which is really not a 1,000-year-old egg. It is actually a duck egg that has been coated with a mixture of ashes, salt, and lime and buried in the ground for 3 months. The insides of the egg turn into a dark jelly-type solution that can actually be eaten without fear of food poisoning. These eggs can even be stored at room temperature for up to 2 weeks and still be edible. The combination of the ashes, salt, and lime has a drawing effect on the fluids in the egg. This causes the proteins in both the white and the yolk to gel and to be colored by the minerals decomposing and staining the proteins.

Butter: Getting A Good Grade

To be called butter, butter must have a butterfat percentage of 80%. A natural coloring agent called annatto is added to some butters to give them a deeper yellow color. The USFDA grades butter by taste, color, aroma, texture and body. Grading is done on a point system with 100 being the best. Grade AA must have at least 93 points, Grade A at least 92, and Grade B a minimum of 90 points. Salt is added to butter to increase its shelf life.

What Can You Do To Stop Curdling?

There is always the risk of curdling, especially if you are preparing cream soups and sauces. To avoid the problem, you should always wait until you have thickened the mixture with flour or cornstarch before adding any ingredients that are acidic, such as wine, any type of citrus, or tomatoes.

Can Foods Cause Arthritis?

Recent studies are providing some alarming information about a relationship between *Salmonella*, *Campylobacter*, and other bacteria, and arthritis. Recently, 198,000 people became ill from drinking milk contaminated with *Salmonella*. Approximately 2% of the people became arthritis sufferers only 1-4 weeks after consuming the tainted product. The new type of arthritis is called "reactive arthritis." Symptoms include painful inflammation of joints in the knees and ankles, and lower back pain.

Do Cows Have To Give Birth Before Giving Milk?

Few people who were not raised ona farm realize that a cow must give birth before being able to give milk. The mammary glands which give milk become active by special hormones that are produced at the termination of the pregnancy. If the mammary glands are milked regularly they will produce milk for about 10 months. The gestation period for a cow is 282 days, which means that the farmer has a long wait before the cow will produce milk, and after the 10 months the cow must become pregnant again in order to produce more milk. Milk cows are usually bred again about 90 days after calving to get the cycle working again.

Hear Ye, Hear Ye: Flying Fortress Used To Make Ice Cream

A 1943 an article in *The New York Times* titled "Flying Fortress Doubles as Ice-Cream Freezers" stated that airmen were placing special canisters with an ice cream mixture and attaching it to the tail gunner's compartment of Flying Fortresses. The vibration of the plane and the cold temperature of the high altitude made ice cream as they were flying over enemy territory on their missions.

How To Guarantee A Creamy Custard?

The recipe for a basic custard formula calls for 1 egg, 1 cup of milk, and 2 tablespoons of granulated sugar. If you wish to increase the richness you will need to add 2-3 egg yolks, which increases the fat and cholesterol significantly. To avoid a solid custard it will be necessary to continually stir the mixture over a low heat setting.

Milk in a custard is really not the main protein source but contributes salts to assist in producing a gel. Never try to replace the milk with water. The milk and sugar will thin out the proteins and increase the volume. Abide by the recipe and never try speeding up the cooking process by increasing the heat; it will end up ruining the custard. To make the perfect custard takes time and patience.

Can Butter Be Easily Made At Home?

It's really not as hard as you might think. Place the bowl and metal blade unit of a food processor in the freezer for 20 minutes. Measure 2 cups of cold heavy whipping cream (never use ultra-pasteurized) into the ice-cold bowl and metal blade and process for 3-5 minutes, scraping down the sides to make sure that it all gets processed. Be sure to continue processing until all the solids are separated from the liquid. Then pour off the liquid, which is a protein substance called whey. The solids (butter) need to be refrigerated and used within 3-4 days. This will make about 6-7 ounces of butter.

Why Is It Impossible To Buy A Good Brie Cheese In the U.S.?

The finest Brie cheeses that reach their perfection in taste are made in France and are always made from unpasteurized milk. The United States will not allow this "surface-ripened" cheese to be imported unless it is made from pasteurized milk, aged for 60 days, or stored in such a manner that the flavor would be adversely affected during shipping. Natural Brie, if aged for 60 days, would lose its flavor and become overripe. The Brie that we do buy does not have the flavor or quality of the French Brie and has a lower fat content by about 10%.

CHAPTER 13
SUPERMARKETS

Kosher Foods: Better Or Worse?

While kosher foods do not contain any animal-based additives such as lard or edible offal, they still may contain tropical oils (palm and coconut) which are high in saturated fats. Kosher meats usually have a higher sodium content than any other type of meat or meat product due to the heavy salting in their special type of processing. Kosher products for the most part are no more healthful than any other product and the additional cost is just not worth it unless you adhere to the religious restrictions.

Nutrients In Supermarket Foods

The level of nutrients in supermarket products varies to such a degree that trying to calculate whether you really are ingesting the level you think you are is almost impossible. The following are results from one study. The variance in nutritional content was caused by many factors such as storage times, transportation times, original quality of the food, washings in the markets, effects of direct light, packaging, canning procedures, freezing techniques, preservatives used, processing, variations in the nutrient content of the soil or feed, etc.

The following is the vitamin A content in 3½ oz. servings of a few common foods:

Calf Liver	470-41,200IU	Carrots (with skin)	70-18,500IU
Tomatoes	640-3,020IU	White Cheddar Cheese	735-1,590IU
Eggs (without shell)	905-1,220IU		

The following is the vitamin C content in 3½ oz. servings of a few common foods:

Oranges (no skin)	Trace-116mg	Tomatoes (with skin)	9-38mg
Calf Liver	15-36mg	Carrots (with skin)	1-8mg.

Shopping Carts: A Losing Proposition

Shopping carts are a necessity but they are an expensive necessity. Supermarkets lose about 12% of their carts every year, with another 17% wearing out. The cost of the average cart is $100, which is an average cost to the market of $5,000 annually. The number of carts a store has is also an indication of its total dollar business. Most markets average $1,000 for every cart they have in service every week. If the market has 200 carts then it probably does $200,000 per week in business, which equals $10.4 million a year.

Sales Produced From Produce

The produce department in a supermarket is one of the more successful departments. In 1995 produce sales totaled about $32 billion a year. Apples are the most popular item with oranges second, then lettuce, potatoes, and tomatoes. Some of the least popular are broccoli, squash, asparagus, and cauliflower. Fruits account for 44% of the sales, with vegetables accounting for 56%. Tomatoes, which are botanically a fruit, are counted as a vegetable according to law and watermelons, which are actually a vegetable, are counted as a fruit.

What Are The Most Common Items Stolen From supermarkets?

Shoplifting is a real problem in supermarkets. Security cameras are popping up everywhere. The losses are estimated to be $5 billion per year. The most common items stolen are cigarettes, health and beauty aids, meats, fish, and batteries. Two of the most common problems are stock boys that steal and cashiers not ringing up items for friends.

When Were America's Most Popular Foods Introduced?

1691....First Patent For A Food Additive	
1853....Potato Chips	1928....Rice Krispies
1875....Heinz Ketchup	1930....Snickers
1880....Hot Dog	1930....Twinkies
1894....Chocolate Bar	1932....3 Musketeers
1896....Tootsie Roll	1934....Ritz Crackers
1897....Jell-O	1937....Spam
1897....Grape Nuts Cereal	1941....Cheerios
1906....Planter's Peanuts	1941....M & M's
1906....Instant Coffee	1944....Hawaiian Punch
1907....Hershey's Kisses	1946....Minute Rice
1911....Crisco	1946....Frozen French Fries
1912....Goo-Goo Clusters	1947....Almond Joy
1912....Oreos	1948....Cheetos
1912....Life Savers	1950....Sugar Corn Pops
1914....Clark Bar	1952....Sugar Flakes
1914....Mary Jane	1953....Sugar Smacks
1915....Velveeta	1956....Brownie Mix
1916....All Bran	1956....Jif peanut butter
1917....Moon Pie	1958....Tang Orange Drink
1920....Baby Ruth	1965....Shake 'n' Bake
1921....Mounds Candy Bar	1966....Cool Whip
1923....Milky Way	1968....Pringles Chips
1923....Peanut Butter Cup	1976....Country Time Lemonade
1927....Kool-Aid	1978....Weight Watcher's Food

Shopping For A Party?

The following chart is based on 20 guests. Adjust accordingly.

TYPE OF FOOD	SERVING SIZE	AMOUNT NEEDED
Coffee	1 Cup	3/4-1 lb
Soft Drinks	12 Oz.	(4) 2-Liter Bottles
Tea, Iced	1 Cup	1½ Gallons, 30 Bags
Cake	1½ Cake	(2) 13x9" Cakes
Ice Cream	1 Cup	5 Quarts
Pie	1/6 Pie	(4) 9" Pies
Butter/margarine	2 Pats	1 lb
Pizza	⅓ of 12" Pie	(7) 12" Pizzas

TYPE OF FOOD	SERVING SIZE	AMOUNT NEEDED
Potato/Corn Chips	1 oz	1½ lbs
Olives	4	1½ Quarts
Pickles	½ Pickle	10 Medium Pickles
Pasta	1 Cup Cooked	2 lbs, Uncooked
Spaghetti	1½ Cups	3½ lbs, Uncooked
Mashed Potatoes	½ Cup	6½ lbs
Potato Salad/slaw	½ Cup	2½-3 Quarts
Soup	1½ Cups	(3) 50 oz. Cans
Canned Vegetables	½ Cup	6 lbs

Supermarket Statistics

For every $100 spent on food, almost $18.00 is spent on meat, seafood, or poultry. Produce takes almost $10.00, snack foods take just over $5.00, and beans, rice and dried vegetables take $1.00. Potato chips are purchased every two weeks by over 80% of all households.

Supermarket Profits Are On The Edge

Almost 50% of the profit a supermarket makes is from the edges of the store. Most of the money you spend is spent on foods that are placed at the edges, such as produce, meats, dairy, and the salad bar. Breakfast cereals make more money for the store than any interior store product and are given a large amount of space. Shoppers are still beeped out of about $1 billion a year by scanner errors. This problem is being worked on and is improving. The meats are always at the end of the aisles so that you will notice them every time you reach the end of an aisle. Milk is always as far from the entrance as possible since it is such a popular item the market wants you to see other foods. Anchor displays are placed at the end of each aisle. These are products the market needs to sell out, or are a higher profit item. The produce department is the showcase of most stores and you will have to go past the great-looking fruits and vegetables first.

The produce area usually has the most influence on where the shopper shops. Produce is the second highest profit for the market while meat is always first. In supermarket terms, the aisles are called the "prison," since once you enter you cannot get out until you reach the other end. The "prison," however, is where the least profitable foods are found.

Getting Canned

The United States cans over 1,500 different kinds of foods with billions of cans being sold annually. There are over 40 varieties of beans alone, 75 varieties of juices, and over 100 different types of soups. If stored in a cool, dry location, a can of food will last for about 2 years and still retain a reasonable level of nutrients.

Supermarkets Love Pets

Americans spend an unbelievable amount of money on pet foods. In 1996 over $5.9 million was spent per day on cat food and over $8.6 million on dog food. Pet foods are an $8 billion a year industry. The higher quality pet foods contain more protein and less sugar, as well as fewer artificial dyes and additives. Nationally, veterinarians estimate household pets to be about 50% overweight and a study showed that overweight pets had overweight owners. Feeding cats that saucer of milk may not be a real treat since cats have a difficult time digesting lactose and would prefer a lower lactose treat like cottage cheese or yogurt. Too much chocolate can actually kill a dog. Most cats won't even touch it since they don't posses a sweet taste bud.

CHAPTER 14
BEVERAGES

Speedy Iced Beer

Quick-chilling beer has always been a problem. Placing the beer into the freezer usually means a problem since it either explodes or turns into a beer "slushy" if you forget it is in there. The best way to fast-chill beer is to have a cooler chest filled with water and ice and plunge the beer into the chest. In about 20 minutes the beer will be ice cold. The ice water is about 32° F. and of course is warmer than a 0° F. freezer. The ice water, however, absorbs the warmth from the bottle faster and more efficiently than the cold air does.

Hot Water For Ice Cubes?

If someone told you that boiling water would freeze faster than cold water, you would probably tell them that they were crazy or ask them to prove it. Well, actually boiling water does freeze faster than cold water and the reason is that even though cold water is closer to the freezing point than the boiling water, the hot water evaporates faster than the cold water, which leaves less water to freeze. The evaporation also creates an air current over the ice cube tray, which cools the water in a manner similar to blowing on a spoon of hot soup before tasting it.

Are Styrofoam Cups Leaving A Puddle?

Have you ever noticed that there was a puddle under your cup of tea? Recent studies have shown that when hot tea and lemon are placed into a polystyrene cup, the citric and tannic acids combine and, with the addition of heat, will actually eat away the cup, producing a noticeable hole. This puts carcinogens (cancer forming agents) into the tea. This reaction occurs only when the two acids and the heat are present.

At What Temperature Should Tea Be Brewed?

Tea experts agree that green teas should be brewed between 180°-200° F., Oolong teas between 185°-205° F, and black teas between 190°-210° F. The better quality teas should be brewed at lower temperatures since they tend to release their flavor more readily than the lower quality teas. The higher temperature used in the lower quality teas seems to stimulate the tea to release flavor.

Fresh Ground Coffee Beans: Brew It Fast

When coffee beans are ground up, a large percentage of their surface is exposed to air, which allows oxidation to take place at a rapid rate as well as causing some of the natural aromatics to be lost. Another problem is that the longer the fresh-ground beans sit, the more carbon dioxide (which contributes to the coffee's body and aroma) is lost. Coffee beans should be stored in the refrigerator; only the quantity that is needed should be removed and ground. The vacuum packed cans should be stored in the refrigerator, upside down to preserve the taste and flavor longer. By placing the can upside down you reduce the amount of oxygen that has contact with the surface of the coffee, thus slowing down oxidation.

Does A Hot Cup Of Any Beverage Really Warm You Up?

Other than a psychological effect, hot drinks will not raise your body temperature. Research conducted by the U.S. Army Research Institute of Environmental Medicine showed that you would have to drink 1 quart of a liquid at 130° F. to generate any increase in body temperature. They also stated that it would be difficult to keep that much liquid down. Hot liquids do cause a dilation of the surface blood vessels which may make you feel slightly warmer, but actually may lead to a loss of heat.

Are There Any Safe Methods Of Decaffeinating Coffee?

The only safe methods are the Swiss water method and the carbon dioxide method. With the Swiss Water Process method, the green coffee beans are soaked in water for several hours, which removes about 97% of the caffeine as well as a few of the flavor components. The water is then passed through a carbon filter which removes the caffeine and leaves the flavors. The same water is then added back to the beans before they are dried.

In the carbon dioxide method, the green beans are dampened with water, then placed into a pot that is then filled with pressurized carbon dioxide. The carbon dioxide has the ability to draw the caffeine out of the bean and can remove almost 100% of the caffeine. The coffee beans are then dried to remove the excess moisture. Both methods employ only natural elements to decaffeinate the coffee beans.

Does The Grind Size Of Coffee Beans Make A Difference?

The size of the grind does make a difference in the taste and level of caffeine in a cup of coffee. Espresso should be made with a fine ground, and Turkish coffee needs to have an even finer ground. Most American coffee is ground into a "drip grind." This provides the maximum surface area and will brew a rich cup of coffee that is not bitter. However, if the grinds are ulta-fine the water will take longer to filter through and this will result in an increase in polyphenols (tannins) and bitter tasting coffee.

Are They Really Making Caffeinated Water?

Yes, it's true. Sold under the names of "Water Joe" and "Java Johnny," it is being advertised as the latest cure for sleepiness when you are driving. When you go to a restaurant they will soon be asking you whether you want your water "caffeinated or plain."

The Latest Coffee Craze: The Cafetière

The cafetière or French coffee press or plunger pot is the latest craze in the United States. A number of coffee product retailers are touting the cafetière as the "preferred method of brewing." The unit does not use a filter but just presses the coffee and water which is then poured into a cup. Studies, however, indicate that this is not a preferred method, and if people drink 5-6 cups of pressed coffee a day it may increase their cholesterol levels by about 10% and the "bad" cholesterol (LDL) by 14% in some cases. The standard American method of brewing coffee by pouring water through a filter removes two of the risk ingredients that are implicated in raising cholesterol: cafestol and kahweol. These compounds are also found in other non-filtered coffee products such as espresso, which is produced by forcing steam or water through finely ground coffee.

Coffee Bitter?

The best flavor will be from freshly ground coffee Always use filtered water. Coffee should never be boiled. The longer it is boiled the more tannins are released.

Do You Have The Moxie To Order Moxie?

The oldest carbonated soft drink is called "Moxie." It was introduced in the United States in 1884 by Dr. Augustus Thompson in Union, Maine. This drink was originally sold as a nerve tonic and is still available today on the east coast. The soda is formulated using the root of the yellow gentian plant, which was thought to calm frazzled nerves. Moxie is still sold in orange cans with labels that resemble the original bottle. A Miss Moxie Pageant is held annually in Lisbon Falls, Maine. Presently, the Moxie headquarters is in Atlanta, Georgia, within the Monarch Bottling Company. To order your Moxie call (207) 353-8173.

Reducing Acidity In Beverages

Acid levels can easily be reduced in a number of common beverages, since certain people are overly sensitive to these beverages. To reduce the acidity just add a pinch of baking soda to the drink, especially coffee. Baking soda will reduce acid levels in high acid foods as well.

Coffee Is Made From Coffee Cherries

Coffee trees originated in Africa and records show the actual beverage we think of as "coffee" was in use in the Middle East. The coffee bean was so highly prized that the Arabs would not allow the export of the bean. It was finally smuggled to Holland in 1660 and then to Brazil in 1727. Coffee trees need an annual rainfall of over 70 inches of rain. Each tree produces only about 2,000 coffee cherries, which will make one pound of coffee. The United States consumes 50% of the world's coffee which amounts to 400 million cups every day. The average coffee drinker drinks 3 cups per day.

How Are You Able To Drink Burning Hot Coffee?

Drinking coffee that is hot enough to burn your skin but not your mouth is easily explained. When you sip a cup of very hot coffee, you will suck in more cool air than you ordinarily would. This air lowers the temperature through both convection (air current) and evaporation. The other factor involved is that the saliva released partly coats the inside of the mouth, insulating it from being easily burned.

Does Coffee Keep You Up At Night?

In most instances, coffee will only keep you up if you are not used to drinking a large amount. The more coffee you drink, the higher your tolerance will be to caffeine and the more it will take to keep you up. Some individuals are actually born with a high tolerance and are never kept awake. Studies have also found that people who think coffee is supposed to keep them awake, find themselves staying awake after drinking coffee.

Should Your Coffee Maker Have A Thermometer?

The proper temperature for brewing coffee will allow the extraction of the maximum amount of caffeol compounds (taste and aroma enhancer) and the lowest level of polyphenol compounds (tannins) that tend to give coffee an off-taste. A professional coffee brewer will keep the temperature of brewing coffee between 185°-205° F. If the temperature is too low, the coffee grounds will not release adequate caffeol compounds, and if gets too high the tannins are released. Caffeine in coffee has very little to do with the taste.

Does Tea Really Have Less Caffeine Than Coffee?

Actually, a pound of tea has almost twice the amount of caffeine as a pound of roasted coffee. However, one pound of tea will make 160 cups, while one pound of coffee will brew only 40 cups. This is the reason that tea has only about 25% of the caffeine as coffee. One of the absurdities which we all come into contact with on a daily basis is that children are usually not allowed to drink coffee, yet some soft drinks contain up to 25% of the same caffeine found in one cup of coffee.

Crystal-Like Particles On Your Wine Cork?

This phenomenon occurs only when the wine is poorly processed. It is not harmful and is caused by malic acid crystals that have turned into a solid from incomplete processing during the wine-making procedure. This does not make the wine unsafe to drink but I would not purchase that brand again.

Drink A Cup Of Water With Every Soft Drink

When you drink a non-diet soft drink, the sugar must be broken down by the body. This process is normally conducted in the small intestine which requires water to break down the sugar. This may cause you to be thirstier than before you tried to quench your thirst with the soft drink. If you are really thirsty, the best drink is water. Alcoholic drinks also require 1 cup of water per drink to metabolize the alcohol.

Carbonation Lasts Longer In Cold Soft Drinks

Two popular acids are used to make carbon dioxide, the gas that produces the bubbles in a soft drink. Phosphoric acid and citric acid react with water and form carbon dioxide gas. When carbon dioxide is in warm drinks or at a warm temperature, the gas expands and more of it escapes in the form of bubbles. If you add ice cubes to warm soda you will allow the gas to escape from the beverage at a faster rate, since the ice cubes contain more surface (nucleation sites) for the gas bubbles to collect on. This releases more of the carbon dioxide. This is the reason that the beverage goes flat in a very short period of time. To slow down the process, rinse the ice cubes in cold water for about 10 seconds before adding them to the soft drink. This will almost eliminate the "fizzing up" or loss of carbon dioxide in too short a period of time.

How Alcohol Is Distilled

Alcohol is so toxic to all living organisms that even the yeasts that produce fermentation are unable to survive in a solution of more than 15% alcohol. Beer and wine were the only alcoholic products for hundreds of years until the process of distillation was invented. This process is only possible because alcohol boils at 173° F., which is 39° lower than water. When alcohol and water are mixed and brought to a boil, the alcohol will predominate in the vapor. The vapor is then cooled through long curled tubes of cold metal and allowed to drip into a container.

Hear Ye, Hear Ye: Alcohol Kills Antioxidants

According to information released from the American Cancer Society, alcohol has the ability to neutralize the beneficial effects of beta-carotene.

Did The English Or French Invent Champagne?

The English actually invented champagne almost 40 years before the French. The English invented the cork stopper which was made from the inner bark of an oak tree that was native to Spain. The English had been using the cork material to stopper their wine and beer bottles for hundreds of years while the French used plugs of hemp soaked in oil that would seep. When carbon dioxide would build up in the French bottles, it would seep out through the hemp. The English cork held back the carbon dioxide and therefore the carbonation was retained. The English imported still champagne and bottled it, and the yeasts that were left in the wine produced the carbon dioxide in the closed environment. Wine needs to be stored on its side to keep the cork damp and prevent any air from getting into the bottle, which would increase the deterioration. Portugal supplies about 80% of the corks sold worldwide.

Why Do Wine Connoisseurs Swirl The Wine?

People who enjoy wine also enjoy the aroma of the various wines. By swirling the wine around in the glass, you release the full aroma of the wine. Wine may contain 400 hundred different organic molecules, 200 of which have an aroma.

What Are The Classifications Of Champagne?

Brut is the driest and the best grade. Vintage is normally very dry. Sec or just plain Dry is slightly sweet. Extra Sec or Extra Dry is a moderate sweet champagne. Demi-sec falls into the sweet category. Doux is very sweet, and Blanc de blanc and Year mean that the only white grape used was a Chardonnay.

Why is Champagne Always Served In Narrow Glasses?

Champagne is always served in "flutes" (tall, narrow glasses) because these glasses provide less surface from which the carbon dioxide bubbles can escape. Also, they allow a better bouquet to be released more slowly. The older type glasses that were shallow and had a wide brim allowed the bubbles and bouquet to escape at least twice as fast.

Too Much Punch In Your Punch?

If you have added too much alcohol to your punch (by accident, of course), try floating some cucumber slices on the top to absorb the taste of the alcohol.

Why Do We Need To Drink More Water At Higher Elevations?

Where we live will actually have an effect on the amount of water we need to drink to hydrate the body adequately. At higher elevations water tends to evaporate faster through your skin, due to the lower atmospheric pressure that makes the air drier. Since the air is thinner we also tend to increase our rate of breathing and lose additional moisture through exhalation. You will need to consume approximately 3-4 more glasses of water per day if you live in the mile-high city of Denver than if you live in New York.

You Need To Get The Lead Out

Over 5 million private wells in the United States may be exposing millions of people to high levels of lead. A warning has been issued by the Environmental Protection Agency that certain types of submersible pumps may leach lead into the water. The problem pumps have fittings made from brass that contains copper and zinc and 2-7% lead. It is possible to drink water with 51 times the allowable limits of lead in water prescribed by the EPA. Pumps should be made from stainless steel or plastic to eliminate the risk. For more information call the EPA's Safe Drinking Water Hotline at (800) 426-4791.

Scrub Those Ice Cubes

When ice cubes are allowed to remain in the freezer tray more than a few days, they tend to pick up freezer odor from other foods, or even a degree of contamination from the air when the freezer is frequently opened. It would be wise to wash the ice cubes before using them to avoid any contamination or alteration of the flavor of the beverage.

How About A Scuppernong or Muscadine Cocktail?

When the Pilgrims landed, one of their favorite foods was the muscadine berry which was growing wild. It has a great-tasting, tangy, berry flavor and is made into juice, jams, syrup, and jellies in the southern United States. The berries come in two varieties, the white (or scuppernong) and the red muscadines. Muscadine juice is the first new juice introduced to supermarkets since the 1930's. No sugar, coloring agents, or water is added to the juice and it is not bottled as a concentrate. It has a little punch to it and frequently replaces apple cider. To order the juice if it is not available in your area, call (800) 233-1736.

Beer Will Stay Colder In A Bottle Than In A Can

Aluminum cans are very thin and therefore when you hold the can it is easy for the heat to transfer and lower the temperature of the beer. A glass bottle, however, is much thicker, and the heat from your hands can't penetrate as well. Beer in a bottle will stay colder for a considerable length of time.

What Does Wine Have To Do With Making A Toast?

We have all been to a party where the host pops up and says, "Let's make a toast." This saying originated in the 17th century in England when a piece of spiced toast was placed in a carafe of wine or an individual glass to improve the taste. When the "toast" was made it was polite to eat the toast so as not to offend the host. The toast has since been omitted and just the wine consumed.

During World War II, Coke Almost Went Batty

In 1942, caffeine was becoming scarce due to the war and reduction of imports from foreign countries. The Coca Cola company was considering the idea of extracting caffeine from bat guano (bat feces). However, they decided against it since they were afraid that if the public ever found out that Coke had bat excrement in it, Pepsi would have won the cola wars, hands down!

Drinking Milk From The Carton Affects Storage Life

Even if you live alone and no one else drinks from the carton, the bacteria deposited into the carton will cause the milk to sour faster and shorten the storage life of the milk.

Draft Beer vs. Bottle Or Canned

A real beer drinker, one who is knowledgeable in respect to how beer is brewed and stored, will always order a draft beer over a bottle or can. Since all beer is subject to some degree of spoilage by microorganisms, all bottled and canned beer must be pasteurized (sterilized). This high-temperature processing causes a loss of natural flavor which the discerning beer drinker will notice. Draft beer is dispensed from kegs that do not go through the pasteurization process. They are kept cold and are never stored long enough to allow the microorganisms to alter the flavor or spoil the beer.

A Beer A Day Keeps The Doctor Away

New studies are showing that one alcoholic beverage a day (beer, wine, or liquor) may reduce the risk of a heart attack. Alcohol seems to boost the body's natural levels of a clot-dissolving enzyme called TPA. Physicians are using this enzyme to stop heart attacks in progress, according to the *Journal of the American Medical Association.* Other studies are now showing that moderate alcohol consumption also raises the supply of the good cholesterol HDL in the bloodstream.

What Happens When You Cook With Beer?

When you cook with beer, the heat will cause the alcohol to evaporate, leaving the flavoring agents intact. The acid, however, will react with certain metals (especially aluminum and iron) to form a dark compound that will cause a discoloration of the pot. When cooking with beer, always use a glass or enameled pot.

Nature's Carbonated Water

A number of "natural" beverages advertise that their drink contains naturally carbonated water. This water is created underground by the action of a somewhat acidic water. This water comes into contact with limestone, resulting in the production of the gas carbon dioxide. The gas is trapped by the water under the high pressure underground. Artificially, carbonation is helped along with either phosphoric acid or citric acid in most soft drinks. Unfortunately, phosphorus residues may remain in the drink, which may upset the calcium to phosphorus ratio in the body.

Does Blowing On Hot Soup Really Cool It?

Laboratory testing has shown that if a spoonful of very hot soup is held at room temperature for 45 seconds before it is consumed, it will cool down to an acceptable temperature, one that will not burn the mouth. If the same spoonful is blown on to speed up the cooling, it will cool to the same acceptable temperature in 20 seconds. The fast moving air will carry heat away from the soup more efficiently by forcing evaporation from the surface.

Who Put The Pop In Soda Pop?

In 1822, a man by the name of Townsend Speakman in Philadelphia developed the method of adding carbonation artificially to a beverage. He was asked to invent the process by none other than the father of surgery, Dr. Philip Syng Physick, who wanted to give such a beverage to his patients. The doctor charged his patients $1.50 per month for one drink a day. In 1878, the plain beverage was flavored and sold as soda water with a Hutchinson Bottle Stopper made from wire and rubber that would seal the carbonation into the bottle. When the stopper was moved to 1 side, for drinking, the gas escaped and caused the popping sound, hence the nickname soda pop.

Does Country Time Lemonade Mix Contain Lemon?

Lemon Pledge furniture polish contains more actual lemon than Country Time Lemonade Mix.

How Long Will Orange Juice Concentrate Last?

Orange juice has a higher acid content and therefore will last about a week after is reconstituted. However, the nutritional value, especially of the vitamin C, will decrease rapidly and it would be wise to consume the juice within the first 3-4 days. Water contains oxygen, which is the enemy of vitamin C. That, and the aeration of the mixing process, adds a large amount of oxygen to the juice.

Why Ice Floats

When water freezes, its molecules of hydrogen and oxygen combine in a loose fashion, creating air pockets in the structure of the ice cube. When water is in its liquid form, these pockets do not exist, which makes water denser than ice.

Rainbow-Colored Beverages?

In case you haven't noticed, children's foods are changing colors. Beverages now are all different colors, the most popular being blue. Kids will purchase blue drinks over any color and manufacturers are now going to make blue candy, cookies, ice cream, and even some foods. Studies performed at the University of Massachusetts showed that children "are open to the novelty of unnaturally tinted products." It was also discovered that color has an impact on how a food tastes to people. Kool-Aid now markets a green powder called Great Bluedini Punch that changes to blue when you add water.

Can You Get Higher Quicker On Champagne Than On Other Wines?

Yes! Champagne contains carbonation that will speed the absorption of the alcohol into the bloodstream. A wine cooler made with a carbonated beverage will give you the same effect.

Pop Goes The Champagne

Champagne is produced with a high level of trapped carbon dioxide dissolved in the liquid. The pressure in the bottle is sufficient to keep the carbon dioxide in suspension until the bottle is opened and the pressure, immediately drops to room pressure which draws the cork out of the bottle at a high speed. This causes the carbon dioxide to be released in the form of bubbles. This process will continue until all the carbon dioxide is depleted and the champagne goes flat, which will not take very long. The carbon dioxide gas also tends to increase the absorption of alcohol into the bloodstream, allowing you to feel the effects sooner than you would if you were drinking any other type of wine.

Will Coffee Sober You Up?

In many people, alcohol will first provide a feeling of euphoria and then have an opposite effect of making them drowsy and incoherent. Coffee, because of its caffeine, will make you more awake but it will have little to do with sobering you up. The quickest way to sober up is to consume a glass of water for each drink you had and take a multi-vitamin, multi-mineral supplement while you are drinking. This assists the liver in metabolizing the alcohol more efficiently. The hangover effects are reduced or eliminated although these are usually the result of poor quality booze or alcohol that contains too many cogeners (by-products of the processing). High quality alcoholic beverages rarely cause a hangover.

Not All Foods Get Along With Wine

There are a number of foods that do not have an affinity for wine. Foods like vinegar and citrus fruits that have a high acid content will give wine a bad flavor. Egg yolks contain sulfur which tends to have a negative effect on wine's flavor. There is also an assortment of aroma and flavor problems that can be traced to certain ingredients such as asparagus, chocolate, onions, tomatoes, pineapples, and artichokes.

What Is There In Coffee And Tea That Acts As A Diuretic?

Many people switched to decaffeinated beverages so that they would stop running to the bathroom as often and were surprised that the problem was still with them. Unfortunately, many people over a period of years get used to going to the bathroom after drinking coffee and tea. Their bodies just tell them they need to continue doing that even though it isn't necessary. Caffeine does have a diuretic effect on many people. Unfortunately, even when it is removed from tea there remains another diuretic agent called theophylline that may stimulate the bladder.

Getting A Head With Beer

The "head retention" on beer is measured by the "half-life" of the foam which is equal to the number of seconds it takes for the foam to be reduced by half its volume. If the beer has a head half-life of 110 seconds, it is considered to be very good. Foam will last longer if the beer is served in a tall, narrow glass that does not contain even a speck of soap scum.

The Colder The Beer, The Less The Flavor

The colder the beer, the less flavorful it will be, which is why beer is served at room temperature in many countries. If beer is allowed to sit in the sun, however, a chemical change will occur from the intensity of the illumination. Some of the sun's wavelengths tend to react with the hop resin humulone, which in turn reacts with the sulfur-containing molecules in the beer. This produces isopentenyl mercaptan, one of the odor ingredients in skunk spray, resulting in "skunky beer."

The Making Of The Brew

Beer making is a series of steps that eventually lead up to the final product. The first step is to allow dry barley kernels to soak, germinate, and accumulate specific starch-digesting enzymes such as amylase. The second step is to take the partly germinated kernels (or malt), dry them to stop the enzyme activity, and heat them in a kiln until they are the desired color and flavor. The third step is when the malt is mashed in a warm water bath, thus reviving the enzymes. This results in a somewhat sweet, brown liquid called the wort. The fourth step involves adding the hops into the wort and boiling the two to extract the hop resins which are responsible for flavoring the beer. This also inactivates the enzymes, enhances the color, and kills any microbes that may have been present. The fifth step ferments the wort with yeast, producing the desired level of sugar and alcohol. The sixth step is to filter the beer, remove the majority of the yeast, and then age the beer as desired. Finally, the beer is filtered, clarified, possibly pasteurized, packaged and sold.

The Percentage of Alcohol In Beers

BRITISH
Brown Ale..........3.0%
Light Ale............3.5
Lager.................3.5
Stout..................4.8
Strong Ale..........7.0

AMERICAN
Low-Cal..........3.75%
Lager...............4.5
Malt Liquor.....5.6

With What Type Of Water Should Thirst Be Quenched?

There has been a debate going on for years over whether it is best to drink ice water or room-temperature water when you are thirsty. The answer is to drink ice water, which will quench your thirst faster because it will cause the stomach to constrict, thereby forcing the water into the small intestine where it will be absorbed into the bloodstream faster.

Caffeine vs. Calcium

Recent studies released from the University of Washington state that drinking regular coffee will cause calcium to be excreted in the urine. The loss of calcium amounts to approximately 7 mg of calcium for every cup of coffee or two cans of caffeinated soda pop, according to a researcher at the Creighton University's Osteoporosis Unit in Omaha, Nebraska. To replace the calcium losses, it would be wise to add or consume 2 tablespoons of milk for each cup of coffee you drink.

Storing Beer

Beer should always be stored in the upright position, whether it is a can or a bottle. When beer is allowed to lie on its side for any length of time, more of the beer is exposed to any oxygen in the container. The more oxygen it is exposed to, the more oxidation will take place and the sooner the beer will lose its flavor. Also, beer should not be moved from one location in the refrigerator to another since the slightest temperature change will affect the flavor.

How Did Gatorade Originate?

Gatorade originated in 1967, when researchers at the University of Florida decided that their football team, the Gators, needed to replace the minerals and fluids lost through strenuous exercise. In 1983, Quaker Oats purchased the brand name and sold the drink in different flavors. The drink was developed to provide water, sugar (energy), salt (fluid balance), and potassium (nerve transmission). At present Gatorade has about 85% of the sports drink market of over $800 million a year.

Can Corn Silk Be Used To Make Tea?

On almost every continent, corn silk has been used to prepare tea that has a diuretic effect. In fact, it is one of the best diuretics you can prepare from any herb. It was also shown in some studies that corn silk tea even lowered blood pressure, probably by controlling fluid retention. If your doctor ever recommends that you take a diuretic it would be best to ask him if you could try a natural one before a prescribed medication.

Does Dehydration Affect Us More In The Summer Or Winter?

It is a known fact that the human body will lose more water during the summer months, but you are more likely to become dehydrated in the winter. In the winter you lose the conscious need to drink more fluids and water is still lost through sweat. Sweat will not linger and is absorbed more quickly by the dryness of the atmosphere in a heated room and the rate of absorption of heavier clothing.

Avoid The New Beverage Mugs With A Freezable Lining

A number of companies are producing a beverage mug with a walled separation that contains a liquid that will freeze. The mugs are to be kept in the freezer and used for any type of beverage. They are safe to use. However, when a beverage is placed in them, ice crystals are formed in the beverage that reduce the palatability of the beverage. Even alcoholic beverages such as beer will develop ice crystals and reduce the flavor and aroma significantly. Soda will become crunchy and not very pleasant to drink. The mugs are fine if you are going to allow a beverage to sit for some time before you drink it. Standard mugs kept in the freezer do not produce the same problem.

CHAPTER 15
FOOD
SUBSTITUTIONS

Active Dry Yeast (One Package)	1 cake compressed yeast
Agar Agar	Use gelatin
Allspice	¼ teaspoon cinnamon and ½ teaspoon ground cloves or ¼ teaspoon nutmeg for baking only or black pepper other than baking
Anise (Use Equivalent Amount)	fennel or dill or cumin
Apples	1 cup of firm chopped pears 1 one tablespoon of lemon juice. 1 pound of apples = 4 small, 3 medium, or 2 large or 2¾ cups sliced or 2 cups chopped
Arrowroot	flour, just enough to thicken, should take a few tablespoons.
Baking Powder (One Teaspoon, Double-Acting)	½ teaspoon cream of tartar plus ¼ teaspoon of baking soda or ¼ teaspoon baking soda plus ½ cup of sour milk, cream, or buttermilk. Must take the place of other liquid or 4 teaspoons of quick-cooking tapioca
Baking Powder (One Teaspoon, Single-Acting)	¾ teaspoon double-acting baking powder
Basil (Dried)	tarragon or summer savory of equal amounts or thyme or oregano
Bay Leaf	thyme of equal amounts
Black Pepper	allspice in cooking, providing salt is also used in the dish
Borage	cucumber
Brandy	cognac rum
Bread Crumbs (¼ Cup, Dry)	¼ cup cracker crumbs or ½ slice of bread, may be toasted or crumbled or ¼ cup rolled oats or ¼ cup of matzo meal or

¼ cup of sifted flour or
¼ cup of corn flakes

Bulghur (Use Equal Amounts)	cracked wheat kasha brown rice couscous millet quinoa
Butter (In Baking)	hard margarine or shortening (Do not use oil in baked products.) 1 lb = 2 cups 1 cup = 2 sticks 2 tablespoon = ¼ stick or 1 oz 4 tablespoons = ½ stick or 2 oz 8 tablespoons = 1 stick or 4 oz
Buttermilk	1 cup of milk plus 1¾ tablespoons of cream of tartar or equivalent of sour cream
Cake Flour	use 1 cup of all-purpose flour minus 2 tablespoons
Capers	chopped green olives
Caraway Seed	fennel seed or cumin seed
Cardamon	cinnamon or mace
Cayenne Pepper	ground hot red pepper or chili powder
Chervil	parsley or tarragon (use less) or anise (use less)
Chives	onion powder (small amount) or leeks or shallots (small amount)
Chocolate, Baking,	3 tablespoons of unsweetened cocoa plus 1 tablespoon of butter
Unsweetened (1 oz or square)	3 tablespoons of carob powder plus 2 tablespoons of water Chocolate, Baking Unsweetened (1 oz pre-melted) 3 tablespoons of unsweetened cocoa plus 1 tablespoon of corn oil or melted Crisco

Chocolate, Semi-Sweet (6 oz of chips or squares)	9 tablespoons of cocoa plus 7 tablespoons of sugar plus 3 tablespoons of butter
Cilantro	parsley and lemon juice or orange peel and a small amount of sage or lemon grass with a small amount of mint
Cinnamon	allspice (use a small amount) or cardamon
Cloves (ground)	allspice or nutmeg or mace
Club Soda	mineral water or seltzer
Cornmeal	grits (corn) or polenta
Cornstarch	flour, a few tablespoons for thickening, usually no more than 2
Corn Syrup (one cup, light)	1¼ cups granulated sugar or 1 cup granulated sugar plus ¼ cup of liquid
Cream Cheese	cottage cheese mixed with cream or cream with a small amount of butter or milk
Crème Fraîche	sour cream in a recipe ½ sour cream and ½ heavy cream in sauces
Cumin	⅓ anise plus ⅔ caraway or fennel Dill Seed caraway celery seed
Edible Flowers (garnish)	bachelor buttons blue borage calendula petals chive blossoms mini carnations nasturtiums pansies rose petals snap dragon violets

Eggs, Whole	2 tablespoons water plus 2 tablespoons of flour plus ½ tablespoons of Crisco plus ½ teaspoon of baking powder or 2 yolks plus 1 tablespoon of water or 2 tablespoons of corn oil plus 1 tablespoon of water or 1 teaspoon of cornstarch plus 3 tablespoons of water if part of a recipe
Evaporated Milk	light cream or half and half or heavy cream
Flour (thickeners, use up to 2-3 tablespoons only)	Bisquick tapioca, quick cooking cornstarch arrowroot (use small amount) potato starch mashed potato flakes pancake mix
Garlic (equivalent of 1 clove)	¼ teaspoon of minced, dried garlic or ⅛ teaspoon of garlic powder or ¼ teaspoon of garlic juice or ½ teaspoon of garlic salt (omit ½ tsp salt from recipe)
Ghee	clarified butter
Honey (one cup in baked goods)	1¼ cups granulated sugar plus ¼ cup water
Juniper Berries	a small amount of gin
Lemon Grass	lemon or lemon rind or verbena or lime rind
Lovage	celery leaves
Marjoram	oregano (use small amount) or thyme or savory
Masa Harina	corn flour
Mascarpone	cream cheese, whipped with a small amount of butter
Milk, Evaporated	light cream or half and half or heavy cream

Milk *(in baked goods)*	fruit juice plus ½ teaspoon of baking soda mixed in with the flour
Milk (one cup)	½ cup evaporated milk plus ½ cup of water or 3 tablespoons of powdered milk plus 1 cup of water. If whole milk is called for add 2 tablespoons of butter.
Molasses *(one cup)*	1 cup of honey
Nutmeg	allspice or cloves or mace
Nuts (in baked *goods only)*	bran
Oregano	marjoram or rosemary or thyme (fresh only)
Pancetta	lean bacon (cooked) or very thinly sliced ham
Parsley	chervil or cilantro
Polenta	cornmeal or grits (corn)
Poultry Seasoning	sage plus a blend of any of these: thyme, marjoram, savory, black pepper, and rosemary Rosemary thyme or tarragon or savory
Saffron *(1/8 teaspoon)*	1 teaspoon dried yellow marigold petals or 1 teaspoon azafran or 1 teaspoon safflower or ½ to 1 teaspoon turmeric (adds color)
Sage	poultry seasoning or savory or marjoram or rosemary

Self-Rising Flour *(one cup)*	1 cup all-purpose flour plus 1 teaspoon of baking powder, ½ teaspoon of salt, and ¼ teaspoon of baking soda
Shallots	small green onions or leeks or standard onions (use small amount) or scallions (use more than is called for)
Shortening *(one cup in baked goods only)*	1 cup butter or 1 cup hard margarine
Sour Cream *(one cup)*	1 tablespoon of white vinegar plus sufficient milk to make 1 cup. Allow the mixture to stand for 5 minutes before using or 1 tablespoon of lemon juice plus enough evaporated milk to make 1 cup or 1 cup of plain yogurt if it is being used in a dip or cold soup or 6 ounces of cream cheese plus 3 tablespoons of milk or ⅓ cup of melted butter plus ¾ cup of sour milk for baked goods
Tahini	finely ground sesame seeds
Tarragon	anise (use small amount) or chervil (use larger amount) or parsley (use larger amount) or a dash of fennel seed
Tomato Paste	1 tablespoon of ketchup or ½ cup of tomato sauce providing you reduce some of the other liquid
Turmeric	mustard powder
Vanilla Extract *(in baked goods only)*	almond extract or other extracts that will alter the flavor
Vinegar	lemon juice in cooking and salads only or grapefruit juice, in salads or wine, in marinades
Yogurt	sour cream or crème fraîche or buttermilk or heavy cream or mayonnaise (use in small amounts)

CHAPTER 16
COMMON HOUSEHOLD PRODUCTS

How Can I Make An Effective Grout Cleaner?

Cleaning grout around tiles is one of the worst cleaning jobs in the home. Most common products contain sodium hypochlorite (similar to diluted laundry bleach) and/or calcium hypochlorite and some detergent. An inexpensive grout cleaner may be made by mixing together 2 parts of liquid laundry bleach with ½ part of a phosphate-based liquid floor cleaner (or 2 tablespoons of Spic and Span), 3 parts of isopropyl alcohol, and 4½ parts of water. The solution can be placed in a clean plastic pump bottle and used the same as the store cleaners. When mixing chemicals, be sure to not place any near an open flame or heating element. The isopropyl alcohol is flammable.

Should We Use A Phosphate Detergent?

Phosphates increase the alkalinity of wash water and are more effective than the older products that used washing soda. Phosphates tend to bind certain metal salts that are found in hard water and change them into soft water, which makes the fabric more accessible to the detergent. Sometimes phosphates are called sodium triployphosphate (STPP), which is an inexpensive form and harmless to humans.

What Other Chemicals Besides Soap Are In Laundry Detergent?

There are a number of other chemicals in most laundry detergents. These include bleaches, perfumes, enzymes, re-deposition agents, surfactants, and even chemicals to prevent your washer from being damaged. Some products even use optical brighteners, which are dyes that are deposited on your garments that will transmit light to the human eye that would ordinarily be invisible, ultraviolet light rays. When you see an advertising that claims its products will make your clothes "whiter than white," they only appear to be. One of the more interesting agents is the anti-redeposition agents that coat the clothes with a type of cotton-like substance (carboxymetacellulose) that can prevent the dirt and grime that has been washed from the garments from being redeposited back on the clothes during the wash cycle. The agent is easily removed during the rinse cycle. The most difficult stains for a detergent to remove are the protein stains from dairy products, eggs, and blood.

What Do Fabric Softeners Actually Do?

Fabric softeners are made from chemicals called "cationic surfactants" or resins. The cationic surfactants possess a positive charge and have an affinity for wet, negatively charged garments. They form an even layer on the surface of the garment, removing the negative charge which is responsible for a scratchy feeling and roughness of the fabric. The softener will also remove the static electricity from the fabric and generally makes the fabric softer to the touch.

What Causes The Rings On Toilet Bowls?

The ring around the bowl is caused by the accumulation of dirt embedded in minerals from the hard water. Minerals usually found in these residues are either calcium or magnesium carbonate. A mild acid will easily remove the stains. The most common and least expensive is oxalic acid, which is available in a powder or flake form. A cola drink that has gone flat contains phosphoric acid and will also do the job in some instances.

What Is Soap Made From?

Whether you use soft soap or hard soap, they are all made from sodium or ammonium hydroxide and one of the following: an animal fat product (usually tallow), coconut oil (lauric acid), oleic acid (olive oil), cottonseed oil (linoleic acid), or the synthetic substance isethionic acid. Soaps may contain perfumes, skin conditioners, or antibacterial agents. Most are non-irritating to the skin, lather well, and have good cleansing ability.

How Is Tallow Produced?

Tallow is derived by passing steam through animal fat. The lighter fat is stearic acid and the sodium salt of stearic acid is called sodium stearate, which is found in bar soap as sodium tallowate. Coconut oil, because it is a liquid, is more unsaturated than tallow, making it a better choice for a soap product.

Why Does Ivory Soap Float?

Excess air is mixed in with the ingredients. This allows it to float. The floating soap was produced by accident when in 1930 an employee who was supposed to be watching the soap mixture fell asleep and the mixture accidentally filled with air. The company didn't want to discard the batch and found that the public liked the floating soap.

Is Cold Cream The Same As Cleansing Cream?

Cleansing creams and cold creams are basically the same product. They are composed of camphor, cloves oil, menthol, phenol, linseed oil, water, stearic acid, soybean oil, eucalyptus oil, calcium hydroxide, and aluminum hydroxide. The camphor, cloves oil, and eucalyptus oil are aromatics. The menthol has some antibacterial properties as well as being an astringent. Soybean oil adds a smooth texture. Stearic acid prepares the skin so that the cream will penetrate. Linseed oil is a softening agent. Phenol is a relatively strong antibacterial agent. A hydroxide will increase the pH.

Are Shampoos Similar To Liquid Dish Soap?

There are really no similarities between liquid dish soap and shampoo. Shampoos are produced from ammonium lauryl sulfonate and are much safer for your hair. Shampoos contain lauramide for producing a lather; lecithin to give your hair a shine; hydrolyzed animal protein to repair those split ends; glycol stearate to untangle your hair and give it luster; methylparaben to preserve the mixture; methylisothiozoline as an antibacterial agen; Canadian balsam as a lacquer; and some citric acid to make the mixture a bit more acidic with a lower pH. When shampoos are produced, they end up too basic (alkaline) to be used on hair and must have the pH lowered.

How Does Hair Spray Work?

When you spray hair spray, you are depositing a thin layer of resin which is dissolved in a volatile solvent or alcohol which easily evaporates in the air. Once the solvent evaporates it leaves behind a layer of "plastic." Hair sprays in standard pump applicators (non-aerosal type) are really "plasticizers." If you don't believe that there is a thin layer of plastic on your hair, just take a flat glass surface and spray a thick layer on the glass. Allow it to dry for a minute or so, then just peel off the layer in one thin sheet. Mousses, gels, and creams for the hair are also a type of plasticizer.

How Does A Liquid Hair Remover Work?

A hair remover is called a "depilatory." These products remove body hair using a concentrated chemical solution to break the sulfide bonds in hair. The main chemical used is calcium thioglycolate. In high concentrations it is capable of breaking down almost 100% of the disulfide bonds in hair, thus causing the hair to literally fall apart and disintegrate. The minute fragments of hair are then removed with washing.

What Is Toothpaste Composed Of?

There are a number of chemicals that all work together to grind off stains, help prevent cavities, wash away the debris, and add a flavoring. The abrasives to remove stains may include any of the following: hydrated silica, calcium carbonate, baking soda, calcium pyrophosphate, hydrated aluminum oxide, magnesium carbonate, or tricalcium phosphate. The mosturizing agent is usually sorbitol. The chemical that prevents the conversion of plaque to tartar is tetrapotassium pyrophosphate. The sweetener may be sodium saccharin. One of the more popular whiteners is titanium dioxide. A thickening agent, carbomer, is needed. And, of course, a number of artificial dyes: F, D, and C blue #1. Using baking soda after each meal may be just as effective as this chemical smorgasbord.

How Do Antiperspirants And Deodorants Differ?

The first antiperspirant was produced about 1905 and was called "Odo-Ro-No." Early deodorants were actually just underarm perfumes. Antiperspirants are formulated to cause the sweat glands to constrict and actually prevent normal perspiration. Bacteria need a certain amount of moisture to reproduce, and the sweat provides a perfect medium for them to live in and produce offensive odors. Antiperspirants contain chemicals that prevent the problem from occurring. These include aluminum chlorohydrate, aluminum chloride, and zirconium chloride. Sticks are more effective because of their solid composition. Creams and sprays tend to lose effectiveness too soon.

Deodorants do not act to constrict the sweat glands but they do contain antibacterial agents, the most effective being triclosan. The antibacterial effects are only effective for about 2-3 hours and most deodorants contain a perfume to hide the offensive odors. Deodorants are used by people who would prefer a more natural approach, preferring not to have normal bodily process altered.

Why Are Aftershave Lotions Used?

Aftershave lotions tend to cool the skin, tighten the pores, and promote healing from the irritation of shaving. The most common ingredients used to accomplish these tasks are propylene glycol, menthol, and benzoic acid. Pre-shave lotions are used only with electric shavers and are skin lubricants that help the shaver move more easily across the skin. Some have ingredients that may also make the facial hair stand up to be cut.

What Is Vaseline Made Out Of?

Vaseline is produced from a mixture of hydrocarbons that are derived from purified crude oil. Petroleum jelly is excellent for sealing off the skin and protecting it from surface damage, especially from irritations and a mild abrasion.

What Is The Difference In Over-The-Counter Pain Relievers?

The most common analgesics (pain relievers) are aspirin, acetaminophen, ibuprofen, and naproxen. Aspirin has the ability to reduce inflammation in joints and act as an antipyretic (fever reducer). Ibuprofen is supposed to be more effective for deep muscle pain; however, it has yet to be clinically proven to the satisfaction of the medical community. Naproxen is similar in action to ibuprofen but tends to remain in the bloodstream for about 2-3 hours longer, which may provide a benefit. Acetaminophen (known as paracetamol in England) does not seem to offer any relief for inflammation and is not as good a pain reliever as aspirin, but it does not irritate the stomach, which aspirin may do. A relative newcomer is naproxen sodium, sold under the brand name of Aleve. Naproxen sodium may irritate the stomach just as much as aspirin and is sold to relieve pain, backache, muscle pain, discomfort of arthritis, and menstrual cramping.

Aspirin works by slowing the transmission of nerve impulses to the brain, thus reducing the sensation of pain. It also interferes with prostaglandins, which (in excess) tend to dilate the small vessels in the brain and cause headaches by localized inflammation. *Stomach irritation by aspirin is usually the result of not drinking a full glass of water when taking the product.*

Why Are So Many Hospitals Using Tylenol?

Tylenol is selling the hospitals their product below cost to promote it as one of the more popular analgesics used by the medical community. Bayer is also trying this method and is making some inroads. Once the patient leaves the hospital, most physicians advise their patients to purchase any over-the-counter pain reliever.

Why Do Liniments Reduce Pain?

Liniment have been used for hundreds of years on both animals and humans to relieve pain, especially pain related to muscle overuse. They are mainly in cream form although there are still a few that are in liquid form. The creams tend to stay on better and allow the chemicals to do their job more efficiently. Liniments work by a process called counterirritation. They actually irritate the skin to such a degree that they cause a mild pain which causes the pain receptors in the area to be "switched off"'" A common liniment for horses, DMSO is not recommended for humans; it tends to dilate surface blood vessels and will allow almost any medication or chemical to enter circulation.

Why Can't I Keep That New Car Smell Longer?

A number of products have that same "new car" smell for a short period of time, especially new carpets. During the manufacture of plastics, oils are added to the plastic to keep it from drying out. These special oils are absorbed into the plastic and over a short period of time their vapors come into the air. The oils that are left on the surface are the ones you smell when you purchase a new item. Over a period of time, the deeper internal oils come to the surface but are not strong enough to create a noticeable odor.

Are Oven Cleaners Dangerous?

The majority of aerosol oven cleaners contain sodium hydroxide (lye) which is also found in drain cleaners. Spraying lye on burnt fats and carbohydrates converts them into a soap that is easily wiped off with a damp cloth. It would be best to use a number of the newer products that use organic salts and are less dangerous. With any type of oven cleaner, make sure that there is good ventilation or it may burn the lining of your mouth and throat.

How Does Antifreeze Work?

Antifreeze is composed mainly of propylene alcohol; which when added to water, lowers the freezing point and also increases the boiling point. Therefore water can't freeze at 32° F. and it will not boil at 212° F. The coolant is circulated through the engine by the water pump. The engine heat is transferred to the coolant which returns to the radiator. The radiator is cooled by the outside air which cools the antifreeze, preventing boil-overs.

Can Coca-Cola Really Clean My Car Battery?

Carbonated beverages, especially those that are carbonated using phosphoric acid, will dissolve metal oxides that cake on battery terminals. However, the best way to clean the terminals is with a metal brush, with some baking soda sprinkled on first to neutralize the acid. Never clean the battery terminals with water, or the battery may short out and explode.

Why Don't Cars Want To Start On Cold Days?

The problem usually has nothing to do with the battery but with the oil. Freezing temperatures tend to turn your oil into a thick syrup, making your battery work harder to turn the engine over. Manufacturers make higher-amp batteries that may help alleviate this problem, or you may want to consider a heated blanket to keep the motor oil from becoming a semi-solid.

What Is The Difference Between A Car Polish And A Wax?

A car polish is only meant to enhance and restore the luster to a wax coating. It removes dirt and debris trapped in the wax and restores a smooth finish to the surface. The polish will not provide any protection; it will just keep the wax clean.

What Is The Difference Betweem Cement And Concrete?

Cement is mainly composed of limestone (calcium carbonate), calcium oxide, clay, and usually shale. The ingredients absorb water, which turns it into a paste. Concrete is cement with the addition of sand, gravel, and crushed rock. The addition of these ingredients lowers the cost since pure cement is very expensive. The hardening process of cement is somewhat complicated, however. The moistened mixture containing calcium, aluminum, and silicon salts tends to interact and produce new substances called tricalcium aluminates. These are inorganic compounds that, after a few days, form interlocking crystals that produce the concrete's strength.

What Is Stainless Steel Made Of?

When stainless steel is produced, iron and chromium are mixed together. The percentage of chromium is about 12%. As long as the alloy contains this 12%, a percentage of the chromium will rise to the surface of the metal and will form a thin coating of chromium oxide, which protects the iron from rusting and gives it a shiny surface. Other metals such as nickel are sometimes added to increase the strength of the stainless steel.

What Makes A Disinfectant Different From An Antiseptic?

Antiseptics are chemical agents that kill a percentage of bacteria. Although they don't kill all bacteria, they are effective in preventing the growth of most. Antiseptics are mainly used on a cut or abrasion. Disinfectants are formulated to kill all bacteria and viruses but are too harsh to be applied to your skin.

How Do The Instant Hot Shaving Creams Work?

A number of shaving creams advertise that they heat up on your face to provide a more comfortable shaving experience. These products use compounds such as methyl salicitate or salicylic acid to actually irritate the skin. This causes the sensation of heat by increasing the circulation of blood in that area where it is applied. The same ingredients can be found in a number of liniments.

What Happens When You Have Your Hair Straightened?

Hairs are linked together by a chemical bond called a disulfide bond. These sulfur atoms are attracted to each other and form a bond which can be broken using a chemical called thioglycolic acid. When this is applied, the bonds release and become free, allowing the hair to relax.

Do I Need A Special Detergent For Cold Water Washing?

It is not necessary to purchase a special cold water detergent. The difference between hot and cold water detergents is so insignificant that it a waste of money if there is a difference in cost. There is only 1 compound that is capable of changing the effectiveness of any detergent when it is used in cold water and that is the amount of surfactant they use. Almost all products are at the same level. A surfactant will actually make the water "wetter" by changing the surface tension. This allows the water and detergent to more freely enter the garment.

Do Dry Bleaches Work Better Than Liquid Bleaches?

There is a misconception that bleaches remove stains. Bleaches do not remove stains. They only mask the stain so that you will not see it. This process is known as oxidation and utilizes one of two types of bleach. The dry bleach is composed of sodium perborate which is converted to hydrogen peroxide, which continues to break down, liberating oxygen gas which then oxidizes the clothing. Liquid bleach contains the chemical sodium hypochlorite which cause the release of chlorine gas that oxidizes the clothing, thus bleaching the stain out. The more powerful of the two bleaching agents is the liquid bleach.

What Is The Secret Formula Of Those Magical Spot Removers?

The TV commercials and newspaper ads announcing a cleaner that will take any spot or stain out of any fabric are just commercials for a combination of detergent and bleach. Most of these are sold through good advertising and sales techniques. Most do work well. However, you could probably make them with two or three ingredients you already have at home.

What Is The Difference Between Synthetic And Natural Fibers?

Synthetic or permanent press fabrics are produced from either 100% synthetic or natural fibers that contain sufficient quantities of plastic to give the qualities the manufacturer requires. Permanent press fabrics will retain their shape up to the point that they will start to melt, which is a very high temperature and never achieved when they are washed or dry cleaned. Because of the plastic, the synthetic fabric is very dense and will not lose its shape. Garments made of natural fibers are not very dense; therefore, they are unable to retain their shape or crease as well.

Are The Expensive Bathtub Cleaners Really Necessary?

Most advertisements for bathtub cleaners state that they contain powerful disinfectants that will kill bacteria as well as cleaning off the soap scum and dirt residues. While they do contain disinfectants, the bacteria-killing action only lasts for about 3-4 hours. Then the bacteria come right back. The best cleaner for tubs is diluted laundry bleach. If you can't handle the smell, purchase one that is scented. Be sure to wear gloves and ventilate the room well when using bleach of any type.

What Do Those Large Toilet-Cleaning Tablets Really Do?

The bowl-cleaning tablets that are placed into the toilet tank are not going to clean your toilet. They are only designed to slow down the process of hard-water buildup which contains imbedded dirt and debris. They contain a strong chlorine bleach compound or quaternary ammonium chloride. Both are strong disinfectants and have good cleaning properties. Some products, however, may be so strong that they will cause scaling of any metal surface in the tank and may cause the toilet to clog up.

Do The Colored Ribbons Of Toothpaste Contain Different Ingredients?

Toothpastes that come out of the tube in different colors are all the same product, dyed red and green. Recently, a new product did come on the market with a plunger and two compartments in the container that provide you with two different ingredients to care for your teeth and gums. Check with your dentist before using the product, since it contains hydrogen peroxide.

What's In A Breath Mint And How Does It Work?

Breath mints contain sweeteners and moisturizers, and may contain a germ killer. Most brands contain sorbitol as the sweetener, which may cause diarrhea if too much is consumed by susceptible individuals. The odor eaters are probably chlorophyll and "Retsyn," which is another name for cuprous (copper) gluconate.

What Are The Differences Among Perfume, Cologne, And Toilet Water?

The main difference is the concentration of the compounds that are responsible for the aroma of each product. Perfumes are produced with the highest concentrations and therefore last longer. If you place a small amount of Vaseline on the areas where you are applying the perfume, it will last twice as long. Colognes contain less of the same compound and more fillers, while toilet water is just diluted cologne. The cost of most perfumes is determined by the amount of money that is spent in advertising and in-store marketing of the product.

What Makes Toilet Tissues Different?

The better brands and, of course, the more expensive ones, are made from purified wood pulp and skin softeners. The other products include only purified wood pulp and they do not go through any softening process. You should have no problem telling the difference. Colored toilet paper contains traces of metals that produce the different colors. Occasionally people with very sensitive skin may experience a reaction from the colored papers.

Do Acne Medications Work?

Acne medications do not cure acne. They only provide a measure of control. Studies show that diet doesn't have much effect, either. Keeping the face clean with soap and water seems to work almost as well as some of the medications. The preparations contain a chemical sponge which may contain sulfur and salicylic creams as the absorbent to soak up the excess skin oils. The oils are actually more related to pimples than acne. One of the more common methods is to soak a cotton ball in alcohol and use that to cleanse the area.

How Do Preparations That Claim To Coat The Stomach Actually Work?

These preparations absorb large quantities of water and waste food materials in the stomach and upper small intestine. This allows these areas to "dry out" and protects the delicate stomach lining against any additional infection. These coating products contain purified clay, aluminum magnesium silicate, bismuth salts, and usually activated charcoal.

Does Coca Cola Really Control Nausea And Vomiting?

Nausea and vomiting can be controlled by medications called antiemetics. Emetrol is one of the most popular. These anti-emetics control the "gag reflex" and are very effective. However, Coca-Cola syrup or almost any other cola syrup which contain sugar and phosphates is every bit as effective in most instances. Your pharmacist may be able to assist you in obtaining a cola syrup. Diet colas will not work since they do not contain sugar.

How Does Baking Soda Remove Odors?

Sodium bicarbonate (baking soda) is an inorganic powder, which simply means that it is not produced from living matter and is sold in very fine particles with a high surface area. House odors are composed of organic oils that become stuck in the powder and are neutralized, as if taken into a sponge. The oils eventually become inactivated permanently, when they remain in the soda.

How Do Electric Air Cleaners Work?

The newer electric air cleaners draw the air over a series of electrically-charged metal plates that attract dust and pollutants. The plates must be removed periodically and cleaned. Another type is the porous silicon plate, which traps the particles like a magnet. This type of unit utilizes a blower motor to pass the air over the filters, which need to be washed occasionally.

Do Windshield De-Icers Really Work?

Most windshield de-icers are made from alcohol and are over-priced products. They do, however, work fairly well, depending on the thickness of the ice. If the ice is very thick, it will take quite a while for it to melt. Never place hot water on your windshield as it may cause the glass to expand and then contract when it cools, cracking the windshield. Most de-icers are similar to antifreeze. You can place a solution of homemade de-icer in your window washer unit. Just mix 1 part of any commercial antifreeze with 9 parts of a 50/50 mixture of alcohol and water.

What Is Paint Primer?

These are usually colorless and will cause paint to adhere to surfaces better. Colored primers hide a color that may bleed through. Primers may also be used to protect a metal surface from corrosion as an undercoat. Since many paints do not adhere well to a number of surfaces, primers are often a necessity.

What Can I Use To Clean Silverstone And Teflon Pots?

For the most part, these plastic-coated pots are easy to keep clean. However, they do stain and may develop a build-up of grease and oil over time. When this occurs it will adversely affect the efficiency of the non-stick surface. To clean the surface, just mix 2 tablespoons of baking soda with ½ cup of white vinegar in 1 cup of water. Put these ingredients into the pot, place the pot on the range, and boil it for about 10 minutes. Wash the pot, then rub vegetable oil on the surface of the plastic coating to re-season it.

How Can I Unclog A Drain Using Ingredients Around The Kitchen?

After trying a plumber's helper with no success, try the following method: Remove all standing water so that you are able to pour the ingredients into the drain. First, pour 1 cup of baking soda, 1 cup of table salt, and ½ cup of white vinegar into the clogged drain. These will start dissolving any organic matter and grease immediately. Next, flush 1-2 quarts of boiling water down the drain.

What Is The Formula For An All-Around Breading For Any Food?

The following blend should make any food taste better and enhance the flavor. Mix all ingredients together well and store in the refrigerator until needed. Allow to stand at room temperature for 20 minutes before using.

   2 cups of whole wheat pastry flour
   ½ tablespoon paprika
   1 tablespoon of dry mustard
   ¾ teaspoon of finely ground celery seed
   1 teaspoon ground black pepper
   1 teaspoon dried basil
   1 teaspoon dried marjoram
   ¾ teaspoon dried thyme

How Do You Clean A Thermos Bottle?

The easiest way to eliminate the odors and stains is to fill the container with hot water and drop in a denture cleaning tablet, then allow it to stand overnight. Baking soda will also work but not as well.

How Do You Make A Candle Almost Dripless?

Prepare a solution of 2 tablespoons of salt per candle in just enough water to cover the candles. Allow the candles to soak in the saltwater solution for about 2-3 hours, then rinse them, let them dry, and wait at least 24 hours before you use them. The salt water hardens the wax and allows it to burn more cleanly, reducing the chance of its dripping on the tablecloth.

All Chopsticks Are Not The Same

If you have ever eaten in a Japanese restaurant, you will notice that the chopsticks are pointed. In a Chinese restaurant the chopsticks are blunt. Many restaurants will Americanize the chopsticks by placing a rubberband around them about ¼ of the way down from the top. This will hold them together and make them easier to handle.

What Is An Easy Method Of Oven Cleaning?

If you have an oven that is not equipped with a self-cleaning feature, just preheat it to 200° F. and turn it off. Place a small bowl containing ½ cup of ammonia on the center shelf, then close the oven and allow it to stand overnight. The next day, open the oven and allow it to air for 30 minutes in a well ventilated kitchen. then wipe up the mess with a warm, damp paper towel.

GLOSSARY OF THE
MORE UNUSUAL

Acid	A sour tasting substance that is soluble in water.
Acidulated Water	A number of fruits and vegetables turn brown easily and need to be sprayed with a solution of ascorbic acid (vitamin C), a mild acid found in fruits. To prepare acidulated water, just mix 1 part of lemon or lime juice to 5 parts of water and place the mixture in a bowl or spray bottle.
Al Dente	This is an Italian term meaning "to the tooth." It is used to describe the cooked pasta when it has reached the stage where it has a slight resistance when you bite down on it.
Alkali	A substance that is capable of neutralizing an acid. Sodium bicarbonate is a good example.
Angelica	This is a sweet aromatic herb whose candied stems are used in cake decorating and to flavor alcoholic beverages.
Antioxidant	A substance that can protect another substance from being destroyed or damaged by oxygen.
Aperitif	Alcoholic beverages such as sweet vermouth, dry sherry, or champagne that are served before a meal to stimulate the appetite.
Astringent	These are compounds that are capable of drawing skin or other soft tissue together. They are used to close the pores of the skin and block toxins from entering surface cells.
Avidin	A protein which is found in egg white and will inactivate biotin.
Average Flour Value	This is derived from four factors: the color of the flour; loaves per barrel; the size of the loaf; and the quality of the bread as compared to any given flour shipment.
Baking Chocolate	This is also called bitter or unsweetened chocolate and is pure chocolate liquor that has been extracted from the cocoa bean. Usually has lecithin and vanilla added for flavor and to keep it in a usable suspension.
Barding	This is the process of covering meats or fowl with added fat to keep the flesh moist. It is usually done to meats that have only a small fat covering and is accomplished by basting the meat with any fat source.
Benzyl Peroxide	A fine powder that is mixed into the flour in very small amounts to bleach it.

Blanch

The process of plunging food into boiling water, usually to remove the skin from fruits and vegetables or to kill bacteria prior to freezing.

Boiled Icing

Made by beating cooked sugar syrup into egg whites that have been firmly whipped. The mixture is then beaten until it is smooth and glossy. Also known as Italian meringue.

Bolting

Removing the bran from ground grain by sifting.

Brix Scale

This is a measurement of the density of sugar that has been dissolved in water to prepare a syrup. The scale is designed to provide a measurement of the amount of water, which will determine whether the syrup is at a low or high density level. The instrument used to accomplish this is called a saccharometer.

Cake Breaker

A comb with 3-4"-long metal teeth that is used to slice angel food and chiffon cakes. Cuts the cakes cleanly instead of tearing it as a knife will do.

Cake Leveler

A U-shaped metal frame that is used to cut cakes into even horizontal layers. It stands on plastic feet and has a thin, very sharp, serrated cutting blade. It will adjust to any size slice. The cake is pushed against the blade. This will cut cakes up to 16 inches in diameter.

Caramel Rulers

Also called chocolate rulers, they are used to contain the hot chocolate or caramel as it cools. They are usually 20-30 inches in length with ½ inch stainless steel or chrome bars. The bars are lightly oiled or dusted with corn starch to keep the product from sticking and are placed on a marble working counter. The hot mixture is then poured into the center of the mold.

Carbon Dioxide

A colorless, odorless gas that is non-combustible. It is commonly used as a pressure-dispensing agent in gassed whipped creams and carbonated beverages. It is also used in the form of dry ice in the frozen food industry. It has been used in stage productions to produce harmless smoke or fumes. However, it may cause shortness of breath, nausea, elevated blood pressure, and disorientation if inhaled in lager quantities.

Carcinogen

A substance that may contribute to producing a cancer cell in the body.

Casein

The main protein in cow's milk is used as a water-absorbing powder with no odor. It is used as a texturizer for a number of dairy products including ice cream and frozen custards. It is also used in hair preparations to thicken thin hair and as an emulsifier in cosmetics.

Cheesecloth
A natural white cotton cloth which is available in either fine or coarse weaves. It is lint-free and maintains its shape when wet. Primarily used for straining jellies or wrapping stuffing in turkeys.

Chelating Agent
A compound that has the capability to bind with and precipitate trace metals from the body. The most common agent is EDTA (ethylenediamine tetraacetic acid).

Chèvre Cheese
Any cheese made from goat's milk, usually found coated with an herb or ash.

Chocolate Bloom
This has also been called "fat bloom." The bloom is actually accomplished when the cocoa butter and the chocolate separate during cooking and the cocoa butter floats to the top and crystallizes. The streaks of fat look like the bloom of a plant, hence the name. As soon as the chocolate melts, the cocoa butter goes back into the mixture.

Choux Paste
The French name for a special pastry dough used in cream puffs and chocolate eclairs.

Clarification
The process of removing small particles of suspended material from a liquid. Butyl alcohol is used to remove particles from shampoos. Traces of copper and iron are removed from certain beverages and vinegar.

Clotted Cream
May also be known as Devonshire cream in recipes. It is a thick, rich, scalded cream that is made by slowly cooking and skimming cream or unpasteurized milk. The thickened cream floats to the surface and is removed after the cream cools. It is traditionally served with scones in England.

Cockle
A very small mollusk that resembles a clam. May be sold either shucked or canned.

Crackling
The crisp, browned pieces that remain in the bottom of the pan after fresh pork fat is rendered into lard. May be added to a number of dishes, especially beans, corn bread, or vegetables.

Cutting
The process of adding fat into a flour mixture with a pastry blender or other mixing utensil.

Demulcent
A thick or creamy substance, usually oily, that is used to relieve pain and inflammation in mucosal membranes. One of the common demulcents is gum acacia.

Docker	This is a tool for making holes in pastry dough, especially puff pastries, so that steam can escape as the dough is baking. It looks like a paint roller with protruding metal or plastic spikes.
Emulsifier	A commonly used substance that is added to stabilize a mixture and to ensure the proper consistency. One of the most common emulsifiers is lecithin, which will keep oil and vinegar in suspension. Cosmetics use stearic acid soaps which include potassium and sodium stearates.
Fermentation	This is the breakdown of starch (grains) using certain enzymes that speed up the reaction. The end product may depend on the particular enzyme that is used. If the enzyme diastase is used, the end product will be maltose.
Filé Powder	A spice made from ground sassafras leaves and used by Cajun chefs to thicken and add a thyme-like flavor to gumbos. Tends to become stringy when boiled and needs to be added just before serving.
Floating Island	A dessert made from chilled custard and topped with a special "poached" meringue. The custard usually contains fruit and the meringue is occasionally drizzled with a thin stream of caramel syrup.
Flummery	A soft custardlike dessert that is served over berries or other types of fruit. Resembles a thickened fruit sauce.
Focaccia	An Italian yeast bread that resembles a deep-dish pizza crust with a breadlike texture. It is usually topped with a variety of toppings.
Frappé	A beverage or slushy dessert that is made with crushed ice. It usually has liquor poured over it.
Glycogen	The body's main storage carbohydrate. Is easily converted into energy.
Gnocchi	A small Italian dumpling made from potatoes and 100% semolina flour. They may be found in many shapes, from squares to balls, and usually are served as an appetizer in better Italian restaurants.
Haricot	A term used to describe a thick meat stew.
Hydrolyzed	To be put into a water form.
Isopropyl Alcohol	This is not an alcohol that can be drunk. It is not for human consumption and is used only for massages, as a disinfectant,

and to remove moisture from gasoline tanks. If you are trying to remove moisture from a gas tank, be sure the isopropyl alcohol is 100%, not 70%, or you will have more problems.

Jaggery

This is also known as palm sugar and is semi-refined sugar which is produced from the sap of the Palmyra palm tree. It may also be made from Hawaiian sugar cane. It looks like a coarse, crumbly, brown sugar with a strong flavor, and is sold in cakes. It is mostly used in Asian and Indonesian dishes.

Leavening

A chemical placed in baked goods to make them lighter and more porous by causing the release of carbon dioxide gas during cooking.

Mary Ann Pan

Also known as the shortcake pan. It is a shallow, round, aluminum pan that looks like a tart pan. It has fluted sides and is made with a deep hollow area around the edges, making the center appear to be raised. Used mainly for sponge cakes and pastry shells.

Metabolize

A substance that undergoes physical and chemical changes when changed into a usable form.

Miso

A fermented soybean paste made from rice, barley or wheat, used mainly in Japanese cooking.

Parch

Browning with a dry heat.

pH

This refers to the scale used to measure acidity and alkalinity. The pH is actually the hydrogen (H) ion concentration of a solution. The small "p" is for the power of the hydrogen ion. The scale is used to determine the level of acidity or alkalinity of a product or solution. The number 14 is the highest level and 7 is a neutral point where the acidity and alkalinity are balanced. Water is 7, and if the number goes above 7, the solution is considered to be alkaline. If the number falls below 7, the solution is considered to be acidic. Human blood has a pH of 7.3, vinegar and lemon juice are 2.3, and common lye is 13.

Phyllo Dough

A very thin pastry dough, usually sold in 1-pound cartons. Sold fresh in the Middle East and sold frozen in the United States. Must be kept wrapped, otherwise the dough will dry out rapidly.

Piquant

Refers to any food that has a sharp flavor. Usually used to describe cheeses.

Quenelle

A small, delicate, round dumpling made from finely chopped fish or meat in a flour and egg mixture. It is poached and served as an appetizer, with a rich sauce.

Raclette	A Swiss cheese snack prepared by placing a piece of cheese near a flame so that it will remain soft enough to scrape a small amount off and use it as a spread on bread or boiled potatoes.
Rice Stick	This is an almost transparent Oriental noodle that is flavorless. It is made from rice flour and may be sold as rice noodles or rice vermicelli. It will expand to 8-10 times its original volume and is usually cooked in liquid or deep fried.
Roux	A special cooked mixture of flour and butter, usually used to thicken sauces and stews.
Rusk	A slice of bread that is crisp and used as a cracker. The bread is baked, sliced very thin, allowed to dry out and then browned.
Sequestrant	A substance that absorbs iron and prevents chemical changes that would affect the flavor, texture, and color of foods. Sodium is an example that is used for water softening.
Shelf Stable	This is a term that is used to describe foods that have been sterilized and sealed in airtight plastic bags, containers, or special paper foil. This type of food preservation of food does not require refrigeration or freezing. It is sometimes referred to as aseptic packaging. The most popular products to be sold in this manner are dairy products, puddings, and sauces.
Suet	This is a semi-hard fat found in the loin and kidney areas of beef and pork. Occasionally beef suet will be used to make mincemeat.
Toxin	An organic poison that is produced in or on living or dead organisms.
Zest	The oil found in the outer yellow or orange rind of citrus fruits.

INDEX

A

B

D

Q

R